An OPUS book

The Russian Revolution

The Russian Revolution had a decisive impact on the history of the twentieth century. Now, following the collapse of the Soviet regime and the opening of its archives, it is possible to step back and see the full picture. In this second, substantially revised edition of Sheila Fitzpatrick's already classic work, *The Russian Revolution*, first published in 1983, the author incorporates data from archives that were previously inaccessible not only to Western but also to Soviet historians, as well as drawing on important recent Russian publications such as the memoirs of one of the great survivors of Soviet politics, Vyacheslav Molotov.

Impeccable in its scholarship and objectivity, the book tells a gripping story of a Marxist revolution that was intended to transform the world, visited enormous suffering on the Russian people, and, like the French Revolution before it, ended up by devouring its own children. In a new concluding section that will be of great interest to scholars in the field as well as the general reader, the author treats the Stalinist Great Purges as the last act of the drama of the Russian Revolution.

Sheila Fitzpatrick is Professor of History at the University of Chicago.

OPUS General Editors

Christopher Butler
Robert Evans
John Skorupski

OPUS books provide concise, original, and authoritative introductions to a wide range of subjects in the humanities and sciences. They are written by experts for the general reader as well as for students.

The Russian Revolution

SECOND EDITION

Sheila Fitzpatrick

Oxford   New York

OXFORD UNIVERSITY PRESS

OXFORD
UNIVERSITY PRESS

Great Clarendon Street, Oxford OX2 6DP

Oxford University Press is a department of the University of Oxford.
It furthers the University's objective of excellence in research, scholarship,
and education by publishing worldwide in

Oxford New York

Athens Auckland Bangkok Bogotá Buenos Aires Calcutta
Cape Town Chennai Dar es Salaam Delhi Florence Hong Kong Istanbul
Karachi Kuala Lumpur Madrid Melbourne Mexico City Mumbai
Nairobi Paris São Paulo Singapore Taipei Tokyo Toronto Warsaw

with associated companies in Berlin Ibadan

Oxford is a registered trade mark of Oxford University Press
in the UK and in certain other countries

British Library Cataloguing in Publication Data

Data available

Library of Congress Cataloging in Publication Data

Fitzpatrick, Sheila.
The Russian revolution / Sheila Fitzpatrick.—2nd ed.
p. cm.
'An Opus book'—Half t.p.
Includes bibliographical references and index.
1. Soviet Union—History—Revolution, 1917-1921. I. Title.
DK265.F48 1994 947.084—dc20 93-46676

ISBN 0-19-289257-6

10 9 8 7 6

Printed in Great Britain by
Cox & Wyman Ltd,
Reading, Berkshire

Acknowledgements

The first draft of this book was written in the summer of 1979, when I was a Visiting Fellow at the Research School of Social Sciences of the Australian National University, Canberra. I would like to express my gratitude to Professor T. H. Rigby, who arranged my invitation to A.N.U. and subsequently made very helpful comments on the manuscript; to Jerry Hough, who was a constant source of intellectual stimulus and encouragement; and to the students in my courses at Columbia University and the University of Texas at Austin, who were the first audience for much of this book.

For help in the preparation of the second edition, I would like to thank Jonathan Bone and Joshua Sanborn, who served as research assistants; Colin Lucas, with whom I taught a course on 'Revolutionary Violence' in 1993; Terry Martin, who raised a question that I tried to answer in revising Chapter 6; William Rosenberg and Arch Getty, who responded promptly to last-minute queries; Michael Danos, who read the revised manuscript; and all the members of the Workshop on Russian/Soviet Studies at the University of Chicago.

Contents

Acknowledgements   v

Introduction   1

1 **The Setting**   15
The society   16
The revolutionary tradition   23
The 1905 Revolution and its aftermath; the First World
    War   31

2 **1917: The Revolutions of February and
    October**   40
The February Revolution and 'dual power'   44
The Bolsheviks   49
The popular revolution   52
The political crises of the summer   57
The October Revolution   61

3 **The Civil War**   68
The Civil War, the Red Army and the Cheka   72
War Communism   78
Visions of the new world   83
The Bolsheviks in power   87

4 **NEP and the Future of the Revolution**   93
The discipline of retreat   96
The problem of bureaucracy   102
The leadership struggle   106
Building socialism in one country   111

5 **Stalin's Revolution**   120
   Stalin versus the Right   124
   The industrialization drive   129
   Collectivization   135
   Cultural Revolution   141

6 **Ending the Revolution**   148
   'Revolution accomplished'   150
   'Revolution betrayed'   156
   Terror   163

   Notes   173
   Select Bibliography   185
   Index   193

Introduction

THIS second edition of *The Russian Revolution* appears in the wake of dramatic events—the fall of the Communist regime and the dissolution of the Soviet Union at the end of 1991. Those events have had all sorts of consequences for historians of the Russian Revolution. In the first place, they have opened archives that were previously closed, brought forth memoirs that were hidden in drawers, and released a flood of new material of every kind. In the second place, they have changed the category of the Russian Revolution. Until December 1991, the Russian Revolution belonged to the category of 'birth of a nation' revolutions—those, like the American Revolution, that left behind them an enduring national and institutional structure and were the focus of a national myth. Now the Soviet nation that was born in the Russian Revolution appears to be dead, and the Revolution has to be reclassified (which means rethought) as an episode in the long sweep of Russian history.

The question is, what kind of episode? In Russia, the Bolsheviks' October Revolution[1] is currently in as deep disrepute as was the French Revolution in France after the fall of Napoleon. Journalists write about it as an aberration, an inexplicable but fatal break with the traditions of 'the real Russia' as well as the mainstream of world civilization. To many Russian intellectuals, it seems, the best thing to do with the Russian Revolution would be to erase it, along with the whole seven decades of the Soviet era, from national memory.

But history is not so obliging. We are all saddled with our pasts, approving or disapproving. Sooner or later the Russians will have to accept the Revolution back into their history—although, on the analogy of the French Revolution, one might expect at least a century of heated debate about its meaning to follow. For the rest of us, the abrupt end of the Soviet Union only makes its beginnings more intriguing. With major historical problems like the Russian Revolution, there are many important questions but no simple answers. It is one of those big ambiguous milestones in human history that we keep coming back to decipher.

Timespan of the revolution

Since revolutions are complex social and political upheavals, historians who write about them are bound to differ on the most basic questions—causes, revolutionary aims, impact on the society, political outcome, and even the timespan of the revolution itself. In the case of the Russian Revolution, the starting-point presents no problem: almost everyone takes it to be the 'February Revolution'[2] of 1917, which led to the abdication of Emperor Nicholas II and the formation of the Provisional Government. But when did the Russian Revolution end? Was it all over by October 1917, when the Bolsheviks took power? Or did the end of the Revolution come with the Bolsheviks' victory in the Civil War in 1920? Was Stalin's 'revolution from above' part of the Russian Revolution? Or should we take the view that the Revolution continued throughout the lifetime of the Soviet state?

In his *Anatomy of Revolution*, Crane Brinton suggested that revolutions have a life cycle passing through phases of increasing fervour and zeal for radical transformation until they reach a climax of intensity, which is followed by the 'Thermidorian' phase of disillusionment, declining revolutionary energy, and gradual moves towards the restoration of order and stability.[3] The Russian Bolsheviks, bearing in mind the same French-Revolution model that lies at the basis of Brinton's analysis, feared a Thermidorian degeneration of their own Revolution, and half suspected that one had occurred at the end of the Civil War, when economic collapse forced them into the 'strategic retreat' marked by the introduction of the New Economic Policy (NEP) in 1921.

Yet at the end of the 1920s, Russia plunged into another upheaval—Stalin's 'revolution from above', associated with the industrialization drive of the First Five-Year Plan, the collectivization of agriculture, and a 'Cultural Revolution' directed primarily against the old intelligentsia—whose impact on society was greater even than that of the February and October Revolutions of 1917 and the Civil War of 1918–20. It was only after this upheaval ended in the early 1930s that signs of a classic Thermidor can be discerned: the waning of revolutionary fervour and belligerence, new policies aimed at restoring order and stability, revival of traditional values and culture, solidification of a new political and social structure. Yet even this Thermidor was not quite the end of the revolutionary upheaval. In a final internal convulsion, even more devastating than earlier surges of revolutionary terror, the Great Purges of 1937–8 swept away many of the surviving Old Bolshevik revolutionaries, effected a wholesale turnover of personnel within the political, administrative, and military elites, and sent more than a million people (by latest counts[4]) to their deaths or imprisonment in Gulag.

In deciding on a timespan for the Russian Revolution, the first issue is the nature of the 'strategic retreat' of NEP in the 1920s. Was it the end of the Revolution, or conceived as such? Although the Bolsheviks' avowed intention in 1921 was to use this interlude to gather strength for a later renewal of the revolutionary assault, there was always the possibility that intentions would change as revolutionary passions subsided. Some scholars think that in the last years of his life, Lenin (who died in 1924) came to believe that for Russia further progress towards socialism could only be achieved gradually, with the raising of the cultural level of the population. Nevertheless, Russian society remained highly volatile and unstable during the NEP period, and the party's mood remained aggressive and revolutionary. The Bolsheviks feared counter-revolution, remained preoccupied with the threat from 'class enemies' at home and abroad, and constantly expressed their dissatisfaction with NEP and unwillingness to accept it as the final outcome of the Revolution.

A second issue that has to be considered is the nature of Stalin's 'revolution from above' that ended NEP in the late 1920s. Some historians reject the idea that there was any real continuity between Stalin's revolution and Lenin's. Others feel that Stalin's 'revolution' does not deserve the name, since they believe it was not a popular uprising but something more like an assault on the society by a ruling party aiming at radical transformation. In this book, I trace lines of continuity between Lenin's revolution and Stalin's. As to the inclusion of Stalin's 'revolution from above' in the Russian Revolution, this is a question on which historians may legitimately differ. But the issue here is not whether 1917 and 1929 were alike, but whether they were part of the same process. Napoleon's revolutionary wars can be included in our general concept of the French Revolution, even if we do not regard them as an embodiment of the spirit of 1789; and a similar approach seems legitimate in the case of the Russian Revolution. In common-sense terms, a revolution is coterminous with the period of upheaval and instability between the fall of an old regime and the firm consolidation of a new one. In the late 1920s, the permanent contours of Russia's new regime had yet to emerge.

The final issue of judgement is whether the Great Purges of 1937-8 should be considered a part of the Russian Revolution. Was this revolutionary terror, or was it terror of a basically different type—totalitarian terror, perhaps, meaning a terror that serves the systemic purposes of a firmly entrenched regime? In my view, neither of these two characterizations fully describes the Great Purges. They were a unique phenomenon, located right on the boundary between revolution and postrevolutionary Stalinism. This was revolutionary terror in its rhetoric, targets, and snowballing progress. But it was totalitarian terror in that it destroyed persons but not structures, and did not threaten the person of the Leader. The fact that it was state terror initiated by Stalin does not dis-qualify it from being part of the Russian Revolution: after all, the Jacobin Terror of 1794 can be described in similar terms.[5] Another important similarity between the two episodes is that in both cases the primary targets for destruction were revolutionaries. For dra-matic reasons alone, the story of the Russian Revolution needs the Great Purges, just as the story of the French Revolution needs the Jacobin Terror.

In this book, the timespan of the Russian Revolution runs from February 1917 to the Great Purges of 1937-8. The different stages— the February and October Revolutions of 1917, the Civil War, the interlude of NEP, Stalin's 'revolution from above', its 'Thermidorian' aftermath, and the Great Purges—are treated as discrete episodes in a twenty-year process of revolution. By the end of that twenty years, revolutionary energy was thoroughly spent, the society was exhausted, and even the ruling Communist Party[6] was tired of upheaval and shared the general longing for a 'return to normalcy'. Normalcy, to be sure, was still unattainable, for German invasion and the beginning of Soviet engagement in the Second World War came only a few years after the Great Purges. The war brought further upheaval, but not more revolution, at least as far as the pre-1939 territories of the Soviet Union were concerned. It was the beginning of a new, postrevolutionary era in Soviet history.

Writings about the revolution

There is nothing like revolutions for provoking ideological contestation among their interpreters. The bicentenary of the French Revolution in 1989, for example, was marked by a spirited attempt by some scholars and publicists to end the long interpretative struggle by consigning the Revolution to the dust-heap of history. The Russian Revolution has a shorter historiography, but probably only because we have had a century and a half less in which to write about it. In the Select Bibliography at the end of this book, I have concentrated on recent scholarly works, reflecting the burgeoning of Western scholarship on the Russian Revolution in the last ten to fifteen years. Here I will outline the most important changes in historical perspective over time and characterize some of the classic works on the Russian Revolution and Soviet history.

Before the Second World War, not much was written on the Russian Revolution by professional historians in the West. There were a number of fine eye-witness accounts and memoirs, of which John Reed's *Ten Days that Shook the World* is the most famous, as well as some good history by journalists like W. H. Chamberlin and Louis Fischer, whose insider's history of Soviet diplomacy, *The Soviets in World Affairs*, remains a classic. The works of interpretation that had most long-term impact were Leon (Lev) Trotsky's *History of the Russian Revolution* and the same author's *The Revolution Betrayed*. The first, written after Trotsky's expulsion from the Soviet Union but not as a political polemic, gives a vivid description and Marxist analysis of 1917 from the perspective of a participant. The second, an indictment of Stalin written in 1936, describes Stalin's regime as Thermidorian, resting on the support of an emergent Soviet bureaucratic class and reflecting its essentially bourgeois values.

Of histories written in the Soviet Union before the war, pride of place must be given to a work written under Stalin's close supervision, the notorious *Short Course in the History of the Soviet Communist Party* published in 1938. As the reader may guess, this was not a scholarly work but one designed to lay down the correct 'party line'—that is, the orthodoxy to be absorbed by all Communists and taught in all schools—on all questions of Soviet history, ranging from the class nature of the Tsarist regime and the reasons for the

Red Army's victory in the Civil War to the conspiracies against Soviet power headed by 'Judas Trotsky' and supported by foreign capitalist powers. The existence of a work like the *Short Course* did not leave much room for creative scholarly research on the Soviet period. Strict censorship and self-censorship was the order of the day in the Soviet historical profession.

The interpretation of the Bolshevik Revolution that became established in the Soviet Union in the 1930s and remained enthroned at least until the mid-1950s might be described as formulaic Marxist. The key points were that the October Revolution was a true proletarian revolution in which the Bolshevik Party served as the vanguard of the proletariat, and that it was neither premature nor accidental—its occurrence was governed by historical law. Historical laws (*zakonomernosti*), weighty but usually ill-defined, determined everything in Soviet history, which meant in practice that every major political decision was right. No real political history was written, since all the revolutionary leaders except Lenin, Stalin, and a few who died young had been exposed as traitors to the Revolution and become 'non-persons', that is, unmentionable in print. Social history was written in class terms, with the working class, the peasantry, and the intelligentsia as virtually the sole actors and subjects.

In the West, Soviet history became a matter of strong interest only after the Second World War, mainly in a Cold War context of knowing the enemy. The two books that set the tone were fiction, George Orwell's *Nineteen Eighty-Four* and Arthur Koestler's *Darkness at Noon* (on the Great Purge trials of Old Bolsheviks in the late 1930s), but in the scholarly realm it was American political science that dominated. The totalitarian model, based on a somewhat demonized conflation of Nazi Germany and Stalin's Russia, was the most popular interpretative framework. It emphasized the omnipotence of the totalitarian state and its 'levers of control', paid considerable attention to ideology and propaganda, and largely neglected the social realm (which was seen as passive, fragmented by the totalitarian state). Most Western scholars agreed that the Bolshevik Revolution was a *coup* by a minority party, lacking any kind of popular support or legitimacy. The Revolution, and for that matter the prerevolutionary history of the Bolshevik Party, were studied mainly to elucidate the origins of Soviet totalitarianism.

Before the 1970s, few Western historians ventured into the study of Soviet history, including the Russian Revolution, partly because the subject was so politically charged, and partly because access to archives and primary sources was very difficult. Two pioneering works by British historians deserve note: E. H. Carr's *The Bolshevik Revolution, 1917–1923*, the beginning of his multi-volume *History of Soviet Russia*, of which the first volume appeared in 1952, and Isaac Deutscher's classic biography of Trotsky, of which the first volume, *The Prophet Armed*, appeared in 1954.

In the Soviet Union, Khrushchev's denunciation of Stalin at the Twentieth Party Congress in 1956 and the partial de-Stalinization that followed opened the door for some historical revaluation and a raising of the level of scholarship. Archive-based studies of 1917 and the 1920s began to appear, although there were still constraints and dogmas that had to be observed, for example, on the Bolshevik Party's status as vanguard of the working class. It became possible to mention non-persons like Trotsky and Zinoviev, but only in a pejorative context. The great opportunity that Khrushchev's Secret Speech offered historians was to decouple Lenin and Stalin. Reform-minded Soviet historians produced many books and articles on the 1920s arguing that 'Leninist norms' in different areas were more democratic and tolerant of diversity and less coercive and arbitrary than the practices of the Stalin era.

For Western readers, the 'Leninist' trend of the 1960s and 1970s was exemplified by Roy A. Medvedev, author of *Let History Judge. The Origins and Consequences of Stalinism*, published in the West in 1971. But Medvedev's work was too sharply and overtly critical of Stalin for the climate of the Brezhnev years, and he was unable to publish it in the Soviet Union. This was the era of the blossoming of *samizdat* (unofficial circulation of manuscripts within the Soviet Union) and *tamizdat* (illegal publication of work abroad). The most famous of the dissident authors emerging at this time was Aleksandr Solzhenitsyn, the great novelist and historical polemicist whose *Gulag Archipelago* was published in English in 1973.

While the works of some dissident Soviet scholars started to reach Western audiences in the 1970s, Western scholarly work on the Russian Revolution was still treated as 'bourgeois falsification' and effectively banned from the USSR (though some works, including Robert Conquest's *The Great Terror* circulated clandestinely along with Solzhenitsyn's *Gulag*). All the same, conditions had improved for Western scholars. They were now able to conduct research in the

Soviet Union, albeit with limited and strictly controlled access to archives, whereas in earlier times conditions had been so difficult that many Western Soviet scholars never visited the Soviet Union at all, and others were summarily expelled as spies or subjected to various kinds of harassment.

As access to archives and primary sources in the Soviet Union improved, increasing numbers of young Western historians chose to study the Russian Revolution and Soviet history; and history started to displace political science as the dominant discipline in American Sovietology. That transition began in the late 1970s, and it presaged the coming of age of Western historical scholarship on the Russian Revolution in the 1980s. The interested reader may gauge the extent of the change by looking at the Bibliography and noting how many of the works listed there were published since the appearance of the first edition of this book in 1982.

Interpreting the revolution

All revolutions have *liberté, égalité, fraternité* and other noble slogans inscribed on their banners. All revolutionaries are enthusiasts, zealots; all are utopians, with dreams of creating a new world in which the injustice, corruption, and apathy of the old world are banished forever. They are intolerant of disagreement; incapable of compromise; mesmerized by big, distant goals; violent, suspicious, and destructive. Revolutionaries are unrealistic and inexperienced in government; their institutions and procedures are extemporized. They have the intoxicating illusion of personifying the will of the people, which means they assume the people is monolithic. They are Manicheans, dividing the world into two camps: light and darkness, the revolution and its enemies. They despise all traditions, received wisdom, icons, and superstition. They believe society can be a *tabula rasa* on which the revolution will write.

It is in the nature of revolutions to end in disillusionment and disappointment. Zeal wanes; enthusiasm becomes forced. The moment of madness and euphoria passes. The relationship of the people and the revolutionaries becomes complicated: it appears that the will of the people is not necessarily monolithic and transparent. The temptations of wealth and position return, along with the recognition that one does not love one's neighbour as oneself, and does not want to. All revolutions destroy things whose loss is soon regretted. What they create is less than the revolutionaries expected, and different.

Beyond the generic similarity, however, every revolution has its own character. Russia's location was peripheral, and its educated classes were preoccupied with the country's backwardness *vis-à-vis* Europe. The revolutionaries were Marxists who often substituted 'the proletariat' for 'the people' and claimed that revolution was historically necessary, not morally imperative. There were revolutionary parties in Russia before there was a revolution; and when the moment came, in the midst of war, these parties competed for the support of ready-made units of popular revolution (soldiers, sailors, workers in the big Petrograd factories), not the allegiance of a milling, spontaneous, revolutionary crowd.

In this book, three motifs have special importance. The first is the modernization theme—revolution as a means of escaping from backwardness. The second is the class theme—revolution as the mission of the proletariat and its 'vanguard', the Bolshevik Party. The third is the theme of revolutionary violence and terror—how the Revolution dealt with its enemies, and what this meant for the Bolshevik Party and Soviet state.

The term 'modernization' has begun to sound *passé* in an age that is often described as post-modern. But that is appropriate for our subject, since the industrial and technological modernity for which the Bolsheviks strove now seems hopelessly outdated: the giant smoke-stacks that clutter the landscape of the former Soviet Union and Eastern Europe like a herd of polluting dinosaurs were, in their time, the fulfilment of a revolutionary dream. Russian Marxists had fallen in love with Western-style industrialization long before the revolution; it was their insistence on the inevitability of capitalism (which primarily meant capitalist industrialization) that was the core of their argument with the Populists in the late nineteenth century. In Russia, as was later to be the case in the Third World, Marxism was both an ideology of revolution and an ideology of economic development.

In theory, industrialization and economic modernization were only means to an end for Russian Marxists, the end being socialism. But the more clearly and single-mindedly the Bolsheviks focused on the means, the more foggy, distant, and unreal the end became. When the term 'building socialism' came into common use in the 1930s, its meaning was hard to distinguish from the actual building of new factories and industrial towns that was currently in progress. To Communists of that generation, the new smoke-stacks puffing away on the steppe were the ultimate demonstration that the Revolution had been victorious. As Adam Ulam puts it, Stalin's forced-pace industrialization, however painful and coercive, was 'the logical complement of Marxism, "revolution fulfilled" rather than "revolution betrayed"'.[7]

Class, the second theme, was important in the Russian Revolution because the key participants perceived it as such. Marxist analytical categories were widely accepted in the Russian intelligentsia; and the Bolsheviks were not exceptional, but representative of a much broader socialist group, when they interpreted the Revolution in terms of class conflict and assigned a special role to the industrial working class. In power, the Bolsheviks assumed that proletarians and poor peasants were their natural allies. They also made the complementary assumption that members of the 'bourgeoisie'—a broad group encompassing former capitalists, former noble landowners and officials, small shopkeepers, kulaks (prosperous peasants), and even in some contexts the Russian intelligentsia—were their natural antagonists. They termed such people 'class enemies', and it was against them that the early revolutionary terror was primarily directed.

The aspect of the class issue that has been most hotly debated over the years is whether the Bolsheviks' claim to represent the working class was justified. This is perhaps a simple enough question if we look only at the summer and autumn of 1917, when the working class of Petrograd and Moscow were radicalized and clearly preferred the Bolsheviks to any other political party. After that, however, it is not so simple. The fact that the Bolsheviks took power with working-class support did not mean that they kept that support forever—or, for that matter, that they regarded their party, either before or after the seizure of power, as a mere mouthpiece of industrial workers.

The accusation that the Bolsheviks had betrayed the working class, first heard by the outside world in connection with the Kronstadt revolt of 1921, was one that was bound to come and likely to be true. But what kind of betrayal—how soon, with whom, with what consequences? In the NEP period, the Bolsheviks patched up the marriage with the working class that had seemed close to dissolution at the end of the Civil War. During the First Five-Year Plan, relations soured again because of falling real wages and urban living standards and the regime's insistent demands for higher productivity. An effective separation from the working class, if not a formal divorce, occurred in the 1930s.

But this is not the whole story. The situation of workers *qua* workers under Soviet power was one thing; the opportunities available to workers to better themselves (become something other than workers) was another. By recruiting party members primarily from the working class for fifteen years after the October Revolution, the Bolsheviks did a good deal to substantiate their claim to be a workers' party. They also created a broad channel for working-class upward mobility, since the recruitment of workers to party membership went hand in hand with the promotion of working-class Communists to white-collar administrative and managerial positions. During the Cultural Revolution at the end of the 1920s, the regime cut open another channel for upward mobility by sending large numbers of young workers and workers' children to higher education. While the policy of high-pressure 'proletarian promotion' was dropped in the early 1930s, its consequences remained. It was not workers that mattered in Stalin's regime but *former* workers—the newly-promoted 'proletarian core' in the managerial and professional elites. From the strict Marxist standpoint, such working-class upward mobility was perhaps of little interest. For the beneficiaries, however, their new elite status was likely to seem irrefutable proof that the Revolution had fulfilled its promises to the working class.

The last theme that runs through this book is the theme of revolutionary violence and terror. Popular violence is inherent in revolution; revolutionaries are likely to regard it very favourably in the early stages of revolution but with increasing reservations thereafter. Terror, meaning organized violence by revolutionary groups or regimes that intimidates and terrifies the general population, has also been characteristic of modern revolutions, with the French Revolution setting the pattern. The main purpose of terror, in the revolutionaries' eyes, is to destroy the enemies of the revolution and the impediments to change; but there is often a secondary purpose of maintaining the purity and revolutionary commitment of the revolutionaries themselves. Enemies and 'counter-revolutionaries' are extremely important in all revolutions. The enemies resist by stealth as well as openly; they foment plots and conspiracies; they often wear the mask of revolutionaries.

Following Marxist theory, the Bolsheviks conceptualized the

enemies of the revolution in terms of class. To be a noble, a capitalist, or a kulak was *ipso facto* evidence of counter-revolutionary sympathies. Like most revolutionaries (perhaps even more than most, given their prewar experience of underground party organization and conspiracy), the Bolsheviks were obsessed with counter-revolutionary plots; but their Marxism gave this a special twist. If there were classes that were innately inimical to the revolution, a whole social class could be regarded as a conspiracy of enemies. Individual members of that class might 'objectively' be counter-revolutionary conspirators, even if subjectively (that is, in their own minds) they knew nothing of the conspiracy and thought themselves supporters of the revolution.

The Bolsheviks used two kinds of terror in the Russian Revolution: terror against enemies outside the party, and terror against enemies within. The former was dominant in the early years of the Revolution, died down in the 1920s, and then flared up again at the end of the decade with collectivization and Cultural Revolution. The latter first flickered as a possibility during the party faction fights at the end of the Civil War, but was quashed until 1927, when a small-scale terror was directed against the Left Opposition.

From then on, the temptation to conduct full-scale terror against enemies within the party was palpable. One reason for this was that the regime was using terror on a considerable scale against 'class enemies' outside the party. Another reason was that the party's periodic purging (*chistki*, literally cleansings) of its own ranks had an effect similar to scratching an itch. These purges, first conducted on a national scale in 1921, were reviews of party membership in which all Communists were summoned individually for public appraisals of their loyalty, competence, background, and connections; and those judged unworthy were expelled from the party or demoted to candidate status. There was a national party purge in 1929, another in 1933–4, and then—as purging the party became an almost obsessive activity—two more party membership reviews in rapid succession in 1935 and 1936. Though the likelihood that expulsion might bring further punishment, such as arrest or exile, was still comparatively low, with each of these party purges it crept upwards.

Terror and party purging (with a small 'p') finally came together on a massive scale in the Great Purges of 1937–8.[8] This was not a purge in the usual sense, since no systematic review of party membership was involved; but it was directed in the first instance against party members, particularly those in high official positions, although arrests and fear quickly spread into the non-party intelligentsia and, to a lesser degree, the broader population. In the Great Purges, which would be more accurately described as the Great Terror,[9] suspicion was often equivalent to conviction, evidence of criminal acts was unnecessary, and the punishment for counter-revolutionary crimes was death or a labour-camp sentence. The analogy to the Terror of the French Revolution has occurred to many historians, and it clearly occurred to the organizers of the Great Purges as well, since the term 'enemies of the people', which was applied to those judged counter-revolutionaries during the Great Purges, was borrowed from the Jacobin terrorists. The significance of that suggestive historical borrowing is explored in the last chapter.

Notes on the second edition

The second edition of this book has benefited considerably from the opening of Soviet party and government archives and the end of Soviet censorship. The topics on which we have most new data are those that were previously proscribed in the Soviet Union: terror, repression, Gulag, censorship, the non-canonical Lenin and Stalin, and so on. The archives have yielded up classified Central Committee minutes and Politburo protocols, a suppressed population census, data on the famine of 1932–3 and the Great Purges, secret police reports, citizens' petitions and denunciations, and a host of other materials that historians are still in the process of digesting. Old political scandals have been exhumed and memoirs published. Our picture of Soviet politics and society, especially in the 1930s, is much richer and more detailed than it was even five years ago.

This is reflected in the new edition, which incorporates as much material from the new sources as could be fitted in without upsetting the balance of the narrative, as well as additional footnote references to important new sources in English and Russian. The Bibliography is largely new because so much English-language scholarship on the Russian Revolution has been published in the last decade; it includes the works of Russian scholars from the Gorbachev and post-Soviet eras where these are available in English. With the exception of the Introduction, the only major structural change is in Chapter 6, which ends with a new section on the Great Purges.

Like the first edition, this second edition is essentially a history of the Russian Revolution as experienced in Russia, not in the non-Russian territories that were part of the old Russian Empire and the Soviet Union.

1 The Setting

AT the beginning of the twentieth century, Russia was one of the great powers of Europe. But it was a great power that was universally regarded as backward by comparison with Britain, Germany, and France. In economic terms, this meant that it had been late to emerge from feudalism (the peasants were freed from legal bondage to their lords or the state only in the 1860s) and late in industrializing. In political terms, it meant that until 1905 there were no legal political parties and no central elected parliament, and the autocracy survived with undiminished powers. Russia's towns had no tradition of political organization or self-government, and its nobility had similarly failed to develop a corporate sense of identity strong enough to force concessions from the throne. Legally, Russia's citizens still belonged to 'estates' (urban, peasant, clergy, and noble), even though the estate system made no provision for new social groups like professionals and urban workers, and only the clergy retained anything like the characteristics of a self-contained caste.

The three decades before the 1917 Revolution saw not impoverishment but an increase in national wealth; and it was in this period that Russia experienced its first spurt of economic growth as a result of the government's industrialization policies, foreign investment, modernization of the banking and credit structure, and a modest development of native entrepreneurial activity. The peasantry, which still constituted 80 per cent of Russia's population at the time of the Revolution, had not experienced a marked improvement in its economic position. But, contrary to some contemporary opinions, there had almost certainly not been a steady deterioration in the peasantry's economic situation either.

As Russia's last Tsar, Nicholas II, sadly perceived, the autocracy was fighting a losing battle against insidious liberal influences from the West. The direction of political change—towards something like a Western constitutional monarchy—seemed clear, though many members of the educated classes were impatient at the slowness of change and the stubbornly obstructionist attitude of the autocracy. After the 1905 Revolution, Nicholas gave in and established a national elected parliament, the Duma, at the same time legalizing political parties and trade unions. But the old arbitrary habits of autocratic rule and the continued activity of the secret police undermined these concessions.

After the Bolshevik Revolution of October 1917, many Russian emigrés looked back on the prerevolutionary years as a golden age of progress which had been arbitrarily interrupted (as it seemed) by the First World War, or the unruly mob, or the Bolsheviks. There was progress, but it contributed a great deal to the society's instability and the likelihood of political upheaval: the more rapidly a society changes (whether that change is perceived as progressive or regressive) the less stable it is likely to be. If we think of the great literature of prerevolutionary Russia, the most vivid images are those of displacement, alienation, and lack of control over one's destiny. To the nineteenth-century writer Nikolai Gogol, Russia was a troika careering in darkness to an unknown destination. To the Duma politician Aleksandr Guchkov, denouncing Nicholas II and his Ministers in 1916, it was a car steered along the edge of a precipice by a mad driver, whose terrified passengers were debating the risk of seizing the wheel. In 1917 the risk was taken, and Russia's headlong movement forward became a plunge into revolution.

The society

The Russian Empire covered a vast expanse of territory, stretching from Poland in the west to the Pacific Ocean in the east, extending into the Arctic north, and reaching the Black Sea and the borders of Turkey and Afghanistan in the south. The hub of the Empire, European Russia (including some of the area that is now Ukraine) had a population of 92 million in 1897, with the total population of the Empire recorded by that year's census at 126 million.[1] But even European Russia and the relatively advanced western regions of the Empire remained largely rural and non-urbanized. There were a handful of big urban industrial centres, most of them the product of recent and rapid expansion: St Petersburg, the imperial capital, renamed Petrograd during the First World War and Leningrad in 1924; Moscow, the old and (from 1918) future capital; Kiev, Kharkov, and Odessa, together with the new mining and metallurgical centres of the Donbass, in what is now Ukraine; Warsaw, Lodz, and Riga in the west; Rostov and the oil city of Baku in the south. But most Russian provincial towns were still sleepy backwaters at the beginning of the twentieth century—local administrative centres with a small merchant population, a few schools, a peasant market, and perhaps a railway station.

In the villages, much of the traditional way of life remained. The peasants still held their land in communal tenure, dividing the village fields into narrow strips which were tilled separately by the various peasant households; and in many villages, the *mir* (village council) would still periodically redistribute the strips so that each household had an equal share. Wooden ploughs were in common use, modern farming techniques were unknown in the villages, and peasant agriculture was not much above subsistence level. The peasants' huts were clustered together along the village street, peasants slept on the stove and kept their animals with them in the house, and the old patriarchal structure of the peasant family survived. The peasants were not much more than a generation away from serfdom: a peasant who was sixty at the turn of the century was already a young adult at the time of the Emancipation of 1861.

Of course the Emancipation had changed peasant life, but it had been framed with great caution so as to minimize the change and spread it over time. Before Emancipation, the peasants worked their strips of the village land, and they also worked the masters' land or paid him the equivalent of their labour in money. After the Emancipation, they continued to work their own land, and sometimes worked for hire on their former masters' land, while making 'redemption' payments to the state to offset the lump sums that had been given the landowners as immediate compensation. The redemption payments were scheduled to last for forty-nine years (although in fact the state cancelled them a few years early), and the village community was collectively responsible for the debts of all members. This meant that individual peasants were still bound to the village, though they were bound by the debt and the *mir*'s collective responsibility instead of by serfdom. The terms of the Emancipation were intended to prevent a mass influx of peasants into the towns and the creation of a landless proletariat which would represent a danger to public order. They also had the effect of reinforcing the *mir* and the old system of communal land tenure, and making it almost impossible for peasants to consolidate their strips, expand or improve their holdings, or make the transition to independent small-farming.

While permanent departure from the villages was difficult in the post-Emancipation decades, it was easy to leave the villages temporarily to work for hire in agriculture, construction, mining, or in the towns. In fact such work was a necessity for many peasant families: the money was needed for taxes and redemption payments. The peasants who worked as seasonal labourers (*otkhodniki*) were often away for many months of the year, leaving their families to till their land in the villages. If the journeys were long—as in the case of peasants from central Russian villages who went to work in the Donbass mines—the *otkhodniki* might return only for the harvest and perhaps the spring sowing. The practice of departing for seasonal work was long-established, especially in the less fertile areas of European Russia where the landlords had exacted payment in money rather than labour from their serfs. But it was becoming increasingly common in the late nineteenth and early twentieth century, partly because more work was available in the towns. In the years immediately before the First World War, about nine million peasants took out passports for seasonal work outside their native village each year, and of these almost half were working outside agriculture.[2]

With one in every two peasant households in European Russia including a family member who left the village for work—and a higher proportion in the Petersburg and Central Industrial Regions and the western provinces—the impression that old Russia survived almost unchanged in the villages may well have been deceptive. Many peasants were in fact living with one foot in the traditional village world and the other in the quite different world of the modern industrial town. The degree to which peasants remained within the traditional world varied not only according to geographical location but also according to age and sex. The young were more likely to go away to work, and in addition the young men came in contact with a more modern world when they were called up for army service. Women and the aged were more likely to know only the village and the old peasant way of life. These differences in peasant experience showed up strikingly in the literacy figures of the 1897 census. The young were very much more literate than the old, men were more literate than women, and literacy was higher in the less fertile areas of European Russia—that is, the areas where seasonal migration was most common—than in the fertile Black Earth region.[3]

The urban working class was still very close to the peasantry. The number of permanent industrial workers (somewhat over three million in 1914) was smaller than the number of peasants who left the villages for non-agricultural seasonal work each year, and in fact it was almost impossible to make a hard-and-fast distinction between permanent urban-dwelling workers and peasants who worked most of the year in the towns. Even among the permanent workers, many retained land in the village and had left their wives and children living there; other workers lived in villages themselves (a pattern that was particularly common in the Moscow area) and commuted on a daily or weekly basis to the factory. Only in St Petersburg had a large proportion of the industrial labour force severed all connection with the countryside.

The main reason for the close interconnection between the urban working class and the peasantry was that Russia's rapid industrialization was a very recent phenomenon. It was not until the 1890s— more than half a century after Britain—that Russia experienced large-scale growth of industry and expansion of towns. Even then, the creation of a permanent urban working class was inhibited by the terms of the peasants' Emancipation in the 1860s, which kept them tied to the villages. First-generation workers, predominantly from the peasantry, formed a large part of the Russian working class; and few were more than second-generation workers and urban dwellers. Although Soviet historians claim that more than 50 per cent of industrial workers on the eve of the First World War were at least second-generation, this calculation clearly includes workers and peasant *otkhodniki* whose fathers had been *otkhodniki*.

Despite these characteristics of underdevelopment, Russian industry was in some respects quite advanced by the time of the First World War. The modern industrial sector was small, but unusually highly concentrated, both geographically (notably in the regions centred on Petersburg and Moscow and the Ukrainian Donbass) and in terms of the size of the industrial plants. As Gerschenkron has pointed out, comparative backwardness had its own advantages: industrializing late, with the aid of large-scale foreign investment and energetic state involvement, Russia was able to skip over some of the early stages, borrow relatively advanced technology and move quickly towards large-scale modern production.[4] Enterprises like the famous Putilov metalworking and machine-building plant in Petersburg and the largely foreign-owned metallurgical plants of the Donbass employed many thousands of workers.

According to Marxist theory, a highly concentrated industrial

proletariat in conditions of advanced capitalist production is likely to
be revolutionary, whereas a pre-modern working class that retains
strong ties to the peasantry is not. Thus the Russian working class
had contradictory characteristics for a Marxist diagnosing its revolutionary potential. Yet the empirical evidence of the period from the
1890s to 1914 suggests that in fact Russia's working class, despite its
close links with the peasantry, was exceptionally militant and revolutionary. Large-scale strikes were frequent, the workers showed
considerable solidarity against management and state authority, and
their demands were usually political as well as economic. In the 1905
Revolution, the workers of St Petersburg and Moscow organized
their own revolutionary institutions, the soviets, and continued the
struggle after the Tsar's constitutional concessions in October and
the collapse of the middle-class liberals' drive against the autocracy.
In the summer of 1914, the workers' strike movement in Petersburg
and elsewhere assumed such threatening dimensions that some
observers thought that the government could not take the risk of
declaring a general mobilization for war.

The strength of working-class revolutionary sentiment in Russia
may be explained in a number of different ways. In the first place,
limited economic protest against employers—what Lenin called
trade unionism—was very difficult under Russian conditions. The
government had a large stake in Russia's native industry and in the
protection of foreign investment, and state authorities were quick to
provide troops when strikes against private enterprise showed signs
of getting out of hand. That meant that even economic strikes
(protests over wages and conditions) were likely to turn political; and
the widespread resentment of Russian workers against foreign managers and technical personnel had a similar effect. Although it was
Lenin, a Russian Marxist, who said that by its own efforts the
working class could develop only a 'trade-union consciousness' rather
than a revolutionary one, Russia's own experience (in contrast to
that of Western Europe) did not bear him out.

In the second place, the peasant component of Russia's working
class probably made it more revolutionary rather than less. Russian
peasants were not innately conservative small proprietors like, for
example, their French counterparts. The Russian peasantry's tradition of violent, anarchic rebellion against landowners and officials,
exemplified in the great Pugachev revolt of the 1770s, was manifest

once again in the peasant uprisings of 1905 and 1906: the Emancipation of 1861 had not permanently quietened the peasants' spirit of
revolt because they did not regard it as a just or adequate emancipation and, increasingly land-hungry, asserted their right to the land
that had been withheld. Moreover, the peasants who migrated to
towns and became workers were often young, freed from family
constraints but still unused to the discipline of the factory, and
bearing the resentments and frustrations that go with dislocation and
incomplete assimilation to an unfamiliar environment.[5] To some
extent, the Russian working class was revolutionary just because it
had not had time to acquire the 'trade-union consciousness' of which
Lenin wrote—to become a settled industrial proletariat, capable of
protecting its interests by non-revolutionary means, and understanding the opportunities for upward mobility that modern urban
societies offer those with some education and skills.

However, the 'modern' characteristics of Russian society, even in
the urban sector and the upper educated strata, were still very
incomplete. It was often said that Russia had no middle class; and
indeed its business and commercial class remained comparatively
weak, and the professions had only recently acquired the status
normal in industrialized societies. Despite increasing professionali-
zation of the state bureaucracy, its upper ranks remained dominated
by the nobility, traditionally the state's service class. Service prerog-
atives were all the more important to the nobility because of its
economic decline as a landowning group after the abolition of
serfdom: only a minority of noble landowners had successfully made
the transition to capitalist, market-oriented agriculture.

The schizoid nature of Russian society in the early twentieth century
is well illustrated by the bewildering variety of self-identifications
offered by subscribers to the city directories of St Petersburg, the
largest and most modern of Russia's cities. Some subscribers kept to
the traditional forms and identified themselves by social estate and
rank ('hereditary noble', 'merchant of the First Guild', 'honoured
citizen', 'State Counsellor'). Others clearly belonged to the new
world, and described themselves in terms of profession and type
of employment ('stockbroker', 'mechanical engineer', 'company
director', or, as representative of Russia's achievements in female
emancipation, 'woman doctor'). A third group consisted of persons
who were uncertain which world they belonged to, identifying

themselves by estate in one year's directory and by profession in the next, or even giving both identifications at once, like the subscriber who listed himself quaintly as 'nobleman, dentist'.

In less formal contexts, educated Russians would often describe themselves as members of the intelligentsia. Sociologically, this was a very slippery concept, but in broad terms the word 'intelligentsia' described a Westernized educated elite, alienated from the rest of Russian society by its education and from Russia's autocratic regime by its radical ideology. However, the Russian intelligentsia did not see itself as an elite, but rather as a classless group united by moral concern for the betterment of society, the capacity for 'critical thought' and, in particular, a critical, semi-oppositionist attitude to the regime. The term came into common use around the middle of the nineteenth century, but the genesis of the concept may be found in the latter part of the eighteenth century, when the nobility was released from the obligation of compulsory service to the state, and some of its members, educated but finding their education under-utilized, developed an alternative ethos of obligation to 'serve the people'.[6] Ideally (though not altogether in practice), intelligentsia membership and bureaucratic service were incompatible. The Russian revolutionary movement of the second half of the nineteenth century, characterized by small-scale conspiratorial organization to fight the autocracy and thus liberate the people, was largely a product of the intelligentsia's radical ideology and political disaffection.

By the end of the century, when the development of high-status professions had provided educated Russians with a broader range of occupational choice than had existed earlier, an individual's self-definition as an *intelligent* often implied relatively passive liberal attitudes rather than active revolutionary commitment to political change. Still, Russia's new professional class inherited enough of the old intelligentsia tradition to feel sympathy and respect for the committed revolutionaries, and lack of sympathy for the regime, even when its officials tried to pursue reforming policies or were assassinated by revolutionary terrorists.

Moreover, some types of professional avocation were peculiarly difficult to combine with total support for the autocracy. The legal profession, for example, blossomed as a result of the reform of the legal system in the 1860s, but the reforms were much less successful in the long term in extending the rule of law in Russian society and administration, particularly in the period of reaction that followed

the assassination of Emperor Alexander II by a group of revolutionary terrorists in 1881. Lawyers whose education had led them to
believe in the rule of law were likely to disapprove of arbitrary
administrative practices, untrammelled police power and governmental attempts to influence the working of the judicial system.[7] A
similar inherent adversary relationship to the regime was associated
with the zemstvos, elected local-government bodies that were insti-
tutionally quite separate from the state bureaucracy and frequently
in conflict with it. In the early twentieth century, the zemstvos
employed around 70,000 professionals (doctors, teachers, agrono-
mists and so on), whose radical sympathies were notorious.

Engineers and other technical specialists working for the state or
in private enterprises had less obvious reason to feel alienated from
the regime, especially given the energetic sponsorship of economic
modernization and industrialization that came from the Ministry of
Finance under Sergei Witte in the 1890s and subsequently from the
Ministry of Trade and Industry. Witte, indeed, made every effort to
rally support for the autocracy and its modernization drive among
Russia's technical specialists and businessmen; but the problem was
that Witte's enthusiasm for economic and technological progress was
obviously not shared by a large part of Russia's bureaucratic elite, as
well as being personally uncongenial to Emperor Nicholas II.
Modernization-minded professionals and entrepreneurs might not
object in principle to the idea of autocratic government (though in
fact many of them did, as a result of their exposure to radical politics
as students of the Polytechnical Institutes). But it was very difficult
for them to see the *Tsarist* autocracy as an effective agent of
modernization: its record was too inconsistent, and its political
ideology too clearly reflected nostalgia for the past rather than any
coherent vision of the future.

The revolutionary tradition

The task which the Russian intelligentsia had taken on itself was the
betterment of Russia—first, drawing up the social and political blue-
prints for the country's future, and then, if possible, taking action to
translate them into reality. The yardstick for Russia's future was
Western Europe's present. Russian intellectuals might decide to accept
or reject different phenomena that were observed in Europe, but all
were on the agenda for Russian discussion and possible inclusion in

the plans for Russia's future. In the third quarter of the nineteenth century, one of the central topics of discussion was Western European industrialization and its social and political consequences.

One view was that capitalist industrialization had produced human degradation, impoverishment of the masses, and destruction of the social fabric in the West, and therefore ought to be avoided at all costs by Russia. The radical intellectuals who held this view have been retrospectively grouped under the heading of 'Populists', though the label implies a degree of coherent organization which did not in fact exist (it was originally used by the Russian Marxists to differentiate themselves from all the various intelligentsia groups that disagreed with them). Populism was essentially the mainstream of Russian radical thought from the 1860s to the 1880s.

The Russian intelligentsia generally accepted socialism (as understood by Europe's pre-Marxist socialists, especially the French 'utopians') as the most desirable form of social organization, though this was not seen as incompatible with the acceptance of liberalism as an ideology of political change. The intelligentsia also reacted to its social isolation by a fervent desire to bridge the gulf between itself and 'the people' (*narod*). The strain of intelligentsia thought described as Populism combined anobjection to capitalist industrialization with an idealization of the Russian peasantry. The Populists saw that capitalism had had a destructive impact on traditional rural communities in Europe, uprooting peasants from the land and forcing them into the cities as a landless and exploited industrial proletariat. They wished to save the Russian peasants' traditional form of village organization, the commune or *mir*, from the ravages of capitalism, because they believed that the *mir* was an egalitarian institution—perhaps a survival of primitive communism—through which Russia might find a separate path to socialism.

In the early 1870s, the intelligentsia's idealization of the peasantry and frustration with its own situation and the prospects for political reform led to the spontaneous mass movement which best exemplifies Populist aspirations—the 'going to the people' of 1873-4. Thousands of students and members of the intelligentsia left the cities to go to the villages, sometimes envisaging themselves as enlighteners of the peasantry, sometimes more humbly seeking to acquire the simple wisdom of the people, and sometimes with the hope of conducting revolutionary organization and propaganda. The movement had no central direction and no clearly defined political intent as far as most of the participants were concerned: its spirit was less that of a political campaign than a religious pilgrimage. But the distinction was hard for either the peasantry or the Tsarist police to grasp. The authorities were greatly alarmed, and made mass arrests. The peasants were suspicious, regarding their uninvited guests as off-spring of the nobility and probable class enemies, and often handing them over to the police. This débâcle produced deep disappointment among the Populists. They did not waver in their determination to serve the people, but some concluded that it was their tragic fate to serve them as outcasts, revolutionary desperadoes whose heroic actions would be appreciated only after their deaths. There was an upsurge of revolutionary terrorism in the late 1870s, motivated partly by the Populists' desire to avenge their imprisoned comrades and partly by the rather desperate hope that a well-placed blow might destroy the whole superstructure of autocratic Russia, leaving the Russian people free to find its own destiny. In 1881, the 'People's Will' group of Populist terrorists succeeded in assassinating Emperor Alexander II. The effect was not to destroy the autocracy, but rather to frighten it into more repressive policies, greater arbitrariness and circumvention of law, and the creation of something close to a modern police state.[8] The popular response to the assassination included anti semitic pogroms in the Ukraine, and rumours in Russia's villages that nobles had murdered the Tsar because he had freed the peasants from serfdom.

It was in the 1880s, in the wake of the two Populist disasters, that the Marxists emerged as a distinct group within the Russian intelligentsia, repudiating the utopian idealism, terrorist tactics, and peasant orientation that had previously characterized the revolutionary movement. Because of the unfavourable political climate in Russia and their own repudiation of terrorism, the Marxists made their initial impact in intellectual debate rather than by revolutionary action. They argued that capitalist industrialization was inevitable in Russia, and that the peasant *mir* was already in a state of internal disintegration, propped up only by the state and its state-imposed responsibilities for the collection of taxes and redemption payments. They asserted that capitalism constituted the only possible path towards socialism, and that the industrial proletariat produced by capitalist development was the only class capable of bringing about true socialist revolution. These premises, they claimed, could be scientifically proven by the objective laws of historical development that Marx and Engels had explained in their writings. The Marxists scoffed at those who chose socialism as an ideology because it was ethically superior (it was, of course, but that was beside the point). The point about socialism was that, like capitalism, it was a predictable stage in the development of human society.

To Karl Marx, an old European revolutionary who instinctively applauded the struggle of 'People's Will' against the Russian autocracy, the early Russian Marxists clustered around Georgii Plekhanov in emigration seemed too passive and pedantic—revolutionaries who were content to write articles about the historical inevitability of revolution while others were fighting and dying for the cause. But the impact on the Russian intelligentsia was different, because one of the Marxists' scientific predictions was quickly realized: they said that Russia *must* industrialize, and in the 1890s, under Witte's energetic direction, it did. True, the industrialization was as much a product of state sponsorship and foreign investment as of spontaneous capitalist development, so that in a sense Russia did take a separate path from the West.[9] But to contemporaries, Russia's rapid industrialization seemed dramatic proof that the Marxists' predictions were right, and that Marxism had at least some of the answers to the Russian intelligentsia's 'great questions'.

Marxism in Russia—as in China, India, and other developing countries—had a meaning rather different from that which it had in the industrialized countries of Western Europe. It was an ideology of modernization as well as an ideology of revolution. Even Lenin, who could scarcely be accused of revolutionary passivity, made his name as a Marxist with a weighty study, *The Development of Capitalism in Russia*, that was both analysis and advocacy of the process of economic modernization; and virtually all the other leading Marxists of his generation in Russia produced similar works. The advocacy, to be sure, is presented in the Marxist manner ('I told you so' rather than 'I support . . .'), and it may surprise modern readers who know Lenin only as an anti-capitalist revolutionary. But capitalism was a 'progressive' phenomenon to ˙Marxists in late nineteenth-century Russia, a backward society that by Marxist definition was still semi-feudal. In ideological terms, they were in favour of capitalism because it was a necessary stage on the way to socialism. But in emotional terms, the commitment went deeper: the Russian Marxists admired the modern, industrial, urban world, and were offended by the backwardness of old rural Russia. It has often been pointed out that Lenin—an activist revolutionary willing to give history a push in the right direction—was an unorthodox Marxist with some of the revolutionary voluntarism of the old Populist tradition. That is true, but it is relevant mainly to his behaviour in times of actual revolution, around 1905 and in 1917. In the 1890s, he chose Marxism rather than Populism because he was on the side of modernization; and that basic choice explains a great deal about the course of the Russian revolution after Lenin and his party took power in 1917.

The Marxists made another important choice in the early controversy with the Populists over capitalism: they chose the urban working class as their base of support and Russia's main potential force for revolution. This distinguished them from the old tradition of the Russian revolutionary intelligentsia (upheld by the Populists and later, from its formation in the early 1900s, by the Socialist-Revolutionary (SR) Party), with its one-sided love affair with the peasantry. It distinguished them also from the liberals (some of them former Marxists), whose Liberation movement was to emerge as a political force shortly before 1905, since the liberals hoped for a 'bourgeois' revolution and won support from the new professional class and the liberal zemstvo nobility.

Initially, the Marxists' choice did not look particularly promising: the working class was tiny in comparison with the peasantry, and, in comparison with the urban upper classes, lacked status, education and financial resources. The Marxists' early contacts with the workers were essentially educational, consisting of circles and study groups in which intellectuals offered the workers some general education plus the elements of Marxism. Historians differ in their assessment of the contribution that this made to the development of a revolutionary labour movement.[10] But the Tsarist authorities took the political threat fairly seriously. According to a police report in 1901,[11]

Agitators, seeking to realize their goals, have achieved some success, unfortunately, in organizing the workers to fight against the government. Within the last three or four years, the easygoing Russian young man has been transformed into a special type of semi-literate *intelligent*, who feels obliged to spurn family and religion, to disregard the law, and to deny and scoff at constituted authority. Fortunately such young men are not numerous in the factories, but this negligible handful terrorizes the inert majority of workers into following it.

Clearly Marxists had an advantage over earlier groups of revolutionary intellectuals seeking contact with the masses: they had found a
section of the masses willing to listen. Although Russian workers
were not far removed from the peasantry, they were a much more
literate group, and at least some of them had acquired a modern,
urban sense of the possibility of 'bettering themselves'. Education
was a means of upward social mobility as well as the path towards
revolution envisaged by both revolutionary intellectuals and the
police. The Marxist teachers, unlike the earlier Populist missionaries
to the peasantry, had something more than the risk of police
harassment to offer their students.

From workers' education, the Marxists—illegally organized from
1898 as the Russian Social-Democratic Labour Party—progressed to
an involvement in more directly political labour organization, strikes
and, in 1905, revolution. The match between party-political organization and actual working-class protest was never an exact one, and
in 1905 the socialist parties had great difficulty keeping up with the
working-class revolutionary movement. Between 1898 and 1914,
nevertheless, the Russian Social-Democratic Labour Party ceased to
be a preserve of the intelligentsia and became in the literal sense a
workers' movement. Its leaders still came from the intelligentsia,
and spent most of their time living outside Russia in European
emigration. But in Russia, the majority of members and activists
were workers (or, in the case of professional revolutionaries, former
workers).[12]

In terms of their theory, the Russian Marxists started off with
what seemed to be a major revolutionary disadvantage: they were
obliged to work not for the coming revolution, but for the revolution
after next. According to orthodox Marxist prediction, Russia's entry
into the capitalist phase (which took place only at the end of the
nineteenth century) would inevitably lead to the overthrow of the
autocracy by a bourgeois liberal revolution. The proletariat might
support this revolution, but it seemed unlikely to have more than a
secondary role. Russia would be ripe for proletarian socialist revolution only after capitalism had reached its maturity, and that time
might be far in the future.

This problem did not seem very pressing before 1905, since no
revolution was in progress and the Marxists were having some
success in organizing the working class. However, a small group—
the 'legal Marxists', headed by Petr Struve—came to identify itself

strongly with the objectives of the first (liberal) revolution on the Marxist agenda, and to lose interest in the ultimate goal of socialist revolution. It was not surprising that modernization-minded opponents of the autocracy like Struve should have joined the Marxists in the 1890s, since there was at that time no liberal movement for them to join; and it was equally natural that around the turn of the century they left the Marxists to participate in the establishment of the liberal Liberation movement. The heresy of legal Marxism was nevertheless roundly denounced by Russian Social-Democratic leaders, especially by Lenin. Lenin's violent hostility to 'bourgeois liberalism' was somewhat illogical in Marxist terms, and caused some perplexity to his colleagues. In revolutionary terms, however, Lenin's attitude was extremely rational.

At around the same time, the Russian Social-Democratic leaders repudiated the heresy of Economism, that is, that the workers' movement should stress economic rather than political goals. There were in fact few articulate Economists in the Russian movement, partly because Russian workers' protests tended to progress very quickly from purely economic issues like wages to political ones. But the emigré leaders, often more sensitive to trends within European Social Democracy than to the situation inside Russia, feared the revisionist and reformist tendencies that had developed in the German movement. In the doctrinal struggles over Economism and legal Marxism, the Russian Marxists were putting clearly on record that they were revolutionaries, not reformists, and that their cause was the socialist workers' revolution and not the revolution of the liberal bourgeoisie.

In 1903, when the Russian Social-Democratic Party held its Second Congress, the leaders fell into dispute over an apparently minor issue—the composition of the editorial board of the party newspaper *Iskra*.[13] No real substantive questions were involved, though to the extent that the dispute revolved around Lenin it might be said that he himself was the underlying issue, and that his colleagues considered that he was too aggressively seeking a position of dominance. Lenin's manner at the congress was overbearing; and he had recently been laying down the law very decisively on various theoretical questions, notably the organization and functions of the party. There was tension between Lenin and Plekhanov, the senior Russian Marxist; and the friendship between Lenin and his contemporary Yulii Martov was on the point of breaking.

The outcome of the Second Congress was a split in the Russian Social-Democratic Labour Party between 'Bolshevik' and 'Menshevik' factions. The Bolsheviks were those who followed Lenin's lead, and the Mensheviks (including Plekhanov, Martov, and Trotsky) constituted a larger and more diverse group of party members who thought Lenin had overreached himself. The split made little sense to Marxists inside Russia, and at the time of its occurrence was not regarded as irrevocable even by the emigrés. It proved, nevertheless, to be permanent; and as time passed the two factions acquired more clearly distinct identities than they had had in 1903. In later years, Lenin was sometimes to express pride in being a 'splitter', meaning by this that he considered large, loosely-knit political organizations to be less effective than smaller, disciplined radical groups demanding a high degree of commitment and ideological unity. But some people also attributed this trait to his difficulty in tolerating disagreement—that 'malicious suspiciousness' that Trotsky called 'a caricature of Jacobin intolerance' in a prerevolutionary polemic.[14]

In the years after 1903, the Mensheviks emerged as the more orthodox in their Marxism (not counting Trotsky, a Menshevik until mid-1917 but always a maverick), less inclined to force the pace of events towards revolution and less interested in creating a tightly organized and disciplined revolutionary party. They had more success than the Bolsheviks in attracting support in the non-Russian areas of the Empire, while the Bolsheviks had the edge among Russian workers. (In both parties, however, Jews and other non-Russians were prominent in the intelligentsia-dominated leadership.) In the last prewar years, 1910–14, the Mensheviks lost working-class support to the Bolsheviks as the workers' mood became more militant: they were perceived as a more 'respectable' party with closer links to the bourgeoisie, whereas the Bolsheviks were seen as more working-class as well as more revolutionary.[15]

The Bolsheviks, unlike the Mensheviks, had a single leader, and their identity was in large part defined by Lenin's ideas and personality. Lenin's first distinctive trait as a Marxist theoretician was his emphasis on party organization. He saw the party not only as the vanguard of proletarian revolution but also in a sense as its creator, since he argued that the proletariat alone could achieve only a trade-union consciousness and not a revolutionary one.

Lenin believed that the core of the party's membership should consist of full-time professional revolutionaries, recruited both from the intelligentsia and the working class, but concentrating on the political organization of workers rather than any other social group. In *What Is To Be Done?* (1902), he insisted on the importance of centralization, strict discipline, and ideological unity within the party. These, of course, were logical prescriptions for a party operating clandestinely in a police state. Nevertheless, it seemed to many of Lenin's contemporaries (and later to many scholars) that Lenin's dislike of looser mass organizations allowing greater diversity and spontaneity was not purely expedient but reflected a natural authoritarian bent.

Lenin differed from many other Russian Marxists in seeming actively to desire a proletarian revolution rather than simply predicting that one would ultimately occur. This was a character trait that would surely have endeared him to Karl Marx, despite the fact that it required some revision of orthodox Marxism. The idea that the liberal bourgeoisie must be the natural leader of Russia's anti-autocratic revolution was never really acceptable to Lenin; and in *Two Tactics of Social Democracy*, written in the midst of the 1905 Revolution, he insisted that the proletariat—allied with Russia's rebellious peasantry—could and should play a dominant role. Clearly it was necessary for any Russian Marxist with serious revolutionary intentions to find a way round the doctrine of bourgeois revolutionary leadership, and Trotsky was to make a similar and perhaps more successful effort with his theory of 'permanent revolution'. In Lenin's writing from 1905, the words 'dictatorship', 'insurrection', and 'civil war' appeared increasingly frequently. It was in these harsh, violent, and realistic terms that he conceived the future revolutionary transfer of power.

The 1905 Revolution and its aftermath; the First World War

Late Tsarist Russia was an expanding imperial power with the largest standing army of any of the great powers of Europe. It strength *vis-à-vis* the outside world was a source of pride, an achievement that could be set against the country's internal political and social problems. In the words attributed to an early twentieth-century Minister of Interior, 'a small victorious war' was the best remedy for Russia's domestic unrest. Historically, however, this was a rather dubious proposition. Over the past half century, Russia's wars had tended neither to be successful nor to strengthen society's confidence in the government. The military humiliation of the Crimean War had precipitated the radical domestic reforms of the 1860s. The diplomatic defeat that Russia suffered after its military involvement in the Balkans in the late 1870s produced an internal political crisis that ended only with Alexander II's assassination. In the early 1900s, Russian expansion in the Far East was pushing it towards a conflict with another expansionist power in the region, Japan. Though some of Nicholas II's ministers urged caution, the prevailing sentiment in court and high bureaucratic circles was that there were easy pickings to be made in the Far East, and that Japan—an inferior, non-European power, after all—would not be a formidable adversary. Initiated by Japan, but provoked almost equally by Russian policy in the Far East, the Russo-Japanese War broke out in January 1904.

For Russia, the war turned out to be a series of disasters and humiliations on land and at sea. The early patriotic enthusiasm of respectable society quickly soured, and—as had also happened during the 1891 famine—attempts by public organizations like the zemstvos to help the government in an emergency only led to conflicts with the bureaucracy and frustration. This fuelled the liberal movement, since autocracy always seemed least tolerable when it was most clearly perceived as incompetent and inefficient; and the zemstvo nobility and professionals rallied behind the illegal Liberation movement, directed from Europe by Petr Struve and other liberal activists. In the last months of 1904, with the war still in progress, the liberals in Russia organized a banquet campaign (modelled on that used against the French King, Louis Philippe, in 1847), through which the social elite demonstrated support for the idea of constitutional reform. At the same time, the government was under other kinds of pressure, including terrorist attacks on officials, student demonstrations and workers' strikes. In January 1905, Petersburg workers held a peaceful demonstration—organized not by militants and revolutionaries, but by a renegade priest with police connections, Father Gapon—to bring their economic grievances to the attention of the Tsar. On Bloody Sunday (9 January), troops fired on the demonstrators outside the Winter Palace, and the 1905 Revolution had begun.

The spirit of national solidarity against the autocracy was very strong during the first nine months of 1905. The liberals' claim to leadership of the revolutionary movement was not seriously challenged; and their bargaining position with the regime was based not only on support from the zemstvos and the new unions of middle-class professionals but also on the heterogeneous pressures coming from student demonstrations, workers' strikes, peasant disorders, mutinies in the armed forces, and unrest in the non-Russian regions of the Empire. The autocracy, for its part, was consistently on the defensive, seized by panic and confusion, and apparently unable to restore order. Its prospects for survival improved markedly when Witte managed to negotiate peace with Japan (the Treaty of Portsmouth) on remarkably advantageous terms in late August 1905. But the regime still had a million of its troops in Manchuria, and they could not be brought home on the Trans-Siberian Railway until the striking railwaymen were brought back under control.

The culmination of the liberal revolution was Nicholas II's October Manifesto (1905), in which he conceded the principle of a constitution and promised to create a national elected parliament, the Duma. The Manifesto divided the liberals: the Octobrists accepted it, while the Constitutional Democrats (Cadets) formally withheld acceptance and hoped for further concessions. In practice, however, the liberals withdrew from revolutionary activity at this time, and concentrated their energies on organizing the new Octobrist and Cadet parties and preparing for the forthcoming Duma elections.

However, the workers remained actively revolutionary until the end of the year, achieving greater visibility than before and becoming increasingly militant. In October, the workers of Petersburg organized a 'soviet' or council of workers' representatives elected in the factories. The practical function of the Petersburg Soviet was to provide the city with a kind of emergency municipal government at a time when other institutions were paralysed and a general strike was in progress. But it also became a political forum for the workers, and to a lesser extent for socialists from the revolutionary parties (Trotsky, then a Menshevik, became one of the Soviet's leaders). For a few months, the Tsarist authorities handled the Soviet in a gingerly manner, and similar bodies emerged in Moscow and other cities. But early in December it was dispersed by a successful police operation. The news of the attack on the Petersburg Soviet led to an armed uprising by the Moscow Soviet, in which the Bolsheviks had gained considerable influence. This was put down by troops, but the workers fought back and there were many casualties.

The urban revolution of 1905 stimulated the most serious peasant uprisings since the Pugachev revolt in the late eighteenth century. But the urban and rural revolutions were not simultaneous. Peasant rioting—consisting of the sacking and burning of manor houses and attacks on landowners and officials—began in the summer of 1905 and rose to a peak in the late autumn, subsided, and then resumed on a large scale in 1906. But even in late 1905 the regime was strong enough to begin using troops in a campaign of village-by-village pacification. By the middle of 1906, all the troops were back from the Far East, and discipline had been restored in the armed forces. In the winter of 1906–7, much of rural Russia was under martial law, and summary justice (including over a thousand executions) was dispensed by field courts martial.

Russia's landowning nobility learnt a lesson from the events of 1905–6, namely that its interests lay with the autocracy (which could perhaps shield it from a vengeful peasantry) and not with the liberals.[16] But in urban terms, the 1905 Revolution did not produce such clear consciousness of class polarization: even for most socialists, this was not a Russian 1848, revealing the treacherous nature of liberalism and the essential antagonism of bourgeoisie and proletariat. The liberals—representing a professional rather than capitalist middle class—had stood aside in October, but they had not joined the regime in an onslaught on the workers' revolution. Their attitude to the workers' and socialist movements remained much more benign than that of liberals in most European countries. The workers, for their part, seem to have perceived the liberals rather as a timorous ally than a treacherous one.

The political outcome of the 1905 Revolution was ambiguous, and in some ways unsatisfactory to all concerned. In the Fundamental Laws of 1906—the closest Russia came to a constitution—Nicholas made known his belief that Russia was still an autocracy. True, the autocrat now consulted with an elected parliament, and political parties had been legalized. But the Duma had limited powers; Ministers remained responsible solely to the autocrat; and, after the first two Dumas proved insubordinate and were arbitrarily dissolved, a new electoral system was introduced which virtually disfranchised some social groups and heavily over-represented the landed nobility. The Duma's main importance, perhaps, lay in providing a public forum for political debate and a training-ground for politicians. The political reforms of 1905–7 bred parliamentary politicians just as the legal reforms of the 1860s had bred lawyers; and both groups had an inherent tendency to develop values and aspirations that the autocracy could not abide.

One thing that the 1905 Revolution did *not* change was the police regime that had come to maturity in the 1880s. Due process of law was still suspended (as in the case of the field courts martial dealing with the rebellious peasantry in 1906–7) for much of the population much of the time. Of course there were understandable reasons for this: the fact that in 1908, a comparatively quiet year, 1,800 officials were killed and 2,083 were wounded in politically motivated attacks[17] indicates how tumultuous the society remained, and how much the regime remained on the defensive. But it meant that in many respects the political reforms were only a façade. Trade unions, for example, had been made legal in principle, but individual unions were frequently closed down by the police. Political parties were legal, and even the revolutionary socialist parties could contest the Duma elections and win a few seats—yet the members of revolutionary socialist parties were no less liable to arrest than in the past, and the party leaders (most of whom returned to Russia during the 1905 Revolution) were forced back into emigration to avoid imprisonment and exile.

With hindsight, it might seem that the Marxist revolutionaries, with 1905 under their belts and 1917 already looming on the horizon, should have been congratulating themselves on the workers' spectacular revolutionary début and looking confidently towards the future. But in fact their mood was quite different. Neither Bolsheviks nor Mensheviks had got more than a toehold in the workers' revolution of 1905: the workers had not so much rejected as outpaced them, and this was a very sobering thought, particularly for Lenin. Revolution had come, but the regime had fought back and survived. Within the intelligentsia, there was much talk about abandoning the revolutionary dream and the old illusions of social perfectibility. From the revolutionary standpoint, it was no gain to have a façade of legal political institutions and a new breed of self-important, chattering liberal politicians (to summarize Lenin's view of them, which did not greatly differ from Nicholas II's). It was also deeply, almost unbearably disappointing for the revolutionary leaders to return to the familiar dreariness of emigré life. The emigrés were never more prickly and contentious than in the years between 1905 and 1917; indeed, the Russians' continual petty bickering became one of the scandals of European Social Democracy, and Lenin was one of the very worst offenders.

Among the bad news of the prewar years was that the regime was embarking on a major programme of agrarian reform. The peasant revolts of 1905–7 had persuaded the government to abandon its earlier premise that the *mir* was the best guarantee of rural stability. Its hopes now lay in the creation of a class of small independent farmers—a wager on 'the sober and the strong', as Nicholas's chief Minister, Petr Stolypin, described it. Peasants were now encouraged to consolidate their holdings and separate from the *mir*, and land commissions were established in the provinces to facilitate the process. The assumption was that the poor would sell up and go to the towns, while the more prosperous would improve and expand their holdings and acquire the conservative petty-bourgeois mentality of, say, the French peasant farmer. By 1914, about 40 per cent of peasant households in European Russia had formally separated from the *mir*, although, given the legal and practical complexity of the process, only a relatively small number had completed the later steps towards establishing themselves as proprietors farming their own consolidated and self-contained blocks of land.[18] The Stolypin reforms were 'progressive' in Marxist terms, since they laid the basis for capitalist development in agriculture. But, in contrast to the development of urban capitalism, their short- and medium-range implications for Russian revolution were highly depressing. Russia's traditional peasantry was prone to revolt. If the Stolypin reforms worked (as Lenin, for one, feared that they might), the Russian proletariat would have lost an important revolutionary ally.

In 1906, the Russian economy was bolstered by an enormous loan (two and a quarter billion francs) which Witte negotiated with an international banking consortium; and both native and foreign-owned industry expanded rapidly in the prewar years. This meant, of course, that the industrial working class also expanded. But labour unrest dropped down sharply for some years after the savage crushing of the workers' revolutionary movement in the winter of 1905–6, picking up again only around 1910. Large-scale strikes became increasingly common in the immediate prewar years, culminating in the Petrograd general strike of the summer of 1914, which was sufficiently serious for some observers to doubt that Russia could risk mobilizing its army for war. The workers' demands were political as well as economic; and their grievances against the regime included its responsibility for foreign domination of many sectors of Russian industry as well as its use of coercion against the workers themselves. In Russia, the Mensheviks were conscious of losing support as the workers became more violent and belligerent, and the Bolsheviks were conscious of gaining it. But this did not noticeably raise the spirits of the Bolshevik leaders in emigration: because of poor communications with Russia, they were probably not fully aware of it, and their own position in the emigré Russian and socialist community in Europe was increasingly weak and isolated.[19]

When war broke out in Europe in August 1914, with Russia allied with France and England against Germany and Austria-Hungary, the political emigrés became almost completely cut off from Russia, as well as experiencing the normal problems of alien residents in wartime. In the European socialist movement as a whole, large numbers of former internationalists became patriots overnight when war was declared. The Russians were less inclined than others to outright patriotism, but most took the 'defensist' position of supporting Russia's war effort as long as it was in defence of Russian territory. Lenin, however, belonged to the smaller group of 'defeatists' who repudiated their country's cause entirely: it was an imperialist war, as far as Lenin was concerned, and the best prospect was a Russian defeat which might provoke civil war and revolution. This was a very controversial stand, even in the socialist movement, and the Bolsheviks found themselves very much cold-shouldered. In Russia, all known Bolsheviks—including Duma deputies—were arrested for the duration of the war.

As in 1904, Russia's declaration of war produced a public surge of patriotic enthusiasm, much jingoistic flag-waving, a temporary moratorium on internal strife, and earnest attempts by respectable society and non-governmental organizations to assist the government's war effort. But once again, the mood quickly turned sour. The Russian Army suffered crushing defeats and losses (a total of five million casualties for 1914–17), and the German Army penetrated deep into the western territories of the Empire, causing a chaotic outflow of refugees into central Russia. Defeats bred suspicion of treason in high places, and one of the main targets was Nicholas's wife, Empress Alexandra, who was a German princess by birth. Scandal surrounded Alexandra's relationship with Rasputin, a shady but charismatic character whom she trusted as a true man of God who could control her son's haemophilia. When Nicholas assumed the responsibilities of Commander in Chief of the Russian Army, which took him away from the capital for long periods, Alexandra and Rasputin began to exercise a disastrous influence over ministerial appointments. Relations between the government and the Fourth Duma deteriorated drastically: the mood in the Duma and among the educated public as a whole was captured in the phrase with which the Cadet Pavel Milyukov punctuated a speech on the government's shortcomings—'Is this stupidity or is it treason?' Late in 1916, Rasputin was murdered by some young nobles close to the court and a right-wing Duma deputy, whose motives were to save the honour of Russia and the autocracy.

The pressures of the First World War—and, no doubt, the personalities of Nicholas and his wife, and the family tragedy of their young son's haemophilia[20]—threw the anachronistic traits of the Russian autocracy into sharp relief, and made Nicholas seem less like an upholder of the autocratic tradition than an unwitting satirist of it. The 'ministerial leapfrog' of incompetent favourites in the Cabinet, the illiterate peasant faith-healer at court, the intrigues of the high nobility leading to Rasputin's murder, and even the epic story of Rasputin's stubborn resistance to death by poison, bullets, and drowning—all these seemed to belong to an earlier age, to be a bizarre and irrelevant accompaniment to the twentieth-century realities of troop-trains, trench warfare, and mass mobilization. Russia not only had an educated public to perceive this, but also possessed institutions like the Duma, the political parties, the zemstvos, and the industrialists' War Industries Committee which were potential agents of transition from the old regime to the modern world.

The autocracy's situation was precarious on the eve of the First World War. The society was deeply divided, and the political and bureaucratic structure was fragile and overstrained. The regime was so vulnerable to any kind of jolt or setback that it is hard to imagine that it could have survived long, even without the War, although clearly change might in other circumstances have come less violently and with less radical consequences than was the case in 1917.

The First World War both exposed and increased the vulnerability of Russia's old regime. The public applauded victories, but would not tolerate defeats. When defeats occurred, the society did not rally behind its government (a relatively normal reaction, especially if the enemy becomes an invader of the homeland, and the reaction of Russian society in 1812 and again in 1941–2), but instead turned sharply against it, denouncing its incompetence and backwardness in tones of contempt and moral superiority. This suggests that the regime's legitimacy had become extremely shaky, and that its survival was very closely related to visible achievements or, failing that, sheer luck. The old regime had been lucky in 1904–6, an earlier occasion when war defeats had plunged it into revolution, because it got out of the war relatively quickly and honourably, and was able to obtain a very large postwar loan from Europe, which was then at peace. It was not so lucky in 1914–17. The war lasted too long, draining not only Russia but the whole of Europe. More than a year before the Armistice in Europe, Russia's old regime was dead.

2 1917: The Revolutions of February and October

In February 1917, the autocracy collapsed in the face of popular demonstrations and the withdrawal of elite support for the regime. In the euphoria of revolution, political solutions seemed easy. Russia's future form of government would, of course, be democratic. The exact meaning of that ambiguous term and the nature of Russia's new constitution would be decided by a Constituent Assembly, to be elected by the Russian people as soon as circumstances permitted. In the meantime, the elite and popular revolutions—liberal politicians, the propertied and professional classes, and the officer corps in the first category; socialist politicians, the urban working class, and rank-and-file soldiers and sailors in the second—would coexist, as they had done in the glorious days of national revolutionary solidarity in 1905. In institutional terms, the new Provisional Government would represent the elite revolution, while the newly revived Petrograd Soviet would speak for the revolution of the people. Their relationship would be complementary rather than competitive, and 'dual power' (the term applied to the coexistence of the Provisional Government and the Soviet) would be a source of strength, not of weakness. Russian liberals, after all, had traditionally tended to see the socialists as allies, whose special interest in social reform was comparable to and compatible with the liberals' own special interest in political democratization. Most Russian socialists, similarly, were prepared to see the liberals as allies, since they accepted the Marxist view that the bourgeois liberal revolution had first place on the agenda and the socialists were bound to support it in the struggle against autocracy.

Yet within eight months the hopes and expectations of February lay in ruins. 'Dual power' proved an illusion, masking something very like a power vacuum. The popular revolution became progressively more radical, while the elite revolution moved towards an anxious conservative stance in defence of property and law and order. The Provisional Government barely survived General Kornilov's attempted *coup* from the right before succumbing in October to the Bolsheviks' successful *coup* from the left, popularly associated with the slogan of 'All power to the soviets'. The long-awaited Constituent Assembly met but accomplished nothing, being unceremoniously dispersed by the Bolsheviks in January 1918. On the peripheries of Russia, officers of the old Tsarist Army were mustering their forces to fight the Bolsheviks, some under the monarchist banner that had seemed banished forever in 1917. The Revolution had not brought liberal democracy to Russia. Instead, it had brought anarchy and civil war.

The headlong passage from democratic February to Red October astonished victors and vanquished alike. For Russian liberals, the shock was traumatic. The revolution—*their* revolution by right, as the history of Western Europe demonstrated and even right-thinking Marxists agreed—had finally occurred, only to be snatched from their grasp by sinister and incomprehensible forces. Mensheviks and other non-Bolshevik Marxists were similarly outraged: the time was not yet ripe for proletarian socialist revolution, and it was inexcusable that a Marxist party should break the rules and seize power. The Allies, Russia's partners in the war in Europe, were aghast at the débâcle and refused to recognize the new government, which was preparing to pull Russia out of the war unilaterally. The diplomats barely even knew the names of Russia's new rulers, but suspected the worst and prayed for a speedy resurrection of the democratic hopes they had welcomed in February. Western newspaper readers learned with horror of Russia's descent from civilization into the barbarous depths of atheistic Communism.

The scars left by the October Revolution were deep, and made more painful and visible to the outside world by the emigration of large numbers of educated Russians during and immediately after the Civil War that followed the Bolshevik victory. To the emigrés, the Bolshevik Revolution was not so much a tragedy in the Greek sense as an unexpected, undeserved, and essentially unfair disaster. To the Western and especially the American public, it seemed that the Russian people had been cheated of the liberal democracy for which it had so long and nobly struggled. Conspiracy theories explaining the Bolshevik victory gained widespread credence: the most popular of these was that of international Jewish conspiracy, since Trotsky, Zinoviev, and a number of other Bolshevik leaders were Jewish; but another theory, revived in Solzhenitsyn's *Lenin in Zurich*, pictured the Bolsheviks as pawns of the Germans in a successful plot to take Russia out of the war. Historians, of course, tend to be sceptical of conspiracy theories. But the attitudes that enabled such theories to flourish may also have influenced Western scholarly approaches to the problem. Until quite recently, most historical explanations of the Bolshevik Revolution emphasized its illegitimacy in one way or the other, as if seeking to absolve the Russian people of any responsibility for the event and its consequences.

In the classic Western interpretation of the Bolshevik victory and subsequent evolution of Soviet power, the *deus ex machina* was the Bolsheviks' secret weapon of party organization and discipline. Lenin's pamphlet *What Is To Be Done?* (see above, p. 31), setting out the prerequisites for the successful organization of an illegal, conspiratorial party, was usually cited as the basic text; and it was argued that the ideas of *What Is To Be Done?* moulded the Bolshevik Party in its formative years and continued to determine Bolshevik behaviour even after the final emergence from underground in February 1917. The open, democratic, and pluralist politics of the post-February months in Russia were thus subverted, culminating in the Bolsheviks' unlawful seizure of power by a conspiratorially organized *coup* in October. The Bolshevik tradition of centralized organization and strict party discipline led the new Soviet regime towards repressive authoritarianism and laid the foundations for Stalin's later totalitarian dictatorship.[1]

Yet there have always been problems in applying this general concept of the origins of Soviet totalitarianism to the specific historical situation unfolding between February and October 1917. In the first place, the old underground Bolshevik Party was swamped by an influx of new members, outstripping all other political parties in recruitment, especially in the factories and the armed forces. By the middle of 1917, it had become an open mass party, bearing little resemblance to the disciplined elite organization of full-time revolutionaries described in *What Is To Be Done?* In the second place, neither the party as a whole nor its leadership were united on the most basic policy questions in 1917. In October, for example, disagreements within the party leadership on the desirability of insurrection were so acute that the issue was publicly debated by Bolsheviks in the daily press.

It may well be that the Bolsheviks' greatest strength in 1917 was not strict party organization and discipline (which scarcely existed at this time) but rather the party's stance of intransigent radicalism on the extreme left of the political spectrum. While other socialist and liberal groups jostled for position in the Provisional Government and Petrograd Soviet, the Bolsheviks refused to be co-opted and denounced the politics of coalition and compromise. While other formerly radical politicians called for restraint and responsible, statesmanlike leadership, the Bolsheviks stayed out on the streets with the irresponsible and belligerent revolutionary crowd. As the 'dual power' structure disintegrated, discrediting the coalition parties represented in the Provisional Government and Petrograd Soviet leadership, only the Bolsheviks were in a position to benefit. Among the socialist parties, only the Bolsheviks had overcome Marxist scruples, caught the mood of the crowd, and declared their willingness to seize power in the name of the proletarian revolution.

The 'dual power' relationship of the Provisional Government and Petrograd Soviet was usually seen in class terms as an alliance between the bourgeoisie and the proletariat. Its survival depended on continued co-operation between these classes and the politicians claiming to represent them; but it was clear by the summer of 1917 that the shaky consensus of February had been seriously undermined. As urban society became increasingly polarized between a law-and-order right and a revolutionary left, the middle ground of democratic coalition started to crumble. In July, crowds of workers, soldiers, and sailors came on to the Petrograd streets demanding that the Soviet take power in the name of the working class and repudiate the 'ten capitalist ministers' of the Provisional Government. In August, the month of General Kornilov's abortive *coup*, a leading industrialist urged the liberals to be more decisive in defence of their class interests:[2]

We ought to say . . . that the present revolution is a bourgeois revolution, that the bourgeois order which exists at the present time is inevitable, and since it is inevitable, one must draw the completely logical conclusion and insist that those who rule the state think in a bourgeois manner and act in a bourgeois manner.[2]

The 'dual power' was conceived as an interim arrangement pending the summoning of a Constituent Assembly. But its disintegration under attack from left and right and the growing polarization of Russian politics raised disturbing questions about the future as well as the present in mid-1917. Was it still reasonable to hope that Russia's political problems could be resolved by a popularly elected

Constituent Assembly and the formal institutionalization of parliamentary democracy on the Western model? The Constituent Assembly solution, like the interim 'dual power', required a degree of political consensus and agreement on the necessity of compromise. The perceived alternatives to consensus and compromise were dictatorship and civil war. It seemed, nevertheless, that these alternatives were likely to be chosen by a turbulent and sharply polarized society which had thrown off the reins of government.

The February Revolution and 'dual power'

In the last week of February, bread shortages, strikes, lock-outs and finally a demonstration in honour of International Women's Day by female workers of the Vyborg district brought a crowd on to the streets of Petrograd that the authorities could not disperse. The Fourth Duma, which had reached the end of its term, petitioned the Emperor once again for a responsible cabinet and asked to remain in session for the duration of the crisis. Both requests were refused; but an unauthorized Duma Committee, dominated by liberals of the Cadet Party and the Progressive Bloc, did in fact remain in session. The Emperor's Ministers held one last, indecisive meeting and then took to their heels, the more cautious of them immediately quitting the capital. Nicholas II himself was absent, visiting Army Headquarters in Mogilev; his response to the crisis was a laconic instruction by telegraph that the disorders should be ended immediately. But the police was disintegrating, and troops from the Petrograd garrison brought into the city to control the crowd had begun to fraternize with it. By the evening of 28 February, Petrograd's Military Commander had to report that the revolutionary crowd had taken over all railway stations, all artillery supplies and, as far as he knew, the whole city; very few reliable troops remained at his disposal, and even his telephones were no longer working.

The Army High Command had two options, either to send in fresh troops who might or might not hold firm, or to seek a political solution with the help of the Duma politicians. It chose the latter alternative. At Pskov, on the return journey from Mogilev, Nicholas's train was met by emissaries from the High Command and the Duma who respectfully suggested that the Emperor should abdicate. After some discussion, Nicholas mildly agreed. But, having initially accepted the suggestion that he should abdicate in favour of his son, he thought further about Tsarevich Aleksei's delicate health and decided instead to abdicate on his own behalf and that of Aleksei in favour of his brother, Grand Duke Michael. Always a family man, he spent the remainder of the journey thinking with remarkable calm and political innocence about his future as a private citizen:

He said he would go abroad for the duration of hostilities [in the war against Germany] and then return to Russia, settle in the Crimea and devote himself completely to the education of his son. Some of his advisors doubted whether he would be allowed to do this, but Nicholas replied that nowhere were parents denied the right to care for their children.[3]

(After reaching the capital, Nicholas was sent to join his family outside Petrograd, and thereafter remained quietly under house arrest while the Provisional Government and the Allies tried to decide what to do with him. No solution was reached. Later, the whole family was sent to Siberia and then to the Urals, still under house arrest but in increasingly difficult circumstances which Nicholas bore with fortitude. In July 1918, after the outbreak of the Civil War, Nicholas and his family were executed on orders of the Bolshevik Urals Soviet. From the time of his abdication to his death, Nicholas did indeed behave as a private citizen, playing no active political role whatsoever.)

In the days following Nicholas's abdication, the politicians of Petrograd were in a state of high excitement and frenetic activity. Their original intention had been to get rid of Nicholas rather than the monarchy. But Nicholas's abdication on behalf of his son had removed the possibility of a regency during Aleksei's minority; and Grand Duke Michael, being a prudent man, declined the invitation to succeed his brother. *De facto*, therefore, Russia was no longer a monarchy. It was decided that the country's future form of government would be determined in due course by a Constituent Assembly, and that in the meantime a self-appointed 'Provisional Government' would take over the responsibilities of the former imperial Council of Ministers. Prince Georgii Lvov, head of the Zemstvo League and a moderate liberal, became head of the new government. His cabinet included Pavel Milyukov, historian and Cadet Party theoretician, as Foreign Minister, two prominent industrialists as Ministers of Finance and Trade and Industry, and the socialist lawyer Aleksandr Kerensky as Minister of Justice.

The Provisional Government had no electoral mandate, deriving its authority from the now defunct Duma, the consent of the Army High Command, and informal agreements with public organizations like the Zemstvo League and the War Industries Committee. The old Tsarist bureaucracy provided its executive machinery but, as the result of the earlier dissolution of the Duma, it had no supporting legislative body. Given its fragility and lack of formal legitimacy, the new government's assumption of power seemed remarkably easy. The Allied Powers recognized it immediately. Monarchist sentiment seemed to have disappeared overnight in Russia: in the entire Tenth Army, only two officers refused to swear allegiance to the Provisional Government. As a liberal politician later recalled,

Individuals and organizations expressed their loyalty to the new power. The Stavka [Army Headquarters] as a whole, followed by the entire commanding staff, recognized the Provisional Government. The Tsarist Ministers and some of the assistant Ministers were imprisoned, but all the other officials remained at their posts. Ministries, offices, banks, in fact the entire political mechanism of Russia never ceased working. In that respect, the [February] *coup d'état* passed off so smoothly that even then one felt a vague presentiment that this was not the end, that such a crisis could not pass off so peacefully.[4]

Indeed, from the very beginning there were reasons to doubt the effectiveness of the transfer of power. The most important reason was that the Provisional Government had a competitor: the February Revolution had produced not one but two self-constituted authorities aspiring to a national role. The second was the Petrograd Soviet, formed on the pattern of the 1905 Petersburg Soviet by workers, soldiers and socialist politicians. The Soviet was already in session in the Tauride Palace when the formation of the Provisional Government was announced on 2 March.

The 'dual power' relationship of the Provisional Government and the Petrograd Soviet emerged spontaneously, and the government accepted it largely because it had no choice. In the most immediate practical terms, a dozen Ministers with no force at their disposal could scarcely have cleared the Palace (the initial meeting-place of both the government and the Soviet) of the scruffy throng of workers, soldiers, and sailors who were tramping in and out to make speeches, eat, sleep, argue, and write proclamations; and the mood of the crowd, intermittently bursting into the Soviet Chamber with a captive policeman or former Tsarist Minister to leave at the deputies' feet, must have discouraged the attempt. In broader terms, as War Minister Guchkov explained to the Army's Commander-in-Chief early in March,

The Provisional Government does not possess any real power; and its directives are carried out only to the extent that it is permitted by the Soviet of Workers' and Soldiers' Deputies, which enjoys all the essential elements of real power, since the troops, the railroads, the post and telegraph are all in its hands. One can say flatly that the Provisional Government exists only so long as it is permitted by the Soviet.[5]

In the first months, the Provisional Government consisted mainly of liberals, while the Soviet's Executive Committee was dominated by socialist intellectuals, mainly Mensheviks and SRs by party affiliation. Kerensky, a Provisional Government member but also a socialist, who had been active in setting up both institutions, served as liaison between them. The socialists of the Soviet intended to act as watch-dogs over the Provisional Government, protecting the interests of the working class until such time as the bourgeois revolution had run its course. This deference to the bourgeoisie was partly the result of the socialists' good Marxist education and partly a product of caution and uncertainty. As Nikolai Sukhanov, one of the Soviet's Menshevik leaders, noted, there was likely to be trouble ahead, and better that the liberals take the responsibility and, if necessary, the blame:

The Soviet democracy had to entrust the power to the propertied elements, its class enemy, without whose participation it could not now master the technique of administration in the desperate conditions of disintegration, nor deal with the forces of Tsarism and the bourgeoisie, united against it. But the *condition* of this transfer had to assure the democracy of a complete victory over the class enemy in the near future.[6]

But the workers, soldiers, and sailors who made up the Soviet's rank and file were not so cautious. On 1 March, before the formal establishment of the Provisional Government or the emergence of 'responsible leadership' in the Soviet, the notorious Order No. 1 was issued in the name of the Petrograd Soviet. Order No. 1 was a revolutionary document and an assertion of the Soviet's power. It called for democratization of the Army by the creation of elected soldiers' committees, reduction of officers' disciplinary powers and, most importantly, recognition of the Soviet's authority on all policy questions involving the armed forces: it stated that no governmental order to the Army was to be considered valid without the counter-signature of the Soviet. While Order No. 1 did not actually mandate the holding of elections to confirm officers in their positions, such elections were in fact being organized in the more unruly units; and there were reports that hundreds of naval officers had been arrested or killed by the sailors of Kronstadt and the Baltic Fleet during the February Days. Order No. 1 therefore had strong overtones of class war, and totally failed to offer reassurance about the prospects for class co-operation. It presaged the most unworkable form of dual power, that is, a situation in which the enlisted men in the armed forces recognized only the authority of the Petrograd Soviet, while the officer corps recognized only the authority of the Provisional Government.

The Executive Committee of the Soviet did its best to retreat from the radical position implied by Order No. 1. But in April Sukhanov commented on the 'isolation from the masses' produced by the Executive Committee's *de facto* alliance with the Provisional Government. It was, of course, only a partial alliance. There were recurrent conflicts between the Soviet Executive Committee and the Provisional Government on labour policy and the problem of peasant land claims. There were also important disagreements about Russia's participation in the European war. The Provisional Government remained firmly committed to the war effort; and Foreign Minister Milyukov's Note of 18 April even implied a continued interest in extending Russian control over Constantinople and the Straits (as agreed in the Secret Treaties signed by the Tsarist government and the Allies), before a public outcry and renewed street demonstrations forced him to resign. The Soviet Executive Committee took the 'defensist' position, favouring continuation of the war as long as Russian territory was under attack but opposing annexationist war aims and the Secret Treaties. But on the floor of the Soviet—and in the streets, the factories, and especially the garrisons—the attitude to the war tended to be simpler and more drastic: stop fighting, pull out of the war, bring the troops home.

The relationship that developed between the Soviet Executive Committee and the Provisional Government in the spring and summer of 1917 was intense, intimate, and quarrelsome. The Executive Committee guarded its separate identity jealously, but ultimately the two institutions were too closely bound to be indifferent to each other's fate, or to dissociate themselves in the event of disaster. The link was strengthened in May, when the Provisional Government ceased to be a liberal preserve and became a coalition of liberals and socialists, drawing in representatives of the major socialist parties (Mensheviks and SRs) whose influence was predominant in the Soviet Executive Committee. The socialists were not eager to enter the government, but concluded that it was their duty to strengthen a tottering regime at a time of national crisis. They continued to regard the Soviet as their more natural sphere of political action, especially when it became clear that the new socialist Ministers of Agriculture and Labour would be unable to implement their policies because of liberal opposition. Nevertheless, a symbolic choice had been made: in associating themselves more closely with the Provisional Government, the 'responsible' socialists were separating themselves (and, by extension, the Soviet Executive Committee) from the 'irresponsible' popular revolution.

Popular hostility to the 'bourgeois' Provisional Government mounted in the late spring, as war weariness increased and the economic situation in the towns deteriorated. During the street demonstrations that occurred in July (the July Days), demonstrators carried banners calling for 'All power to the soviets', which in effect meant the removal of power from the Provisional Government. Paradoxically—though logically in terms of its commitment to the Government—the Executive Committee of the Petrograd Soviet rejected the slogan of 'All power to the soviets'; and in fact the demonstration was directed as much against the existing Soviet leadership as against the Government itself. 'Take power, you son of a bitch, when it's given you!' shouted one demonstrator, shaking his fist at a socialist politician.[7] But this was an appeal (or perhaps a threat?) to which those who had pledged themselves to 'dual power' could not respond.

The Bolsheviks

At the time of the February Revolution, virtually all leading Bolsheviks were in emigration abroad or in exile in remote regions of the Russian Empire, arrested *en masse* after the outbreak of war because the Bolsheviks not only opposed Russia's participation but also argued that a Russian defeat would be in the interests of the revolution. The Bolshevik leaders who had been exiled in Siberia, including Stalin and Molotov, were among the first to return to the capitals. But those in emigration in Europe found it much more difficult to return, for the simple reason that Europe was at war. To return via the Baltic was dangerous and required Allied co-operation, while the land routes ran across enemy territory. Nevertheless, Lenin and other members of the emigré community in neutral Switzerland were very anxious to return; and, after negotiations conducted by intermediaries, the German government offered them the chance to cross Germany by sealed train. It was clearly in Germany's interest to let Russian revolutionaries opposed to the war return to Russia, but the revolutionaries themselves had to weigh the desirability of returning against the risk of compromising themselves politically. Lenin, together with a small contingent of mainly Bolshevik emigrés, decided to take the risk, and set off towards the end of March. (A much larger group of Russian revolutionaries in Switzerland, including almost all the Mensheviks, decided that it was more prudent to wait—a shrewd move, since they avoided all the controversy and accusations that Lenin's trip provoked. This group followed in a second sealed train, by similar arrangement with the Germans, a month later.)

Before Lenin's return to Petrograd early in April, the former Siberian exiles had already begun to rebuild the Bolshevik organization and publish a newspaper. At this point the Bolsheviks, like other socialist groups, showed signs of drifting into the loose coalition around the Petrograd Soviet. But the Menshevik and SR leaders of the Soviet had not forgotten what a troublemaker Lenin could be, and awaited his arrival with apprehension. It turned out to be justified. On 3 April, when Lenin stepped off the train at the Finland Station in Petrograd, he responded curtly to the Soviet's welcoming committee, addressed a few remarks to the crowd in the rather harsh voice that always grated on his opponents, and departed abruptly for a private celebration and conference with his Bolshevik Party colleagues. Clearly Lenin had not lost his old sectarian habits. He showed no signs of the joyous emotions that, in these early months, often led old political antagonists to embrace as brothers in honour of the revolutionary victory.

Lenin's appraisal of the political situation, known to history as the April Theses, was belligerent, uncompromising, and distinctly disconcerting to the Petrograd Bolsheviks who had tentatively accepted the Soviet line of socialist unity and critical support for the new government. Scarcely pausing to acknowledge the achievements of February, Lenin was already looking forward to the second stage of revolution, the overthrow of the bourgeoisie by the proletariat. No support should be given to the Provisional Government, Lenin stated. Socialist illusions of unity and the 'naïve confidence' of the masses in the new regime must be destroyed. The present Soviet leadership, having succumbed to bourgeois influence, was useless (in one speech, Lenin borrowed Rosa Luxemburg's characterization of German Social Democracy and called it 'a stinking corpse').

Nevertheless, Lenin predicted that the soviets—under revitalized revolutionary leadership—would be the key institutions in transferring power from the bourgeoisie to the proletariat. 'All power to the soviets!', one of the slogans of Lenin's April Theses, was in effect a call for class war. 'Peace, land, and bread', another of Lenin's April slogans, had similarly revolutionary implications. 'Peace', in Lenin's usage, meant not only withdrawal from the imperialist war but also recognition that such withdrawal '*is impossible* . . . without the overthrow of capital'. 'Land' meant confiscation of the landowners' estates and their redistribution by the peasants themselves—something very close to spontaneous peasant land seizures. No wonder that a critic accused Lenin of 'plant[ing] the banner of civil war in the midst of revolutionary democracy'.[8]

The Bolsheviks, respectful as they were of Lenin's vision and leadership, were shocked by his April Theses: some were inclined to think that he had lost touch with the realities of Russian life during his years in emigration. But in the following months, under Lenin's exhortations and reproaches, the Bolsheviks did move into a more intransigent position, isolating themselves from the socialist coalition. However, without a Bolshevik majority in the Petrograd Soviet, Lenin's slogan of 'All power to the soviets!' did not provide the Bolsheviks with a practical guide to action. It remained an open question whether Lenin's strategy was that of a master politician or simply that of a cranky extremist—a left-wing counterpart of the old socialist Plekhanov, whose unreserved patriotism on the war issue had taken him out of the mainstream of Russian socialist politics.

The need for socialist unity seemed self-evident to most of the politicians associated with the Soviet, who prided themselves on submerging their old sectarian disagreements. In June, at the First

National Congress of Soviets, a speaker asked rhetorically whether any political party was prepared to take on the responsibilities of power alone, assuming that the answer was negative. 'There is such a party!' Lenin interjected. But to most of the delegates, it sounded more like bravado than a serious challenge. It was a serious challenge, however, because the Bolsheviks were gaining popular support and the coalition socialists losing it.

The Bolsheviks were still in a minority at the June Congress of Soviets, and they had yet to win a major city election. But their growing strength was already evident at the grass-roots level—in the workers' factory committees, in the committees of soldiers and sailors in the armed forces, and in local district soviets in the big towns. Bolshevik Party membership was also increasing spectacularly, although the Bolsheviks never made any formal decision to launch a mass recruitment drive, and seemed almost surprised by the influx. The party's membership figures, shaky and perhaps exaggerated as they are, give some sense of its dimensions: 24,000 Bolshevik Party members at the time of the February Revolution (though this figure is particularly suspect, since the Petrograd party organization could actually identify only about 2,000 members in February, and the Moscow organization 600); more than 100,000 members by the end of April; and in October 1917 a total of 350,000 members, including 60,000 in Petrograd and the surrounding province and 70,000 in Moscow and the adjacent Central Industrial Region.[9]

The popular revolution

Seven million men were under arms at the beginning of 1917, with two million in the reserve. The armed forces had suffered tremendous losses, and war weariness was evident in the increasing desertion rate and the soldiers' responsiveness to German fraternization at the front. To the soldiers, the February Revolution was an implicit promise that the war would soon end, and they waited impatiently for the Provisional Government to achieve this—if not on its own initiative, then under pressure from the Petrograd Soviet. In the early spring of 1917, the Army, with its new democratic structure of elected committees, its old problems of inadequate supplies, and its restless and uncertain mood, was at best a doubtfully effective fighting force. At the front, morale had not totally disintegrated. But the situation in the garrisons around the country, where reserve troops were stationed, was much uglier.

Traditionally, Russia's soldiers and sailors of ´917 have been categorized as 'proletarians', regardless of their occupation out of uniform. In fact most of the enlisted men were peasants, although workers were disproportionately represented in the Baltic Fleet and the armies of the Northern and Western Fronts, since their recruitment area was relatively industrialized. It can be argued in Marxist terms that the men in the armed forces were proletarian by virtue of their current occupation, but the more important thing is that this is evidently how they regarded themselves. As Wildman's study indicates,[10] front-line soldiers in the spring of 1917—even when prepared to co-operate with officers who accepted the Revolution and the new norms of behaviour—saw the officers and the Provisional Government as belonging to one class, that of the 'masters', and identified their own interests as those of the workers and the Petrograd Soviet. By May, as the Commander-in-Chief reported with alarm, 'class antagonism' between officers and men had made deep inroads on the Army's spirit of patriotic solidarity.

The Petrograd workers had already demonstrated a revolutionary spirit in February, although they had not then been sufficiently militant or psychologically prepared to resist the creation of a 'bourgeois' Provisional Government. In the first months after the February Revolution, the main grievances expressed by workers in Petrograd and elsewhere were economic, focusing on bread-and-butter issues like the eight-hour day (which the Provisional Government rejected on the grounds of the wartime emergency), wages, overtime, and protection against unemployment.[11] But there was no guarantee that this situation would continue, given the tradition of political militancy in the Russian working class. It was true that the war had changed the composition of the working class, greatly increasing the percentage of women as well as somewhat increasing the total number of workers; and it was usually believed that women workers were less revolutionary than men. Yet it was women workers whose strike on International Women's Day had precipitated the February Revolution; and those who had husbands at the front were particularly likely to object strongly to continuation of the war. Petrograd, as a centre of the munitions industry in which many skilled male workers had been exempted from military conscription, retained a comparatively large proportion of its prewar male working class in the factories. Despite the police round-up of Bolsheviks at the beginning of the war, and the subsequent arrest or military drafting of large numbers of other political troublemakers in the factories, Petrograd's major metallurgical and defence plants were employing a surprisingly large number of workers who belonged to the Bolshevik and other revolutionary parties, and even Bolshevik professional revolutionaries who had come to the capital from Ukraine and other parts of the Empire after the outbreak of war. Other revolutionary workers returned to their factories after the February Revolution, increasing the potential for further political unrest.

The February Revolution had given birth to a formidable array of workers' organizations in all Russia's industrial centres, but especially in Petrograd and Moscow. Workers' soviets were created not only at the city level, like the Petrograd Soviet, but also at the lower level of the urban district, where the leadership usually came from the workers themselves rather than the socialist intelligentsia and the mood was often more radical. New trade unions were established; and at the plant level, workers began to set up factory committees (which were not part of the trade-union structure, and sometimes coexisted with local trade-union branches) to deal with management. The factory committees, closest to the grass roots, tended to be the most radical of all workers' organizations. In the factory committees of Petrograd, the Bolsheviks had assumed a dominant position by the end of May 1917.

The factory committees' original function was to be the workers' watch-dog over the plant's capitalist management. The term used for this function was 'workers' control' (*rabochii kontrol'*), which implied supervision rather than control in the managerial sense. But in practice the factory committees often went further and started to take over managerial functions. Sometimes this was related to disputes over control of hiring and firing, or was the product of the kind of class hostility that led workers in some plants to put unpopular foremen and managers into wheelbarrows and dump them in the river. In other instances, the factory committees took over to save the workers from unemployment, when the owner or manager abandoned the plant or threatened to close it because it was losing money. As such events became more common, the definition of 'workers' control' moved closer to something like workers' self-management.

This change took place as the workers' political mood was becoming more militant, and as the Bolsheviks were gaining influence in the factory committees. Militancy meant hostility to the bourgeoisie and assertion of the workers' primacy in the revolution: just as the revised meaning of 'workers' control' was that workers should be masters in their own plants, so there was an emerging sense in the working class that 'soviet power' meant that the workers should be sole masters in the district, the city, and perhaps the country as a whole. As political theory, this was closer to anarchism or anarcho-syndicalism than to Bolshevism, and the Bolshevik leaders did not in fact share the view that direct workers' democracy through the factory committees and the soviets was a plausible or desirable alternative to their own concept of a party-led 'proletarian dictatorship'. Nevertheless, the Bolsheviks were realists, and the political reality in Petrograd in the summer of 1917 was that their party had strong support in the factory committees and did not want to lose it. Accordingly, the Bolsheviks were in favour of 'workers' control', without defining too closely what they meant by it.

Rising working-class militancy alarmed the employers: a number of plants were closed down, and one prominent industrialist cautiously expressed his opinion that 'the bony hand of hunger' might ultimately be the means of bringing the urban workers back to order. But in the countryside, the landowners' alarm and fear of the peasantry was much greater. The villages were quiet in February, and many of the young peasant men were absent because of conscription for military service. But by May, it was clear that the countryside was sliding into turmoil as it had done in 1905 in response to urban revolution. As in 1905–6, manor houses were being sacked and burned. In addition, the peasants were seizing private and state land for their own use. During the summer, as the disturbances mounted, many landowners abandoned their estates and fled from the countryside.

Although Nicholas II had clung even after the 1905–6 revolts to the idea that Russian peasants loved the Tsar, whatever their opinion of local officials and landed nobles, the peasants responded to news of the downfall of the monarchy and the February Revolution in a quite different way. It seems to have been assumed throughout peasant Russia that this new revolution meant—or should be made to mean—that the nobles' old illegitimate title to the land was revoked. Land should belong to those who tilled it, peasants wrote in their numerous petitions to the Provisional Government in the spring.[12] What that seems to have meant to the peasants in concrete terms was that they should get the land which they had tilled as serfs for the nobles, and which had been retained by the noble landowners in the Emancipation settlement. (Much of this land was currently leased from the landowners by peasants; in other cases, the landowners cultivated it, using the local peasants as hired labour.)

If the peasants still held assumptions about the land that went back more than half a century to the time of serfdom, it is scarcely surprising that the agrarian reforms carried out by Stolypin in the years before the First World War had made little impact on peasant consciousness. Still, the evident vitality of the peasant *mir* in 1917 came as a shock to many people. The Marxists had been arguing since the 1880s that the *mir* had essentially disintegrated internally, surviving only because the state found it a useful instrument. On paper, the effect of Stolypin's reforms had been to dissolve the *mir* in a high proportion of the villages of European Russia. Yet for all this, the *mir* was clearly a basic factor in peasant thinking about the land in 1917. In their petitions, the peasants asked for an egalitarian redistribution of lands held by the nobility, the state, and the Church—that is, the same kind of equal allocation among village households that the *mir* had traditionally organized with regard to the village fields. When unauthorized land seizures began on a large scale in the summer of 1917, the seizures were conducted on behalf of village communities, not individual peasant households, and the general pattern was that the *mir* subsequently divided up the new lands among the villagers as it had traditionally divided up the old ones. Moreover, the *mir* often reasserted its authority over former members in 1917–18: the Stolypin 'separators', who had left the *mir* to set themselves up as independent small farmers in the prewar years, were in many cases forced to return and merge their holdings once again in the common village lands.

Despite the seriousness of the land problem and the reports of land seizures from the early summer of 1917, the Provisional Government procrastinated on the issue of land reform. The liberals were not on principle against expropriation of private lands, and generally seem to have regarded the peasants' demands as just. But any radical land reform would clearly pose formidable problems. In the first place, the Government would have to set up a complicated official mechanism of expropriation and transfer of lands, which was almost certainly beyond its current administrative capacities. In the second place, it could not afford to pay the large compensation to the landowners that most liberals considered necessary. The Provisional Government's conclusion was that it would be best to shelve the problems until they could be properly resolved by the Constituent Assembly. In the meantime, it warned the peasantry (though to little avail) not on any account to take the law into its own hands.

The political crises of the summer

In mid-June, Kerensky, now the Provisional Government's Minister of War, encouraged the Russian Army to mount a major offensive on the Galician Front. It was the first serious military undertaking since the February Revolution, as the Germans had been content to watch the disintegration of the Russian forces without engaging themselves further in the east, and the Russian High Command, fearing disaster, had earlier resisted Allied pressure to take the initiative. The Russians' Galician offensive, conducted in June and early July, failed with an estimated 200,000 casualties. It was a disaster in every sense. Morale in the armed forces disintegrated further, and the Germans began a successful counter-attack that continued throughout the summer and autumn. Russian desertions, already rising as peasant soldiers responded to news of the land seizures, grew to epidemic proportions. The Provisional Government's credit was undermined, and tension between government and military leaders increased. At the beginning of July, a governmental crisis was precipitated by the withdrawal of all the Cadet (liberal) ministers and the resignation of the head of the Provisional Government, Prince Lvov.

In the midst of this crisis, Petrograd erupted once again with the mass demonstrations, street violence, and popular disorder of 3–5 July known as the July Days.[13] The crowd, which contemporary witnesses put as high as half a million, included large organized contingents of Kronstadt sailors, soldiers, and workers from the Petrograd plants. To the Provisional Government, it looked like a Bolshevik attempt at insurrection. The Kronstadt sailors, whose arrival in Petrograd set off the disorders, had Bolsheviks among their leaders, carried banners with the Bolshevik slogan 'All power to the soviets', and made Bolshevik Party headquarters at the Kseshinskaya Palace their first destination. Yet when the demonstrators reached the Kseshinskaya Palace, Lenin's greeting was subdued, almost curt. He did not encourage them to take violent action against the Provisional Government or the present Soviet leadership; and, although the crowd moved on to the Soviet and milled around in a threatening manner, no such action was taken. Confused and lacking leadership and specific plans, the demonstrators roamed the city, fell to drinking and looting, and finally dispersed.

In one sense, the July Days were a vindication of Lenin's intransigent stand since April, for they indicated strong popular sentiment against the Provisional Government and the dual power, impatience with the coalition socialists, and eagerness on the part of the Kronstadt sailors and others for violent confrontation and probably insurrection. But in another sense, the July Days were a disaster for the Bolsheviks. Clearly Lenin and the Bolshevik Central Committee had been caught off balance. They had talked insurrection, in a general way, but not planned it. The Kronstadt Bolsheviks, responding to the sailors' revolutionary mood, had taken an initiative which, in effect, the Bolshevik Central Committee had disowned. The whole affair damaged Bolshevik morale and Lenin's credibility as a revolutionary leader.

The damage was all the greater because the Bolsheviks, despite the leaders' hesitant and uncertain response, were blamed for the July Days by the Provisional Government and the moderate socialists of the Soviet. The Provisional Government decided to crack down, withdrawing the 'parliamentary immunity' that politicians of all parties had enjoyed since the February Revolution. Several prominent Bolsheviks were arrested, along with Trotsky, who had taken a position close to Lenin's on the extreme left since his return to Russia in May and was to become an official Bolshevik Party member in August. Orders were issued for the arrest of Lenin and one of his closest associates in the Bolshevik leaderships, Grigorii Zinoviev. During the July Days, moreover, the Provisional Government had intimated that it had evidence to support the rumours that Lenin was a German agent, and the Bolsheviks were battered by a wave of patriotic denunciations in the press that temporarily eroded their popularity in the armed forces and the factories. The Bolshevik Central Committee (and no doubt Lenin himself) feared for Lenin's life. He went into hiding, and early in August, disguised as a workman, he crossed the border and took refuge in Finland.

If the Bolsheviks were in trouble, however, this was also true of the Provisional Government, headed from early July by Kerensky. The liberal–socialist coalition was in constant turmoil, with the socialists pushed to the left by their Soviet constituency and the liberals moving to the right under pressure from the industrialists, landowners, and military commanders, who were all increasingly alarmed by the collapse of authority and the popular disorders. Kerensky, despite an exalted sense of his mission to save Russia, was essentially a go-between and negotiator of political compromises, not greatly trusted or respected, and lacking a political base in any of the major parties. As he sadly complained, 'I struggle with the Bolsheviks of the left and the Bolsheviks of the right, but people demand that I lean on one or the other . . . I want to take a middle road, but nobody will help me.'[14]

It seemed increasingly likely that the Provisional Government would fall one way or the other, but the question was, which? The threat from the left was a popular uprising in Petrograd and/or Bolshevik *coup*. Such a challenge had failed in July, but German activity on the north-western fronts was heightening tension in the armed forces surrounding Petrograd in a most ominous way, and the influx of deserters who were aggrieved, armed, and unemployed presumably increased the danger of street violence in the city itself. The other threat to the Provisional Government was the possibility of a *coup* from the right to establish a law-and-order dictatorship. By the summer, this course was being discussed in high military circles and had support from some of the industrialists. There were signs that even the Cadets, who would obviously have to oppose such a move before the fact and in public statements, might accept a *fait accompli* with considerable relief.

In August, the *coup* from the right was finally attempted by General Lavr Kornilov, whom Kerensky had recently appointed Commander-in-Chief with a mandate to restore order and discipline in the Russian Army. Kornilov was evidently not motivated by personal ambition but by his sense of the national interest. He may, in fact, have believed that Kerensky would welcome an Army intervention to create a strong government and deal with left-wing troublemakers, since Kerensky, partially apprised of Kornilov's intentions, dealt with him in a peculiarly devious way. Misunderstandings between the two principal actors confused the situation, and the Germans' unexpected capture of Riga on the eve of Kornilov's move added to the mood of panic, suspicion and despair that was spreading among Russia's civilian and military leaders. In the last week of August, baffled but determined, General Kornilov dispatched troops from the front to Petrograd, ostensibly to quell disorders in the capital and save the Republic.

The attempted *coup* failed largely because of the unreliability of the troops and the energetic actions of the Petrograd workers. Railway-men diverted and obstructed the troop-trains; printers stopped publication of newspapers supporting Kornilov's move; metalworkers rushed out to meet the oncoming troops and explain that Petrograd was calm and their officers had deceived them. Under this pressure, the troops' morale disintegrated, the *coup* was aborted outside Petrograd without any serious military engagement, and General Krymov, the commanding officer acting under Kornilov's orders, surrendered to the Provisional Government and then committed suicide. Kornilov himself was arrested at Army Headquarters, offering no resistance and taking full responsibility.

In Petrograd, politicians of the centre and right rushed to reaffirm their loyalty to the Provisional Government, which Kerensky continued to head. But Kerensky's standing had been further damaged by his handling of the Kornilov affair, and the government weakened. The Executive Committee of the Petrograd Soviet also emerged with little credit, since the resistance to Kornilov had been organized largely at the local union and factory level; and this contributed to an upsurge of support for the Bolsheviks which almost immediately enabled them to displace the Soviet's old Menshevik–SR leadership. The Army High Command was hit hardest of all, since the arrest of the Commander-in-Chief and failure of the *coup* left it demoralized and confused; relations between officers and men deteriorated sharply; and, as if this were not enough, the German advance was continuing, with Petrograd the apparent objective. In mid-September, General Alekseev, Kornilov's successor, abruptly resigned as Commander-in-Chief, prefacing his statement with an emotional tribute to Kornilov's high motives. Alekseev felt he could no longer take responsibility for an army in which discipline had collapsed and 'our officers are martyrs'.

Practically speaking, in this hour of terrible danger, I can state with horror that we have no army (at these words the General's voice trembled and he shed a few tears), while the Germans are prepared, at any moment, to strike the last and most powerful blow against us.[15]

The left gained most from the Kornilov affair, since it gave substance to the previously abstract notion of a counter-revolutionary threat from the right, demonstrated working-class strength, and at the same time convinced many workers that only their armed vigilance could save the revolution from its enemies. The Bolsheviks, with many of their leaders still gaoled or in hiding, played no special role in the actual resistance to Kornilov. But the new swing of popular opinion towards them, already discernible early in August, greatly accelerated after Kornilov's aborted *coup*; and in a practical sense they were to reap future benefit from the creation of workers' militia units or 'Red Guards' which began in response to the Kornilov threat. The Bolsheviks' strength was that they were the only party uncompromised by association with the bourgeoisie and the February regime, and the party most firmly identified with ideas of workers' power and armed uprising.

The October Revolution

From April to August, the Bolsheviks' slogan 'All power to the soviets' was essentially provocative—a taunt directed at the moderates who controlled the Petrograd Soviet and did not want to take all power. But the situation changed after the Kornilov affair, when the moderates lost control. The Bolsheviks gained a majority in the Petrograd Soviet on 31 August and a majority in the Moscow Soviet on 5 September. If the second national Congress of Soviets, scheduled to meet in October, followed the same political trend as the capitals, what were the implications? Did the Bolsheviks want a quasi-legal transfer of power to the soviets, based on a decision by the Congress that the Provisional Government had no further mandate to rule? Or was their old slogan really a call for insurrection, or an affirmation that the Bolsheviks (unlike the rest) had the courage to take power?

In September, Lenin wrote from his hiding-place in Finland urging the Bolshevik party to prepare for an armed insurrection. The revolutionary moment had come, he said, and must be seized before it was too late. Delay would be fatal. The Bolsheviks must act *before* the meeting of the Second Congress of Soviets, pre-empting any decision that the Congress might make.

Lenin's advocacy of immediate armed uprising was passionate, but not entirely convincing to his colleagues in the leadership. Why should the Bolsheviks take a desperate gamble, when the tide was so clearly running their way? Moreover, Lenin himself did not return and take charge: surely he would have done this if he were really serious? No doubt the accusations against him in the summer had left him overwrought. Possibly he had been brooding about his and the Central Committee's hesitation during the July Days, convincing himself that a rare chance to seize power had been lost. In any case, Lenin was temperamental, like all great leaders. This mood might pass.

Lenin's behaviour at this time was certainly contradictory. On the one hand, he insisted on a Bolshevik insurrection. On the other, he remained for some weeks in Finland, despite the fact that the Provisional Government had released the left politicians imprisoned in July, the Bolsheviks now controlled the Soviet, and the time of acute danger to Lenin had surely passed. When he did return to Petrograd, probably at the end of the first week of October, he stayed in hiding, isolated even from the Bolsheviks, and communicated with his Central Committee through a series of angry, exhortatory letters.

On 10 October, the Bolshevik Central Committee agreed that an uprising was desirable in principle. But clearly many of the Bolsheviks were inclined to use their position in the Soviet to achieve a quasi-legal, non-violent transfer of power. According to the later recollections of a member of the Petrograd Bolshevik Committee,

Hardly any of us thought of the beginning as an armed seizure of all the institutions of government at a specific hour . . . We thought of the uprising as the simple seizure of power by the Petrograd Soviet. The Soviet would cease complying with the orders of the Provisional Government, declare itself to be the power, and remove anyone who tried to prevent it from doing this.[16]

Trotsky, recently released from prison and admitted to Bolshevik Party membership, was now the leader of the Bolshevik majority in the Petrograd Soviet. He had also been one of the Soviet's leaders in 1905. Although he did not openly disagree with Lenin (and later claimed that their views had been identical), it seems probable that he too had doubts about insurrection, and thought that the Soviet could and should handle the problem of dislodging the Provisional Government.[17]

Strong objections to a Bolshevik-led insurrection came from two of Lenin's old Bolshevik comrades, Grigorii Zinoviev and Lev Kamenev. They thought it irresponsible for the Bolsheviks to seize power by a *coup*, and unrealistic to think that they could hold power alone. When Zinoviev and Kamenev published these arguments under their own names in a non-Bolshevik daily newspaper (Maxim Gorky's *Novaya zhizn'*), Lenin's anger and frustration rose to new heights. This was understandable, since it was not only an act of defiance but also a public announcement that the Bolsheviks were secretly planning an insurrection.

It may seem remarkable, under these circumstances, that the Bolsheviks' October *coup* actually came off. But in fact the advance publicity probably helped Lenin's cause rather than hindered it. It put the Bolsheviks in a position where it would have been difficult *not* to act, unless they had been arrested beforehand, or received strong indications that the workers, soldiers, and sailors of the Petrograd area would repudiate any revolutionary action. But Kerensky did not take decisive counter-measures against the Bolsheviks, and their control of the Petrograd Soviet's Military-Revolutionary Committee made it comparatively easy to organize a *coup*. The Military-Revolutionary Committee's basic purpose was to organize the workers' resistance to counter-revolution *à la* Kornilov, and Kerensky was clearly not in a position to interfere with that. The war situation was also an important factor: the Germans were advancing, and Petrograd was threatened. The workers had already rejected a Provisional Government order to evacuate the major industrial plants from the city: they did not trust the Government's intentions towards the revolution, and for that matter they did not trust its will to fight the Germans. (Paradoxically, given the workers' approval of the Bolshevik 'peace' slogan both they and the Bolsheviks reacted belligerently when the German threat was immediate and actual: the old peace slogans were scarcely heard in the autumn and winter of 1917, after the fall of Riga.) Had Kerensky tried to disarm the workers as the Germans approached, he would probably have been lynched as a traitor and capitulationist.

The insurrection began on 24 October, the eve of the meeting of the Second Congress of Soviets, when the forces of the Soviet's Military-Revolutionary Committee began to occupy key governmental institutions, taking over the telegraph offices and the railway stations, setting up roadblocks on the city's bridges and surrounding the Winter Palace, where the Provisional Government was in session.

They encountered almost no violent resistance. The streets remained calm, and citizens continued to go about their everyday business. On the night of 24–25 October, Lenin came out of hiding and joined his comrades at the Smolny Institute, a former school for young ladies which was now the headquarters of the Soviet; he too was calm, having apparently recovered from his bout of nervous anxiety, and he resumed his old position of leadership as a matter of course.

By the afternoon of the 25th, the *coup* was all but accomplished—except, provokingly, for the taking of the Winter Palace, which was still under siege with the Provisional Government members inside. The Palace fell late in the evening, in a rather confused assault against a dwindling body of defenders. It was a less heroic occasion than later Soviet accounts suggest: the battleship *Aurora*, moored opposite the Palace in the River Neva, did not fire a single live shot, and the occupying forces let Kerensky slip out a side entrance and successfully flee the city by car. It was also slightly unsatisfactory in terms of political drama, since the Congress of Soviets—having delayed its first session for some hours, on Bolshevik insistence—finally began proceedings before the Palace fell, thus frustrating the Bolsheviks' wish to make a dramatic opening announcement. Still, the basic fact remained: the February regime had been overthrown, and power had passed to the victors of October.

Of course, this did leave one question unanswered. Who *were* the victors of October? In urging the Bolsheviks towards insurrection before the Congress of Soviets, Lenin had evidently wanted this title to go to the Bolsheviks. But the Bolsheviks had in fact organized the uprising through the Military-Revolutionary Committee of the Petrograd Soviet; and, by accident or design, the Committee had procrastinated until the eve of the meeting of the national Congress of Soviets. (Trotsky later described this as a brilliant strategy—presumably his own, since it was clearly not Lenin's—of using the soviets to legitimate a Bolshevik seizure of power.[18]) As the news went out to the provinces, the most common version was that the soviets had taken power.

The question was not wholly clarified at the Congress of Soviets which opened in Petrograd on 25 October. As it turned out, a clear majority of the Congress delegates had come with a mandate to support transfer of all power to the soviets. But this was not an exclusively Bolshevik group (300 of the 670 delegates were Bolsheviks, which gave the party a dominant position but not a majority), and such a mandate did not necessarily imply approval of the Bolsheviks' pre-emptive action. That action was violently criticized at the first session by a large group of Mensheviks and SRs, who then quit the Congress in protest. It was questioned in a more conciliatory manner by a Menshevik group headed by Martov, Lenin's old friend; but Trotsky consigned these critics, in a memorable phrase, to 'the dust-heap of history'.

At the Congress, the Bolsheviks called for the transfer of power to workers', soldiers', and peasants' soviets throughout the country. As far as central power was concerned, the logical implication was surely that the place of the old Provisional Government would be taken by the standing Central Executive Committee of the soviets, elected by the Congress and including representatives from a number of political parties. But this was not so. To the surprise of many delegates, it was announced that central governmental functions would be assumed by a new Council of People's Commissars, whose all-Bolshevik membership was read out to the Congress on 26 October by a spokesman for the Bolshevik Party. The head of the new government was Lenin, and Trotsky was People's Commissar (Minister) of Foreign Affairs.

Some historians have suggested that the Bolsheviks' one-party rule emerged as the result of historical accident rather than intention[19]—that is, that the Bolsheviks did not mean to take power for themselves alone. But if the intention in question is Lenin's, the argument seems dubious; and Lenin overrode the objections of other leading members of the party. In September and October, Lenin seems clearly to have wanted the Bolsheviks to take power, not the multi-party soviets. He did not even want to use the soviets as camouflage, but would apparently have preferred to stage an unambiguous Bolshevik *coup*. In the provinces, certainly, the immediate result of the October Revolution was that the soviets took power; and the local soviets were not always dominated by Bolsheviks. Although the Bolsheviks' attitude to the soviets after October is open to different interpretations,[20] it is perhaps fair to say that they had no objection in principle to the soviets exercising power at a local level, as long as the soviets were reliably Bolshevik. But this requirement was difficult to square with democratic elections contested by other political parties.

Certainly Lenin was quite firm on the issue of coalition in the new central government, the Council of People's Commissars. In November 1917, when the Bolshevik Central Committee discussed the possibility of moving from an all-Bolshevik government to a broader socialist coalition, Lenin was adamantly against it, even though several Bolsheviks resigned from the government in protest. Later a few 'left SRs' (members of a splinter group of the SR Party that had accepted the October *coup*) were admitted to the Council of People's Commissars, but they were politicians without a strong party base. They were dropped from the government in mid-1918, when the left SRs staged an uprising in protest against the peace treaty recently signed with Germany. The Bolsheviks made no further effort to form a coalition government with other parties.

Had the Bolsheviks a popular mandate to rule alone, or did they believe that they had one? In the elections for the Constituent Assembly (held, as scheduled before the October *coup*, in November 1917), the Bolsheviks won 25 per cent of the popular vote. This put them second to the SRs, who won 40 per cent of the vote (left SRs, who supported the Bolsheviks on the issue of the *coup*, were not differentiated in the voting lists). The Bolsheviks had expected to do better, and this is perhaps explicable if one examines the vote in more detail.[21] The Bolsheviks took Petrograd and Moscow, and probably won in urban Russia as a whole. In the armed forces, whose five million votes were counted separately, the Bolsheviks had an absolute majority in the Armies of the Northern and Western Fronts and the Baltic Fleet—the constituencies they knew best, and where they were best known. On the southern fronts and in the Black Sea Fleet, they lost to the SRs and Ukrainian parties. The SRs' overall victory was the result of winning the peasant vote in the villages. But there was a certain ambiguity in this. The peasants were probably single-issue voters, and the SR and Bolshevik programmes on the land were virtually identical. The SRs, however, were much better known to the peasantry, their traditional constituency. Where the peasants knew the Bolshevik programme (usually as a result of proximity to towns, garrisons or railways, where the Bolsheviks had done more campaigning), their votes were split between the Bolsheviks and the SRs.

In democratic electoral politics, nevertheless, a loss is a loss. The Bolsheviks did not take that view of the elections to the Constituent Assembly: they did not abdicate because they had failed to win (and, when the Assembly met and proved hostile, they unceremoniously dispersed it). However, in terms of the mandate to rule, they could and did argue that it was not the population as a whole that they claimed to represent. They had taken power in the name of the working class. The conclusion to be drawn from the elections to the Second Congress of Soviets and the Constituent Assembly was that, as of October to November 1917, they were drawing more working-class votes than any other party.

But what if at some later time the workers should withdraw their support? The Bolsheviks' claim to represent the will of the proletariat was based on faith as well as observation: it was quite possible, in Lenin's terms, that at some time in the future the workers' proletarian consciousness might prove inferior to that of the Bolshevik Party, without necessarily removing the party's mandate to rule. Probably the Bolsheviks did not expect this to happen. But many of their opponents of 1917 did, and they assumed that Lenin's party would not give up power even if it lost working-class support. Engels had warned that a socialist party taking power prematurely might find itself isolated and forced into repressive dictatorship. Clearly the Bolshevik leaders, and Lenin in particular, were willing to take that risk.

3 The Civil War

THE October seizure of power was not the end of the Bolshevik Revolution but the beginning. The Bolsheviks had taken control in Petrograd and, after a week of street-fighting, in Moscow. But the soviets that had sprung up in most provincial centres still had to follow the capitals' lead in overthrowing the bourgeoisie (often, at local level, this meant ousting a 'Committee of Public Safety' set up by the solid citizenry of the town); and, if a local soviet was too weak to take power, support was unlikely to be forthcoming from the capitals. Bolsheviks in the provinces, as well as at the centre, had to work out their attitude to local soviets which successfully asserted their authority but happened to be dominated by Mensheviks and SRs. Rural Russia, moreover, had largely thrown off the yoke of authority imposed from the towns. The outlying and non-Russian areas of the old Empire were in various conditions of complex turmoil. If the Bolsheviks had taken power with the intention of governing the country in any conventional sense, some long and difficult struggles against anarchic, decentralizing, and separatist tendencies lay ahead.

In fact, Russia's future form of government remained an open question. Judging by the October *coup* in Petrograd, the Bolsheviks had reservations about their own slogan of 'All power to the soviets'. On the other hand, the slogan seemed to fit the mood of the provinces in the winter of 1917–18—but this, perhaps, is only another way of saying that central governmental authority had temporarily collapsed. It remained to be seen just what the Bolsheviks meant by their other slogan of 'dictatorship of the proletariat'. If, as Lenin had strongly suggested in his recent writings, it meant crushing the counter-revolutionary efforts of the old possessing classes, the new dictatorship would have to establish coercive organs comparable in function to the Tsarist secret police; if it meant a dictatorship of the Bolshevik Party, as many of Lenin's political opponents suspected, the continued existence of other political parties raised major problems. Yet could the new regime allow itself to act as repressively as the old Tsarist autocracy, and could it retain popular support if it did? A 'dictatorship of the proletariat', more-over, appeared to imply broad powers and independence for all proletarian institutions, including trade unions and factory commit-tees. What happened if the trade unions and factory committees had different concepts of the workers' interests? If 'workers' control' in the factories meant worker self-management, was this compatible with the centralized planning of economic development that the Bolsheviks saw as a basic socialist objective?

Russia's revolutionary regime had also to consider its position in the wider world. The Bolsheviks considered themselves to be part of an international proletarian revolutionary movement, and hoped that their success in Russia would spark similar revolutions throughout Europe; they did not originally think of the new Soviet Republic as a nation state which would have to have conventional diplomatic relations with other states. When Trotsky was appointed Commissar of Foreign Affairs, he expected to issue a few revolutionary procla-mations and then 'close up shop'; as Soviet representative in the Brest-Litovsk peace negotiations with Germany early in 1918, he attempted (unsuccessfully) to subvert the whole diplomatic process by speaking past Germany's official representatives to the German people, particularly the German soldiers on the Eastern Front. Recognition of the need for conventional diplomacy was delayed by the Bolshevik leaders' deep belief in the early years that Russia's Revolution could not survive long without the support of workers' revolutions in the more advanced capitalist countries of Europe. Only as the fact of revolutionary Russia's isolation gradually became clear did they begin to reassess their position *vis-à-vis* the outside world, and by that time the habit of combining revolutionary appeals with more conventional state-to-state contacts was firmly entrenched.

The territorial boundaries of the new Soviet Republic and policy towards non-Russian nationalities constituted another major prob-lem. Before the war, Lenin had cautiously endorsed a principle of national self-determination. For Marxists, however, the class ques-tion was always more important than the national one; and the Bolsheviks found it very difficult to believe that national separatist movements directed against a 'capitalist' or 'autocratic' state were in any sense comparable to separatist movements which involved repudiation of the internationalist revolutionary cause that the Bol-sheviks and the new Soviet Republic represented.

It was as natural for the Bolsheviks in Petrograd to hope for a revolutionary victory of soviet power in Azerbaijan as to hope for it in Hungary—though the Azerbaijanis, as former subjects of Imperial Petersburg, were not very likely to appreciate this. It was also natural for the Bolsheviks to support workers' soviets in Ukraine and oppose the 'bourgeois' Ukrainian nationalists, regardless of the fact that the soviets (reflecting the ethnic composition of Ukraine's working class) tended to be dominated by Russians, Jews, and Poles who were 'foreigners' not only to the nationalists but also to the Ukrainian peasantry. The Bolsheviks' dilemma—most dramatically illustrated when the Red Army marched into Poland in 1920 and the workers of Warsaw resisted the 'Russian invasion'—was that policies of proletarian internationalism in practice had a disconcerting similarity to the policies of old-style Russian imperialism.[1]

But the Bolsheviks' behaviour and policies after the October Revolution were not formed in a vacuum, and the factor of civil war is almost always crucial in explaining them. The Civil War broke out in the middle of 1918, only a few months after the formal conclusion of the Brest-Litovsk peace between Russia and Germany and Russia's definitive withdrawal from the European war. It was fought on many fronts, against a variety of White (that is, anti-Bolshevik) Armies, which had the support of a number of foreign powers including Russia's former Allies in the European war. The Bolsheviks saw it as a class war, both in domestic and international terms: Russian proletariat against Russian bourgeoisie; international revolution (as exemplified by the Soviet Republic) against international capitalism. The Red (Bolshevik) victory in 1920 was therefore a proletarian triumph, but the bitterness of the struggle had indicated the strength and determination of the proletariat's class enemies. Although the interventionist capitalist powers had withdrawn, the Bolsheviks did not believe that this withdrawal was permanent. They expected that at a more opportune moment the forces of international capitalism would return, and crush the international workers' revolution at its source.

The Civil War undoubtedly had an enormous impact on the Bolsheviks and the young Soviet Republic. It polarized the society, leaving lasting resentments and scars; and foreign intervention created a permanent Soviet fear of 'capitalist encirclement' which had elements of paranoia and xenophobia. The Civil War devastated the economy, bringing industry almost to a standstill and emptying the towns. This had political as well as economic and social implications, since it meant at least a temporary disintegration and dispersal of the industrial proletariat—the class in whose name the Bolsheviks had taken power.

It was in the context of civil war that the Bolsheviks had their first experience of ruling, and this undoubtedly shaped the party's subsequent development in many important respects.[2] Over half a million Communists served in the Red Army at some time during the Civil War (and, of this group, roughly half joined the Red Army before joining the Bolshevik Party). Of all members of the Bolshevik Party in 1927, 33 per cent had joined in the years 1917–20, while only 1 per cent had joined before 1917.[3] Thus the underground life of the prerevolutionary party—the formative experience of the 'old guard' of Bolshevik leaders—was known to most party members in the 1920s only through hearsay. For the cohort that had joined the party during the Civil War, the party was a fighting brotherhood in the most literal sense. The Communists who had served in the Red Army brought military jargon into the language of party politics, and made the army tunic and boots—worn even by those who had stayed in civilian posts or been too young to fight—almost a uniform for party members in the 1920s and early 1930s.

In the judgement of one historian, the Civil War experience 'militarized the revolutionary political culture of the Bolshevik movement', leaving a heritage that included 'readiness to resort to coercion, rule by administrative fiat (*administrirovanie*), centralized administration [and] summary justice'.[4] This view of the origins of Soviet (and Stalinist) authoritarianism is in many ways more satisfactory than the traditional Western interpretation, which stressed the party's prerevolutionary heritage and Lenin's advocacy of centralized party organization and strict discipline. Nevertheless, other factors reinforcing the party's authoritarian tendencies must also be taken into account. In the first place, a minority dictatorship was almost bound to be authoritarian, and those who served as its executants were extremely likely to develop the habits of bossing and bullying that Lenin often criticized in the years after 1917. In the second place, the Bolshevik Party owed its success in 1917 to the support of Russia's workers, soldiers, and sailors; and such people were much less inclined than the Old Bolshevik intellectuals to worry about crushing opposition or imposing their authority by force rather than by tactful persuasion.

Finally, in considering the link between the Civil War and

authoritarian rule, it must be remembered that there was a two-way relationship between the Bolsheviks and the political environment of 1918–20. The Civil War was not an unforeseeable act of God for which the Bolsheviks were in no way responsible. On the contrary, the Bolsheviks had associated themselves with armed confrontation and violence in the months between February and October 1917; and, as the Bolshevik leaders knew perfectly well before the event, their October *coup* was seen by many as an outright provocation to civil war. The Civil War certainly gave the new regime a baptism by fire, and thereby influenced its future development. But it was the kind of baptism the Bolsheviks had risked, and may even have sought.[5]

The Civil War, the Red Army and the Cheka

In the immediate aftermath of the Bolsheviks' October *coup*, Cadet newspapers issued a call to arms for the salvation of the revolution, General Krasnov's loyalist troops unsuccessfully engaged pro-Bolshevik forces and Red Guards in the battle of Pulkovo Heights outside Petrograd, and there was heavy fighting in Moscow. In this preliminary round, the Bolsheviks were the victors. But almost certainly they were going to have to fight again. In the large Russian armies on the southern fronts of the war against Germany and Austria-Hungary, the Bolsheviks were much less popular than in the north-west. Germany remained at war with Russia and, despite the advantages to the Germans of peace on the Eastern Front, Russia's new regime could no more count on German benevolence than it could on sympathy from the allied powers. As the commander of German forces on the Eastern Front wrote in his diary early in February 1918, on the eve of a renewed German offensive after the breakdown of peace negotiations at Brest-Litovsk,

No other way out is possible, otherwise these brutes [the Bolsheviks] will wipe up the Ukrainians, the Finns and the Balts, and then quietly get together a new revolutionary army and turn the whole of Europe into a pig-sty . . . The whole of Russia is no more than a vast heap of maggots—a squalid, swarming mass.[6]

During the peace negotiations at Brest in January, Trotsky had refused the terms offered by the Germans and attempted a strategy of 'No war, no peace', meaning that the Russians would neither continue the war nor sign a peace on unacceptable terms. This was pure bravado, since the Russian Army at the front was melting away, while the German Army, despite Bolshevik appeals to working-class brotherhood, was not. The Germans called Trotsky's bluff and advanced, occupying large areas of Ukraine.

Lenin regarded it as imperative that a peace should be concluded. This was very rational, given the state of Russia's fighting forces and the likelihood that the Bolsheviks would soon be fighting a civil war; and, in addition, the Bolsheviks had repeatedly stated before the October Revolution that Russia should withdraw immediately from the European imperialist war. However, it would be rather misleading to see the Bolsheviks as a 'peace party' in any meaningful sense by October. The Petrograd workers who had been ready to fight for the Bolsheviks against Kerensky in October had also been ready to fight for Petrograd against the Germans. This belligerent mood was strongly reflected in the Bolshevik Party in the early months of 1918, and was subsequently to be a great asset to the new regime in fighting the Civil War. At the time of the Brest negotiations, Lenin had the greatest difficulty in persuading even the Bolshevik Central Committee of the need to sign a peace with Germany. The Party's 'left Communists'—a group which included the young Nikolai Bukharin, later to earn a place in history as Stalin's last major opponent in the leadership—advocated a revolutionary war of guerrilla resistance to the German invaders; and the left SRs, who were currently in alliance with the Bolsheviks, took a similar position. Lenin finally forced the decision through the Bolshevik Central Committee by threatening to resign, but it was a hard-fought battle. The terms which the Germans imposed after their successful offensive were considerably harsher than those they had offered in January. (But the Bolsheviks were lucky: Germany subsequently lost the European war, and as a result lost its conquests in the East.)

The Peace of Brest-Litovsk provided only a brief respite from military threat. Officers of the old Russian Army were gathering forces in the south, in the Cossack territory of the Don and the Kuban, while Admiral Kolchak was establishing an anti-Bolshevik government in Siberia. The British had landed troops at Russia's two northern ports, Arkhangelsk and Murmansk, ostensibly to fight the Germans but in fact also with the intention of supporting local opposition to the new Soviet regime.

By a strange fluke of war, there were even non-Russian troops passing through Russian territory—the Czech Legion, numbering about 30,000 men, which was hoping to get to the Western Front before the European war ended, so that they could reinforce their claim to national independency by fighting on the Allied side against their old Austrian masters. Unable to cross the battlelines from the Russian side, the Czechs were making an improbable journey *east* on the Trans-Siberian Railway, planning to reach Vladivostok and return to Europe by ship. The Bolsheviks had sanctioned the trip, but this did not prevent local soviets from reacting with hostility to the arrival of contingents of armed foreigners at railway stations along the way. In May 1918, the Czechs had their first clash with a Bolshevik-dominated soviet in the Urals town of Chelyabinsk. Other Czech units supported Russian SRs in Samara when they rose up against the Bolsheviks to establish a short-lived Volga Republic. The Czechs ended up more or less fighting their way out of Russia, and it was only after many months that they were all evacuated from Vladivostok and shipped back to Europe.

The Civil War proper—Bolshevik 'Reds' against Russian anti-Bolshevik 'Whites'—began in the summer of 1918. At that time, the Bolsheviks moved their capital to Moscow, since Petrograd had escaped the threat of capture by the Germans only to come under attack by a White Army under General Yudenich. But large areas of the country were not effectively under Moscow's control (these included Siberia, southern Russia, the Caucasus, Ukraine, and even much of the Urals and Volga region, where local Bolsheviks intermittently dominated many of the urban soviets), and White Armies threatened the Soviet Republic from the east, the north-west, and the south. Of the Allied Powers, Britain and France were extremely hostile to the new regime in Russia and supported the Whites, though their direct military involvement was on a fairly small scale. Both the US and Japan sent troops to Siberia—the Japanese hoping for territorial gains, the Americans in a muddled effort to restrain the Japanese, police the Trans-Siberian Railway and perhaps support Kolchak's Siberian government if it measured up to American democratic standards.

Although the Bolsheviks' situation seemed desperate indeed in 1919, when the territory firmly under their control was roughly that of Muscovite Russia in the sixteenth century, their opponents also had formidable problems. In the first place, the White Armies operated largely independently of each other, without central direction or co-ordination. In the second place, the Whites' control over their territorial bases was even more tenuous than the Bolsheviks'. Where they set up regional governments, the administrative machinery had to be created almost from scratch, and the results were extremely unsatisfactory. Russia's transport and communications systems, historically highly centralized on Moscow and Petersburg, did not facilitate White operations around the periphery. The White forces were harassed not only by the Reds but also the so-called 'Green Armies'—peasant and Cossack bands that gave allegiance to neither side but were most active in the outlying areas in which the Whites were based. The White Armies, well supplied with officers from the old Tsarist Army, had difficulty keeping up the numbers of recruits and conscripts for them to command.

The Bolsheviks' fighting force was the Red Army, organized under the direction of Trotsky, who became Commissar for War in the spring of 1918. The Red Army had to be built up from the beginning, since the disintegration of the old Russian Army had gone too far to be halted (the Bolsheviks announced its total demobilization shortly after taking power). The nucleus of the Red Army, formed at the beginning of 1918, consisted of Red Guards from the factories and pro-Bolshevik units from the old Army and Fleet. This was expanded by voluntary recruitment and, from the summer of 1918, selective conscription. Workers and Communists were the first to be drafted, and throughout the Civil War provided a high proportion of the combat troops. But by the end of the Civil War, the Red Army was a massive institution with an enlistment of over five million, mainly peasant conscripts. Only about a tenth of these were fighting troops (the forces deployed by either Reds or Whites on a given front rarely exceeded 100,000), while the rest were in supply, transport, or administrative work. To a considerable extent, the Red Army had to fill the gap left by the breakdown of civilian administration: it was the largest and best-functioning bureaucracy the Soviet regime possessed in the early years, with first claim on all available resources.

Although many Bolsheviks had an ideological preference for militia-type units like the Red Guards, the Red Army was organized from the first on regular army lines, with the soldiers subject to military discipline and the officers appointed and not elected. Because of the shortage of trained military professionals, Trotsky and Lenin insisted on using officers from the old Tsarist Army, although this policy was much criticized in the Bolshevik Party, and the Military Opposition faction tried to get it reversed at two successive party congresses. By the end of the Civil War, the Red Army had over 50,000 former Tsarist officers, most of them conscripted; and the great majority of its senior military commanders came from this group. To ensure that the old officers remained loyal, they were paired with political commissars, usually Communists, who had to countersign all orders and shared final responsibility with the military commanders.

In addition to its military forces, the Soviet regime quickly created a security force—the All-Russian Extraordinary Commission for Struggle against Counter-Revolution, Sabotage, and Speculation, known as the Cheka. When this institution was founded in December 1917, its immediate task was to control the outbreak of banditry, looting, and raiding of liquor stores that followed the October seizure of power. But it soon assumed the broader functions of a security police, dealing with anti-regime conspiracies and keeping watch on groups whose loyalty was suspect, including bourgeois 'class enemies', officials of the old regime and Provisional Government and members of the opposition political parties. After the outbreak of the Civil War, the Cheka became an organ of terror, dispensing summary justice including executions, making mass arrests, and taking hostages at random in areas that had come under White control or were suspected of leaning towards the Whites. According to Bolshevik figures for twenty provinces of European Russia in 1918 and the first half of 1919, at least 8,389 persons were shot without trial by the Cheka, and 87,000 arrested.[7]

The Bolsheviks' Red terror had its equivalent in the White terror practised by the anti-Bolshevik forces in the areas under their control, and the same kind of atrocities were attributed to each side by the other. However, the Bolsheviks were forthright about their own use of terror (which implies not only summary justice but also random punishment, unrelated to individual guilt, whose purpose is the intimidation of a specific group or the population as a whole); and they took pride in being tough-minded about violence, avoiding the mealy-mouthed hypocrisy of the bourgeoisie and admitting that the rule of any class, including the proletariat, involves coercion of other classes. Lenin and Trotsky expressed contempt for socialists who could not understand the necessity of terror. 'If we are not ready to shoot a saboteur and White Guardist, what sort of revolution is that?' Lenin admonished his colleagues in the new government.[8]

When the Bolsheviks looked for historical parallels for the activities of the Cheka, they normally referred to the revolutionary terror of 1794 in France. They did not see any parallel to the Tsarist secret police, though Western historians have often drawn one. The Cheka, in fact, operated much more openly and violently than the old police: its style had more in common with the 'class vengeance' of Baltic sailors dealing with their officers in 1917, on the one hand, or Stolypin's armed pacification of the countryside in 1906–7, on the other. The parallel with the Tsarist secret police became more appropriate after the Civil War, when the Cheka was replaced by the GPU (Chief Political Administration)—a move associated with the abandonment of terror and the extension of legality—and the security organs became more routine, bureaucratic, and discreet in their methods of operation. In this longer perspective, there clearly were strong elements of continuity (though apparently not continuity of personnel) between the Tsarist and Soviet secret police; and the clearer they became, the more evasive and hypocritical were Soviet discussions of the security function.

The Red Army and the Cheka both made important contributions to the Bolshevik victory in the Civil War. However, it would be inadequate to explain that victory simply in terms of military strength and terror, especially as no one has yet found a way of measuring the balance of force between Reds and Whites. Active support and passive acceptance by the society must also be taken into account, and indeed these factors were probably crucial. The Reds had active support from the urban working class, with the Bolshevik Party providing an organizational nucleus. The Whites had active support from the old middle and upper classes, with part of the Tsarist officer corps serving as the main organizing agent. But it was surely the peasantry, constituting the great majority of the population, that tipped the balance.

Both the Red Army and the White Armies conscripted peasants in the territories they controlled, and both had a substantial desertion rate. As the Civil War progressed, however, the Whites' difficulties with the peasant conscripts became markedly greater than the Reds'. The peasants resented the Bolsheviks' policy of grain requisitioning (see below, p. 81), but the Whites were no different in this respect. The peasants also had no great enthusiasm for serving in anyone's army, as the experience of the Russian Army in 1917 had amply demonstrated. However, the mass desertions of peasants in 1917 had been closely related to the land seizures and redistribution by the villages. This process was largely completed by the end of 1918 (which greatly reduced the peasants' objection to army service), and the Bolsheviks had approved it. The Whites, on the other hand, did not approve of land seizures and supported the former landowners' claims. Thus on the crucial issue of land, the Bolsheviks were the lesser evil.[9]

War Communism

The Bolsheviks took over a war economy in a state of near collapse, and their first and overwhelming problem was to keep it running.[10] This was the pragmatic context of the economic policies of the Civil War that were later labelled 'War Communism'. But there was also an ideological context. In the long term, the Bolsheviks aimed to abolish private property and the free market and distribute products according to need, and in the short term, they might be expected to choose policies that would bring these ideals closer to fulfilment. The balance between pragmatism and ideology in War Communism has long been a subject of debate,[11] the problem being that policies like nationalization and state distribution can plausibly be explained either as a pragmatic response to the exigencies of war or as an ideological imperative of communism. It is a debate in which scholars on both sides can quote the pronouncements of Lenin and other leading Bolsheviks, since the Bolsheviks themselves were not sure of the answer. From a Bolshevik perspective of 1921, when War Communism was jettisoned in favour of the New Economic Policy, the pragmatic interpretation was clearly preferable: once War Communism had failed, the less said about its ideological underpinnings the better. But from an earlier Bolshevik perspective—for example, that of Bukharin and Preobrazhensky in their classic *ABC of Communism* (1919)—the opposite was true. While War Communism policies were in force, it was natural for Bolsheviks to give them an ideological justification—to assert that the party, armed with the scientific ideology of Marxism, was in full control of events rather than simply struggling to keep up.

The question lying behind the debate is how quickly the Bolsheviks thought they could move towards communism; and the answer depends on whether we are talking about 1918 or 1920. The Bolsheviks' first steps were cautious, and so were their pronouncements about the future. However, from the outbreak of the Civil War in mid-1918 the Bolsheviks' earlier caution began to disappear. To cope with a desperate situation, they turned to more radical policies and, in the process, tried to extend the sphere of centralized government control much further and faster than they had originally intended. In 1920, as the Bolsheviks headed towards victory in the Civil War and disaster in the economy, a mood of euphoria and desperation took hold. With the old world disappearing in the flames of Revolution and Civil War, it seemed to many Bolsheviks that a new world was about to arise, phoenix-like, from the ashes. This hope, perhaps, owed more to anarchist ideology than to Marxism, but it was nevertheless expressed in Marxist terms: with the triumph of proletarian revolution, the transition to communism was imminent, possibly only weeks or months away.

This sequence is clearly illustrated in one of the key areas of economic policy, nationalization. As good Marxists, the Bolsheviks nationalized banking and credit very quickly after the October Revolution. But they did *not* immediately embark upon wholesale nationalization of industry: the first nationalization decrees concerned only individual large concerns like the Putilov Works that were already closely involved with the state through defence production and government contracts.

A variety of circumstances, however, were to extend the scope of nationalization far beyond the Bolsheviks' original short-term intentions. Local soviets expropriated plants on their own authority. Some plants were abandoned by their owners and managers; others were nationalized on the petition of their workers, who had driven out the old management, or even on the petition of managers who wanted protection against unruly workers. In the summer of 1918, the government issued a decree nationalizing all large-scale industry, and by the autumn of 1919 it was estimated that over 80 per cent of such enterprises had in fact been nationalized. This far exceeded the organizational capacities of the new Supreme Economic Council: in practice, if the workers themselves could not keep the plants going by organizing the supply of raw materials and distribution of finished products, the plants often just closed down. Yet, having gone so far, the Bolsheviks felt impelled to go further. In November 1920, the government nationalized even small-scale industry, at least on paper. In practice, of course, the Bolsheviks were hard put to name or identify their new acquisitions, let alone direct them. But in theory the whole sphere of production was now in the hands of Soviet power, and even artisan workshops and windmills were part of a centrally directed economy.

A similar sequence led the Bolsheviks towards an almost complete prohibition on free trade and a virtually moneyless economy by the end of the Civil War. From their predecessors they inherited rationing in the towns (introduced in 1916) and a state monopoly on grain which in theory required the peasants to deliver their whole surplus (introduced in the spring of 1917 by the Provisional Government). But the towns were still short of bread and other foodstuffs because the peasants were unwilling to sell when there were almost no manufactured goods on the market to buy. Shortly after the October Revolution, the Bolsheviks tried to increase grain deliveries by offering the peasants manufactured goods instead of money in exchange. They also nationalized wholesale trade and, after the outbreak of the Civil War, prohibited free retail trade in most basic foodstuffs and manufactured products and tried to convert the consumer co-operatives into a state distribution network. These were emergency measures to cope with the food crisis in the towns and the problems of Army supply. But obviously the Bolsheviks could— and did—justify them in ideological terms.

As the food crisis in the towns worsened, barter became a basic form of exchange, and money lost its value. By 1920, wages and salaries were being paid partly in kind (food and goods), and there was even an attempt to construct a budget on a commodity rather than a money basis. Urban services, in so far as they still functioned in the decaying cities, no longer had to be paid for by the individual user. Some Bolsheviks hailed this as an ideological triumph—the 'withering away of money' that indicated how close the society had already come to communism. To less optimistic observers, however, it looked like runaway inflation.

Unfortunately for the Bolsheviks, ideology and practical imperatives did not always converge so neatly. The divergences (together with some Bolshevik uncertainties about what their ideology actually meant in concrete terms) were particularly evident in policies affecting the working class. In regard to wages, for example, the Bolsheviks had egalitarian instincts rather than a strictly egalitarian policy in practice. In the interests of maximizing production, they tried to retain piece-work in industry, though the workers regarded this basis of payment as essentially inegalitarian and unfair. Shortages and rationing probably tended to reduce urban inequalities during the Civil War period, but this could scarcely be counted as a Bolshevik achievement. In fact, the rationing system under War Communism favoured certain categories of the population, including Red Army personnel, skilled workers in key industries, Communist administrators, and some groups of the intelligentsia.

Factory organization was another touchy question. Were the factories to be run by the workers themselves (as the Bolsheviks' 1917 endorsement of 'workers' control' seemed to suggest), or by managers appointed by the state, following the directions of central planning and co-ordinating agencies? The Bolsheviks favoured the second, but the effective outcome during War Communism was a compromise, with considerable variation from place to place. Some factories continued to be run by elected workers' committees. Others were run by an appointed director, often a Communist but sometimes the former manager, chief engineer or even owner of the plant. In yet other cases, a worker or group of workers from the factory committee or local trade union was appointed to manage the plant, and this transitional arrangement—halfway between workers' control and appointed management—was often the most successful.

In dealing with the peasantry, the Bolsheviks' first problem was the practical one of getting food. State procurements of grain were not improved either by outlawing private grain trading or by offering manufactured goods instead of money in payment: the state still had too few goods to offer, and the peasants remained unwilling to deliver their produce. Given the urgent necessity of feeding the towns and the Red Army, the state had little choice but to take the peasants' produce by persuasion, cunning, threats, or force. The Bolsheviks adopted a policy of grain requisitioning, sending workers' and soldiers' brigades—usually armed, and if possible provided with some goods for barter—to get the hoarded grain out of the peasants' barns. Obviously this produced strained relations between the Soviet regime and the peasantry. But the Whites did the same thing, as had occupying armies throughout the ages. The Bolsheviks' need to live off the land probably surprised themselves more than it surprised the peasants.

But there were other aspects of Bolshevik policy that evidently did surprise and alarm the peasantry. In the first place, they tried to facilitate grain procurements by splitting the village into opposing groups. Believing that the growth of rural capitalism had already produced significant class differentiation among the peasants, the Bolsheviks expected to receive instinctive support from the poor and landless peasants and instinctive opposition from the richer ones. They therefore began to organize village Committees of the Poor, and encouraged them to co-operate with Soviet authorities in extracting grain from the barns of richer peasants. The attempt proved a dismal failure, partly because of the normal village solidarity against outsiders and partly because many formerly landless and poor peasants had improved their position as a result of the land seizures and redistributions of 1917–18. Worse still, it demonstrated to the peasants that the Bolsheviks' understanding of revolution in the countryside was quite different from their own.

For the Bolsheviks, still thinking in terms of the old Marxist debate with the Populists, the *mir* was a decaying institution, corrupted by the Tsarist state and undermined by emergent rural capitalism, lacking any potential for socialist development. Moreover, the Bolsheviks believed, the 'first revolution' in the countryside—land seizures and egalitarian redistribution—was already being followed by a 'second revolution', a class war of poor peasants against rich peasants, which was destroying the unity of the village community and must ultimately break the authority of the *mir*.[12] For the peasants, on the other hand, the *mir* was perceived as a true peasant institution, historically abused and exploited by the state, which had finally thrown off state authority and accomplished a peasant revolution.

Though the Bolsheviks had let the peasants have their way in 1917–18, their long-term plans for the countryside were quite as disruptive as Stolypin's had been. They disapproved of almost every aspect of the traditional rural order, from the *mir* and the strip system of dividing the land to the patriarchal family (*The ABC of Communism* even looked forward to the time when peasant families would give up the 'barbaric' and wasteful custom of eating supper at home, and join their neighbours at a communal village dining-room[13]). They were meddlers in village affairs, like Stolypin; and although they could not in principle share his enthusiasm for a small-farming petty-bourgeoisie, they still had enough ingrained dislike of peasant backwardness to continue the Stolypin policy of consolidating the households' scattered strips into solid blocks suitable for modern small farming.[14]

But the Bolsheviks' real interest was large-scale agriculture, and only the political imperative of winning over the peasantry had led them to condone the breaking up of large estates that took place in 1917–18. On some of the remaining state lands, they set up state farms (*sovkhozy*)—in effect, the socialist equivalent of large-scale capitalist agriculture, with appointed managers supervising the work of agricultural labourers who worked for wages. The Bolsheviks also believed that collective farms (*kolkhozy*) were preferable in political terms to traditional or individual small-holding peasant farming; and some collective farms were established in the Civil War period, usually by demobilized soldiers or workers fleeing hunger in the towns. The collective farms did not divide their land into strips, like the traditional peasant village, but worked the land and marketed produce collectively. Often, the early collective farmers had an ideology similar to the founders of utopian agricultural communities in the United States and elsewhere, pooling almost all their resources and possessions; and, like the utopians, they rarely made a success of farming or even survived long as harmonious communities. The peasants regarded both state and collective farms with suspicion. They were too few and weak to constitute a serious challenge to traditional peasant farming. But their very existence reminded the peasants that the Bolsheviks had strange ideas and were not to be trusted too far.

Visions of the new world

There was a wildly impractical and utopian streak in a great deal of Bolshevik thinking during the Civil War.[15] No doubt all successful revolutions have this characteristic: the revolutionaries must always be driven by enthusiasm and irrational hope, since they would otherwise make the common-sense judgement that the risks and costs of revolution outweigh the possible benefits. The Bolsheviks thought they were immune from utopianism because their socialism was scientific. But, whether or not they were right about the inherently scientific nature of Marxism, even science needs human interpreters, who make subjective judgements and have their own emotional biases. The Bolsheviks were revolutionary enthusiasts, not laboratory assistants.

It was a subjective judgement that Russia was ready for proletarian revolution in 1917, even though the Bolsheviks cited Marxist social-science theory to support it. It was a matter of faith rather than scientific prediction that world revolution was imminent (in Marxist terms, after all, the Bolsheviks might have made a mistake and taken power too soon). The belief, underlying the later economic policies of War Communism, that Russia was on the brink of the definitive transition to communism had scarcely any justification in Marxist theory. The Bolsheviks' perception of the real world had become almost comically distorted in many respects by 1920. They sent the Red Army to advance on Warsaw because, to many Bolsheviks, it seemed obvious that the Poles would recognize the troops as proletarian brothers rather than Russian aggressors. At home, they confused rampant inflation and currency devaluation with the withering away of money under communism. When war and famine produced bands of homeless children during the Civil War, some Bolsheviks saw even this as a blessing in disguise, since the state could give the children a true collectivist upbringing (in orphanages) and they would not be exposed to the bourgeois influence of the old family.

The same spirit was noticeable in the Bolsheviks' early approach to the tasks of government and administration. The utopian texts here were Marx and Engels's dictum that under communism the state would wither away, and the passages in Lenin's *State and Revolution* (1917) where he suggested that administration would ultimately cease to be the business of full-time professionals and would become a rotating duty of the whole citizenry. In practice, however, Lenin always kept a hard-headed realism about government: he was not among those Bolsheviks who saw the old administrative machinery collapsing in the years 1917–20 and concluded that the state was already withering away as Russia approached communism.

But the Bolshevik authors of *The ABC of Communism* (1919), Bukharin and Preobrazhensky, got much more carried away. They had the kind of vision of a depersonalized, scientifically regulated world that the contemporary Russian writer Evgenii Zamyatin satirized in *We* (written in 1920) and George Orwell later described in *Nineteen Eighty-four*. This world was the antithesis of any actual Russia, past, present, or future; and in the chaos of the Civil War that must have made it particularly appealing. In explaining how it would be possible to run a centrally planned economy after the withering away of the state, Bukharin and Preobrazhensky wrote:

The main direction will be entrusted to various kinds of book-keeping offices or statistical bureaux. There, from day to day, account will be kept of production and all its needs; there also it will be decided whither workers must be sent, whence they must be taken, and how much work there is to be done. And inasmuch as, from childhood onwards, all will have been accustomed to social labour, and since all will understand that this work is necessary and that life goes easier when everything is done according to a pre-arranged plan and when the social order is like a well-ordered machine, all will work in accordance with the indications of the statistical bureaux. There will be no need for special ministers of State, for police or prisons, for laws and decrees—nothing of the sort. Just as in an orchestra all the performers watch the conductor's baton and act accordingly, so here all will consult the statistical reports and will direct their work accordingly.[16]

This may have sinister overtones to us, thanks to Orwell's *Nineteen Eighty-four*, but in contemporary terms it was bold, revolutionary thinking that was as excitingly modern (and remote from mundane reality) as Futurist art. The Civil War was a time when intellectual and cultural experimentation flourished, and an iconoclastic attitude to the past was *de rigueur* among young radical intellectuals. Machines—including the 'well-ordered machine' of future society—fascinated artists and intellectuals. Sentiment, spirituality, human drama, and undue interest in individual psychology were out of fashion, often denounced as 'petty-bourgeois'. Avant-garde artists like the poet Vladimir Mayakovsky and the theatre director Vsevolod Meyerhold saw revolutionary art and revolutionary politics as part of the same protest against the old, bourgeois world. They were among the first members of the intelligentsia to accept the October Revolution and offer their services to the new Soviet government, producing propaganda posters in Cubist and Futurist style, painting revolutionary slogans on the walls of former palaces, staging mass re-enactments of revolutionary victories in the streets, bringing acrobatics as well as politically-relevant messages into the conventional theatre, and designing non-representational monuments to revolutionary heroes of the past. If the avant-garde artists had had their way, traditional bourgeois art would have been liquidated even more quickly than the bourgeois political parties. The Bolshevik leaders, however, were not quite convinced that artistic Futurism and Bolshevism were inseparable natural allies, and took a more cautious position on the classics.

The ethos of revolutionary liberation was more wholeheartedly accepted by the Bolsheviks (or at least by the Bolshevik intellectuals) where women and the family were concerned. The Bolsheviks supported the emancipation of women, as most members of the Russian radical intelligentsia had done since the 1860s. Like Friedrich Engels, who had written that in the modern family the husband is the 'bourgeois' and the wife the 'proletarian', they saw women as an exploited group. By the end of the Civil War, laws had been enacted that made divorce easily attainable, removed the formal stigma from illegitimacy, permitted abortion, and mandated equal rights and equal pay for women.

While only the most radical Bolshevik thinkers talked about destroying the family, there was a general assumption that women and children were potential victims of oppression within the family, and that the family tended to inculcate bourgeois values. The Bolshevik Party established special women's departments (*zhenotdely*) to organize and educate women, protect their interests, and help them to play an independent role. Young Communists had their own separate organizations—the Komsomol for adolescents and young adults, the Young Pioneers (established a few years later) for the ten to fourteen age group—which encouraged their members to watch out for 'bourgeois' tendencies at home and at school, and try to re-educate parents and teachers who looked back nostalgically to the old days, disliked the Bolsheviks and the revolution, or clung to 'religious superstitions'. If one slogan reported during the Civil War, 'Down with the capitalist tyranny of parents!', was a bit on the exuberant side for the older Bolsheviks, the spirit of youthful rebellion was generally prized and respected in the party in the early years.

Sexual liberation, however, was a young-Communist cause that rather embarrassed the Bolshevik leadership. Because of the party's position on abortion and divorce, it was widely assumed that the Bolsheviks advocated 'free love', meaning promiscuous sex. Lenin certainly did not: his generation was against the Philistine morality of the bourgeoisie, but emphasized comradely relations between the sexes and thought promiscuity showed a frivolous nature. Even Aleksandra Kollontai, the Bolshevik leader who wrote most about sexual questions and was something of a feminist, was a believer in love rather than the 'glass of water' theory of sex that was often attributed to her.

But the 'glass of water' approach was popular among young Communists, especially the men who had learnt their ideology in the

Red Army and regarded casual sex almost as a Communist rite of passage. Their attitude reflected a general wartime and postwar relaxation of morals that was even more marked in Russia than in other European countries. The older Communists had to put up with it—they assumed that sex was a private matter and, after all, they were revolutionaries and not bourgeois Philistines—as they had to put up with Cubists, advocates of Esperanto, and the nudists who, as an act of ideological affirmation, occasionally leapt naked on to crowded Moscow trams. But they felt that such things detracted from the high seriousness of the revolution.

The Bolsheviks in power

Having taken power, the Bolsheviks had to learn to govern. Hardly any of them had administrative experience: by previous occupation, most were professional revolutionaries, or workers, or free-lance journalists (Lenin listed his own profession as 'man of letters' [*literator*]). They despised bureaucracies and knew very little about how they worked. They knew nothing about budgets. As Anatolii Lunacharsky, head of the People's Commissariat of Enlightenment, wrote of his first finance officer:

[His] face always bore a mark of deepest astonishment when he brought us money from the bank. It still seemed to him that the Revolution and the organization of the new power were a sort of magical play, and that in a magical play it is impossible to receive real money.[17]

During the Civil War, most of the Bolsheviks' organizational talents went into the Red Army, the Food Commissariat, and the Cheka. Capable organizers from the local party committees and soviets were continually being mobilized for the Red Army or sent on trouble-shooting missions elsewhere. The old central government ministries (now People's Commissariats) were run by a small group of Bolsheviks, mainly intellectuals, and staffed largely by officials who had earlier worked for the Tsarist and Provisional Governments. Authority at the centre was confusingly divided between the government (Council of People's Commissars), the soviets' Central Executive Committee, and the Bolshevik Party's Central Committee, with its Secretariat and bureaux for organizational and political affairs, the Orgburo and the Politburo.

The Bolsheviks described their rule as a 'dictatorship of the proletariat', a concept which in operational terms had much in common with a dictatorship of the Bolshevik Party. It was clear from the first that this left little room for other political parties: those that were not outlawed for supporting the Whites or (in the case of the left SRs) staging a revolt were harassed and intimidated by arrests during the Civil War and forced into self-liquidation in the early 1920s. But it was much less clear what the dictatorship meant in terms of the form of government. The Bolsheviks did not initially think of their own party organization as a potential instrument of government. They seem to have assumed that the party organization would remain separate from government and free of administrative functions, just as it would have done if the Bolsheviks had become the governing party in a multi-party political system.

The Bolsheviks also described their rule as 'soviet power'. But this was never a very accurate description, in the first place because the October Revolution was essentially a party *coup*, not a soviet one, and in the second place because the new central government (chosen by the Bolshevik Central Committee) had nothing to do with the soviets. The new government took over control of the various ministerial bureaucracies from the Provisional Government, which in turn had inherited them from the Tsar's Council of Ministers. But the soviets did acquire a role at local level, where the old administrative machinery had completely collapsed. They (or more precisely their executive committees) became the local organs of the central government, creating their own bureaucratic departments of finance, education, agriculture, and so on. This administrative function gave point to the soviets' existence, even after soviet elections had become little more than a formality.

At first, the central government (Council of People's Commissars) seemed the hub of the new political system. But by the end of the Civil War, there were already signs that the Bolshevik Party's Central Committee and Politburo were tending to usurp the government's powers, while at local level the party committees were becoming dominant over the soviets. This primacy of party over state organs was to become a permanent feature of the Soviet system. It has been argued, however, that Lenin (who became seriously ill in 1921 and died in 1924) would have resisted any such tendency if he had not been removed from the scene by illness, and that he intended that the government rather than the party should play the dominant role.[18]

Certainly for a revolutionary and the creator of a revolutionary party, Lenin had an oddly conservative streak when it came to institutions. He wanted a real government, not some kind of improvised directorate, just as he wanted a real army, real laws, and perhaps even, in the final analysis, a real Russian Empire. However, it must be remembered that the members of this government were always in effect chosen by the Bolshevik Central Committee and its Politburo. Lenin headed the government, but he was also *de facto* head of the Central Committee and the Politburo; and it was these party organs rather than the government that dealt with the crucial military and foreign-policy questions during the Civil War. From Lenin's point of view, the big advantage of the government side of the system was probably that its bureaucracies included many technical experts (specialists on finance, engineering, law, public health, and so on), whose skills Lenin thought it essential to use. The Bolshevik Party was developing a bureaucracy of its own, but it did not employ outsiders who were not party members. In the party, and especially among its working-class members, there was great suspicion of 'bourgeois experts'. This had already been clearly demonstrated in the strong Bolshevik opposition in 1918–19 to the army's use of military professionals (the former Tsarist officers).

The nature of the political system that emerged after the Bolsheviks took power must be explained not only in terms of institutional arrangements but also in terms of the nature of the Bolshevik Party. It was a party with authoritarian tendencies, and one that had always had a strong leader—even, according to Lenin's opponents, a dictatorial one. Party discipline and unity had always been stressed. Before 1917, Bolsheviks who disagreed with Lenin on any important issue usually left the party. In the period 1917–20, Lenin had to deal with dissent and even organized dissident factions within the party, but he seems to have regarded this as an abnormal and irritating situation, and finally took decisive steps to change it (see below pp. 100–101). As to opposition or criticism from outside the party, the Bolsheviks had no tolerance for it either before or after the revolution. As Vyacheslav Molotov, a young associate of Lenin and Stalin, commented admiringly many years later, Lenin was even more tough-minded than Stalin in the early 1920s and 'would not have tolerated any opposition, if that had been an option'.[19]

Another key characteristic of the Bolshevik Party was that it was working-class—by its own self-image, by the nature of its support in the society, and to a substantial degree in terms of party membership. In the folk wisdom of the party, working-class Bolsheviks were 'tough', while Bolsheviks from the intelligentsia tended to be 'soft'. There is probably some truth to this, although Lenin and Trotsky, both intellectuals, were notable exceptions. The party's authoritarian, illiberal, rough, and repressive traits may well have been reinforced by the influx of working-class and peasant members in 1917 and the Civil War years.

The Bolsheviks' political thinking revolved around class. They believed that society was divided into antagonistic classes, that the political struggle was a reflection of the social one, and that members of the urban proletariat and other formerly exploited classes were the revolution's natural allies. By the same token, members of the old privileged and exploiting classes were regarded by the Bolsheviks as natural enemies. While the Bolsheviks' attachment to the proletariat was an important part of their emotional make-up, their hatred and suspicion of 'class enemies'—former nobles, members of the capitalist bourgeoisie, kulaks (prosperous peasants), and others—was equally profound, and perhaps even more significant in the long term. As far as the Bolsheviks were concerned, the old privileged classes were not just counter-revolutionary by definition; the mere fact of their existence constituted a counter-revolutionary conspiracy. This internal conspiracy was all the more threatening because, as both theory and the reality of foreign intervention in the Civil War demonstrated, it was backed by the forces of international capitalism.

In order to consolidate the proletarian victory in Russia, the Bolsheviks believed, it was necessary not only to eliminate the old patterns of class exploitation but also to reverse them. One way of reversing them was to apply principles of 'class justice':

In the old law-courts, the class minority of exploiters passed judgement upon the working majority. The law-courts of the proletarian dictatorship are places where the working majority passes judgement upon the exploiting minority. They are specially constructed for the purpose. The judges are elected by the workers alone. The judges are elected solely from among the workers. For the exploiters, the only right that remains is the right of being judged.[20]

These principles were obviously not egalitarian. But the Bolsheviks never claimed to be egalitarian in the period of revolution and transition to socialism. From the Bolshevik standpoint, it was impossible to regard all citizens as equal when some of them were class enemies of the regime. Thus the 1918 Constitution of the Russian Republic gave the vote to all 'toilers' (regardless of sex and nationality), but removed it from members of the exploiting classes and other identifiable enemies of Soviet power—employers of hired labour, persons living on unearned income or from rent, kulaks, priests, former gendarmes and some other categories of Tsarist official, and officers in the White Armies.

The question 'Who rules?' may be posed in abstract terms, but it also has the concrete meaning of 'Which people get the jobs?' Political power had changed hands, and (as a temporary expedient, the Bolsheviks thought) new bosses had to be found to replace the old ones. Given the Bolshevik cast of mind, class was inevitably a criterion in the selection. Some Bolshevik intellectuals, including Lenin, might argue that education was important as well as class, while a few others worried that workers departing for long periods from the factory bench would lose their proletarian identity. But in the party as a whole, the firm consensus was that the only people who could really be trusted with power by the new regime were proletarians who had been victims of exploitation under the old one.[21]

By the end of the Civil War, tens of thousands of workers, soldiers and sailors—Bolsheviks and those who had fought with them in 1917, in the first instance, but later those who had distinguished themselves in the Red Army or the factory committees, those who were young and comparatively well-educated, or simply those who showed an ambition to rise in the world—had become 'cadres', that is, persons holding responsible, usually administrative, jobs. They were in the Red Army command, the Cheka, the food administration, and the party and soviet bureaucracy. Many were appointed factory managers, usually after working in the local factory committee or trade union. In 1920-1, it was not absolutely clear to the party leaders if and how this process of 'worker promotion' could continue on a large scale, since the party's original pool of worker members had been much depleted, and industrial collapse and urban food shortages during the Civil War had dispersed and demoralized the industrial working class of 1917. Nevertheless, the Bolsheviks had found out by experience what they meant by 'dictatorship of the proletariat'. It was not a collective class dictatorship exercised by workers who remained in their old jobs at the factory bench. It was a dictatorship run by full-time 'cadres' or bosses, in which as many as possible of the new bosses were former proletarians.

4 NEP and the Future of the Revolution

THE Bolsheviks' victory in the Civil War brought them face to face with the country's internal problems of administrative chaos and economic devastation. The towns were hungry and half empty. Coal production had dropped catastrophically, the railways were breaking down, and industry was almost at a standstill. The peasants were mutinously resentful about food requisitioning. Crop sowings had dropped, and two consecutive years of drought had brought the Volga and other agricultural regions to the brink of starvation. Deaths from famine and epidemics in 1921–2 would exceed the combined total of casualties in the First World War and Civil War. In addition, the emigration of about two million persons during the years of revolution and war had removed much of Russia's educated elite.

There were over five million men in the Red Army, and the ending of the Civil War meant that most of them had to be demobilized. This was a much more difficult operation than the Bolsheviks had anticipated: it meant dismantling a large part of what the new regime had managed to build since the October Revolution. The Red Army had been the backbone of Bolshevik administration during the Civil War and of the economy of War Communism. Moreover, the Red Army soldiers constituted the largest body of 'proletarians' in the land. The proletariat was the Bolsheviks' chosen base of social support, and since 1917 they had defined the proletariat for all practical purposes as Russia's workers, soldiers, sailors, and poor peasants. Now a large part of the soldier-and-sailor group was about to disappear; and, worse still, the demobilized soldiers—unemployed, hungry, armed, often stranded far from home by transport breakdowns—were causing turmoil. With over two million demobilized by the early months of 1921, the Bolsheviks had discovered that fighters for the revolution could be transformed overnight into bandits.

The fate of the core proletariat of industrial workers was equally alarming. Industrial closures, military conscription, promotion to administrative work and, above all, flight from the towns because of hunger had reduced the number of industrial workers from 3.6 million in 1917 to 1.5 million in 1920. A substantial proportion of these workers had returned to the villages, where they still had family, and received plots of land as members of the village communities. The Bolsheviks did not know how many workers were in the villages, or how long they would remain there. Perhaps they had simply been reabsorbed into the peasantry and would never come back to the towns. But, whatever the long-term prospects, the immediate situation was clear: over half of Russia's 'dictator class' had vanished.[1]

The Bolsheviks had originally counted on support for the Russian Revolution from the European proletariat, which seemed poised on the brink of revolution at the end of the First World War. But the postwar revolutionary wave in Europe had subsided, leaving the Soviet regime without any European counterparts that could be regarded as permanent allies. Lenin concluded that the lack of support from abroad made it imperative for the Bolsheviks to obtain support from Russia's peasantry. Yet requisitions and the collapse of the market under War Communism had alienated the peasants, and in some regions they were in open revolt. In Ukraine, a peasant army headed by Nestor Makhno was fighting the Bolsheviks. In Tambov, an important agricultural region of central Russia, a peasant revolt was suppressed only after the dispatch of 50,000 Red Army troops.[2]

The worst blow to the new regime came in March 1921 when, after an outbreak of workers' strikes in Petrograd, the sailors at the nearby Kronstadt naval base rebelled.[3] The Kronstadters, heroes of the July Days of 1917 and supporters of the Bolsheviks in the October Revolution, had become almost legendary figures in Bolshevik mythology. Now they were repudiating the Bolsheviks' revolution, denouncing 'the arbitrary rule of the commissars' and calling for a true soviet republic of workers and peasants. The Kronstadt revolt occurred while the Tenth Party Congress was in session, and a number of delegates had to leave abruptly to join the elite units of Red Army and Cheka troops that were sent over the ice to fight the rebels. The occasion could scarcely have been more dramatic, or more calculated to imprint itself on Bolshevik consciousness. The Soviet press, in what seems to have been its first major effort to conceal unpleasant truths, claimed that the revolt was inspired by emigrés and led by a mysterious White general. But the rumours circulating at the Tenth Party Congress said otherwise.

The Kronstadt revolt seemed a symbolic parting of the ways between the working class and the Bolshevik Party. It was a tragedy, both to those who thought that the workers had been betrayed, and to those who thought that the party had been betrayed by the workers. The Soviet regime, for the first time, had turned its guns on the revolutionary proletariat. Moreover, the trauma of Kronstadt occurred almost simultaneously with another disaster for the revolution. German Communists, encouraged by Comintern leaders in Moscow, attempted a revolutionary uprising that failed miserably. Their defeat meant that even the most optimistic Bolsheviks lost hope that European revolution was imminent. The Russian Revolution would have to survive by its own, unaided efforts.

The Kronstadt and Tambov revolts, both fuelled by economic as well as political grievances, drove home the need for a new economic policy to replace the policy of War Communism. The first step, taken in the spring of 1921, was to end requisitioning of peasant produce and introduce a tax in kind. What this meant in practice was that the state took only a fixed quota instead of everything it could lay hands on (later, after the restabilization of the currency in the first half of the 1920s, the tax in kind became a more conventional money tax).

Since the tax in kind presumably left the peasant with a marketable surplus, the next logical step was to permit a revival of legal private trade and try to close down the flourishing black market. In the spring of 1921, Lenin was still strongly opposed to the legalization of trade, regarding it as a repudiation of Communist principles, but subsequently the spontaneous revival of private trade (often sanctioned by local authorities) presented the Bolshevik leadership with a *fait accompli*, which it accepted. These steps were the beginning of the New Economic Policy, known by the acronym NEP.[4] It was an improvised response to desperate economic circumstances, undertaken initially with very little discussion and debate (and little evident dissent) in the party and the leadership. The beneficial impact on the economy was swift and dramatic.

Further economic changes followed, amounting to a wholesale abandonment of the system that in retrospect began to be called 'War Communism'. In industry, the drive for complete nationalization was abandoned and the private sector was allowed to re-form, though the state retained control of the economy's 'commanding heights', including large-scale industry and banking. Foreign investors were invited to take out concessions for industrial and mining enterprises and development projects. The Finance Commissariat and State Bank began to heed the advice of the old 'bourgeois' financial experts, pushing for stabilization of the currency and limitations on government and public spending. The central government budget was severely cut, and efforts were made to increase state revenue from taxation. Services like schools and medical care, previously free, now had to be paid for by the individual user; access to old-age pensions and sickness and unemployment benefits was restricted by putting them on a contributory basis.

From the Communist standpoint NEP was a retreat, and a partial admission of failure. Many Communists felt deeply disillusioned: it seemed that the revolution had changed so little. Moscow, the Soviet capital since 1918 and headquarters of the Comintern, became a bustling city again in the early years of NEP, although to all outward appearances it was still the Moscow of 1913, with peasant women selling potatoes in the markets, churchbells and bearded priests summoning the faithful, prostitutes, beggars and pickpockets working the streets and railway stations, gypsy songs in the nightclubs, uniformed doormen doffing their caps to the gentry, theatre-goers in furs and silk stockings. In this Moscow, the leather-jacketed Communist seemed a sombre outsider, and the Red Army veteran was likely to be standing in line at the Labour Exchange. The revolutionary leaders, quartered incongruously in the Kremlin or the Hotel Luxe, looked to the future with foreboding.

The discipline of retreat

The strategic retreat of NEP, Lenin said, was forced on the Bolsheviks by desperate economic circumstances, and by the need to consolidate the victories that the revolution had already won. Its purpose was to restore the shattered economy and to calm the fears of the non-proletarian population. NEP meant concessions to the peasantry, the intelligentsia, and the urban petty-bourgeoisie; relaxation of controls over economic, social, and cultural life; the substitution of conciliation for coercion in the Communists' dealings with society as a whole. But Lenin made it very clear that the relaxation should not extend into the political sphere. Within the Communist Party, 'the slightest violation of discipline must be punished severely, sternly, ruthlessly':

When an army is in retreat, a hundred times more discipline is required than when the army is advancing, because during an advance everybody presses forward. If everybody started rushing back now, it would spell immediate and inevitable disaster . . . When a real army is in retreat, machine-guns are kept ready, and when an orderly retreat degenerates into a disorderly one, the command to fire is given, and quite rightly, too.

As for other political parties, their freedom to express their views publicly should be even more strictly curtailed than during the Civil War, particularly if they tried to claim the Bolsheviks' new moderate positions as their own.

When a Menshevik says, 'You are now retreating; I have been advocating retreat all the time; I agree with you, I am your man, let us retreat together,' we say in reply, 'For public manifestations of Menshevism our revolutionary courts must pass the death sentence, otherwise they are not our courts, but God knows what.'[5]

The introduction of NEP was accompanied by the arrest of a couple of thousand Mensheviks, including all the members of the Menshevik Central Committee. In 1922, a group of right SRs was put on public trial for crimes against the state: some were given death sentences, although the death sentences were apparently not carried out. In 1922 and 1923, some hundreds of prominent Cadets and Mensheviks were forcibly deported from the Soviet Republic. All political parties other than the ruling Communist Party (as the Bolshevik Party was now usually called) were effectively outlawed from this time on.

Lenin's eagerness to crush actual or potential opposition was startlingly demonstrated in a secret letter to the Politburo of 19 March 1922 in which he urged his colleagues to seize the opportunity offered by the famine to break the power of the Orthodox Church. 'Precisely now and only now, when they are eating human flesh in the famine regions and hundreds if not thousands of corpses are lying on the road, we can (and therefore must) carry out the seizure of church valuables with the most desperate and most ruthless energy . . .' In Shuia, where the campaign to seize church property in aid of famine relief had provoked violent demonstrations, Lenin counselled that 'as many as possible' local clergymen and bourgeois must be arrested and put on trial. The trial must end with the shooting of a very large number of the most influential and dangerous Black Hundreds of the city of Shuia, and . . . also of Moscow and . . . other spiritual centres. The more representatives of the reactionary clergy and reactionary bourgeoisie we manage to shoot on this occasion, the better. Now is the time to teach those types such a lesson that for a few dozen years they won't even be able even to think of resistance.[6]

At the same time, the question of discipline *within* the Communist Party was being re-examined. The Bolsheviks, of course, had always put a strong theoretical emphasis on party discipline, going back to Lenin's 1902 pamphlet *What Is To Be Done?* All Bolsheviks accepted the principle of democratic centralism, which meant that party members could freely debate issues before a policy decision was reached, but were bound to accept the decision once a final vote had been taken at a party congress or in the Central Committee. But the principle of democratic centralism did not in itself determine the party's conventions regarding internal debate—how much debate was acceptable, how sharply the party's leaders could be criticized, whether the critics could organize 'factions' or pressure groups on specific issues, and so on.

Before 1917, internal party debate meant for all practical purposes debate within the emigré community of Bolshevik intellectuals. Because of Lenin's dominant position, the Bolshevik emigrés were a more unified and homogenous group than their Menshevik and SR counterparts, who tended to cluster in a number of small circles with their own individual leaders and political identities. Lenin strongly resisted any such development among the Bolsheviks. When another powerful Bolshevik personality, Aleksandr Bogdanov, started to build a group of disciples who shared his philosophical and cultural approach in the post-1905 emigration, Lenin forced Bogdanov and his group to leave the Bolshevik Party, even though the group did not really constitute a political faction or an internal party opposition.

The situation changed radically after the February Revolution, with the merging of the emigré and underground Bolshevik contingents in a larger and more diverse party leadership, and the enormous increase in total party membership. In 1917, the Bolsheviks were more concerned with riding the wave of popular revolution than with party discipline. Many individuals and groups within the party disagreed with Lenin on major policy issues, both before and after October, and Lenin's opinion did not always prevail. Some groups solidified into semi-permanent factions, even after their platform had been rejected by a majority on the Central Committee or at a party congress. The minority factions (consisting largely of Old Bolshevik intellectuals) did not usually leave the party, as they would have done before 1917. Their party was now in power in a virtually one-party state; and leaving the party therefore meant quitting political life altogether.

Despite these changes, however, Lenin's old theoretical premises on party discipline and organization were still part of Bolshevik ideology at the end of the Civil War, as was clear from the Bolsheviks' handling of the new, Moscow-based international communist organization, the Comintern. In 1920, when the Second Comintern Congress discussed the prerequisites for admission to the Comintern, the Bolshevik leaders insisted on imposing conditions that were clearly based on the model of the pre-1917 Bolshevik Party in Russia, even though this meant excluding the large and popular Italian Socialist Party (which wanted to join the Comintern without first purging itself of its right wing and centrist groups) and weakening the Comintern as a competitor with the revived Socialist International in Europe. The '21 Conditions' for admission adopted by the Comintern required, in effect, that the member parties should be minorities of the far left, recruiting only highly committed revolutionaries, and preferably formed by a split (comparable with the split between Bolsheviks and Mensheviks in 1903) in which the party left had demonstratively separated itself from the 'reformist' centre and right wing. Unity, discipline, intransigence, and revolutionary professionalism were the essential qualities of any Communist party operating in a hostile environment.

Of course, the same rules did not necessarily apply to the Bolsheviks themselves, since they had already taken power. It could be argued that a ruling party in a one-party state must, in the first place, become a mass party, and, in the second place, accommodate and even institutionalize diversity of opinion. This was, in fact, what had been happening in the Bolshevik Party since 1917. Factions had developed within the leadership on specific policy issues and (in violation of the principle of democratic centralism) tended to remain in existence even after losing the final vote. By 1920, the factions participating in the current debate on the status of trade unions had become well-organized groups that not only offered competing policy platforms but also lobbied for support in the local party committees during the discussions and election of delegates that preceded the Tenth Party Congress. The Bolshevik Party, in other words, was developing its own version of 'parliamentary' politics, with the factions playing the role of political parties in a multi-party system.

From the standpoint of later Western historians—and indeed any outside observer with liberal-democratic values—this was obviously an admirable development and a change for the better. But the Bolsheviks were not liberal democrats; and there was considerable uneasiness within the Bolshevik ranks that the party was becoming fragmented, losing its old purposeful unity and sense of direction. Lenin certainly did not approve of the new style of party politics. In the first place, the trade-union debate—which was quite peripheral to the urgent and immediate problems facing the Bolsheviks in the aftermath of the Civil War—was taking up an enormous amount of the leaders' time and energy. In the second place, the factions were implicitly challenging Lenin's personal leadership in the party. One faction in the trade-union debate was led by Trotsky, the biggest man in the party next to Lenin despite his relatively recent admission to membership. Another faction, the 'Workers' Opposition' led by Aleksandr Shlyapnikov, claimed a special relationship with the party's working-class members which was potentially very damaging to the old core leadership of emigré intellectuals headed by Lenin.

Lenin therefore set out to destroy the factions and factionalism within the Bolshevik Party. To do this, he used tactics that were not only factional but downright conspiratorial. Both Molotov and Anastas Mikoyan, a young Armenian member of Lenin's group, later described the gusto and single-mindedness with which he set about the operation at the Tenth Party Congress early in 1921, holding secret meetings of his own supporters, splitting the big provincial delegations that were pledged to opposition factions, and drawing up lists of oppositionists to be voted down in the Central Committee elections. Lenin even wanted to call in 'an old Communist comrade from the underground who has type and a hand printing press' to run off leaflets for secret distribution—a suggestion that Stalin opposed on the grounds that it might be interpreted as factionalism.[7] (This was not the only time in the early Soviet years that Lenin reverted to the conspiratorial habits of the past. At a dark moment of the Civil War, Molotov recalled, Lenin summoned the leaders and told them that the fall of the Soviet regime was imminent.

False identity documents and secret addresses had been prepared for them: 'The party is going underground.'[8])

Lenin defeated Trotsky's faction and the Workers' Opposition at the Tenth Congress, securing a Leninist majority on the new Central Committee, and replacing two Trotskyist members of the Central Committee Secretariat with a Leninist, Molotov. But this was not all, by any means. In a move that stunned the factional leaders, Lenin's group introduced and the Tenth Party Congress approved a resolution 'On party unity', which ordered the existing factions to disband and forbade any further factional activity within the party.

Lenin described the ban on factions as temporary. This may conceivably have been sincere, but it is more likely that Lenin was simply giving himself room to back off if the ban turned out to be unacceptable to party opinion. As it happened, this was not the case: the party as a whole seemed quite prepared to sacrifice factions in the interests of unity, probably because the factions had not sunk deep roots in the party rank-and-file and were regarded by many as a prerogative of intellectual *frondeurs*.

The resolution 'On party unity' contained a secret clause allowing the party to expel persistent factionalists and the Central Committee to remove any of its own elected members who were judged guilty of factionalism. But there were strong reservations about this clause in the Politburo, and it was not formally invoked during Lenin's lifetime. In the autumn of 1921, however, a full-scale purge of the party was conducted on Lenin's initiative. That meant that in order to retain party membership, every Communist had to appear before a purge commission, justify his revolutionary credentials, and if necessary defend himself against criticism. The main alleged purposes of the 1921 party purge were to weed out 'careerists' and 'class enemies'; it was not formally directed against supporters of the defeated factions. Nevertheless, Lenin emphasized that 'all members of the Russian Communist Party who are in the slightest degree suspicious or unreliable . . . should be got rid of' (that is, expelled from the party); and, as T. H. Rigby comments, it is difficult to believe that no Oppositionists were among the almost 25 per cent of party members judged unworthy.[9]

While no prominent Oppositionists were expelled from the party in the purge, members of the opposition factions of 1920–1 did not all escape without punishment. The Central Committee's Secretariat, now headed by one of Lenin's men, had charge of appointments and distribution of party personnel; and it proceeded to send a number of prominent Workers' Oppositionists on assignments that kept them far from Moscow and thus effectively excluded them from active participation in leadership politics. The practice of using such 'administrative methods' to reinforce unity in the leadership was later greatly developed by Stalin, after he became General Secretary of the party (that is, head of the Central Committee's Secretariat) in 1922; and scholars have often regarded it as the real death-knell of internal democracy within the Soviet Communist Party. But it was a practice that originated with Lenin and arose out of the conflicts at the Tenth Party Congress, when Lenin was still the master strategist and Stalin and Molotov were his faithful henchmen.

The problem of bureaucracy

As revolutionaries, all Bolsheviks were against 'bureaucracy'. They could happily see themselves as party leaders or military commanders, but what true revolutionary could admit to becoming a bureaucrat, a *chinovnik* of the new regime? When they discussed administrative functions, their language became full of euphemisms: Communist officials were 'cadres' and Communist bureaucracies were 'apparats' and 'organs of Soviet power'. The word 'bureaucracy' was always pejorative: 'bureaucratic methods' and 'bureaucratic solutions' were to be avoided at all costs, and the revolution must be protected from 'bureaucratic degeneration'.

But all this should not obscure the fact that the Bolsheviks had established a dictatorship with the intention of ruling over the society and also transforming it. They could not achieve these objectives without administrative machinery, since they rejected from the start the idea that the society was capable of self-rule or spontaneous transformation. Thus the question was, what kind of administrative machinery did they need? They had inherited a large central government bureaucracy whose roots in the provinces had crumbled. They had soviets, which had partly taken over the functions of local government in 1917. Finally, they had the Bolshevik Party itself— an institution whose previous function of preparing and carrying out a revolution was clearly inappropriate to the situation after October.

The old government bureaucracy, now under Soviet control, still employed many officials and experts inherited from the Tsarist regime, and the Bolsheviks feared its capacity to undermine and sabotage their revolutionary policies. Lenin wrote in 1922 that the 'conquered nation' of old Russia was already in the process of imposing its values on the Communist 'conquerors':

If we take Moscow, with its 4,700 Communists in responsible positions, and if we take that huge bureaucratic machine, that gigantic heap, we must ask: Who is directing whom? I doubt very much whether it can truthfully be said that the Communists are directing that heap. To tell the truth, they are not directing, they are being directed . . . [The] culture [of the old bureaucracy] is miserable, insignificant, but it is still on a higher level than ours. Miserable and low as it is, it is higher than that of our responsible Communist administrators, for the latter lack administrative ability.[10]

Although Lenin saw the danger that Communist values would be swamped by the old bureaucracy, he believed that the Communists had no alternative to working with it. They needed the technical expertise of the old bureaucracy—not just administrative expertise, but also specialized knowledge in fields like government finance, railway administration, weights and measures, or geological survey-ing which the Communists themselves could not hope to supply. In Lenin's view, any party member who did not appreciate the new regime's need for 'bourgeois experts'—including those who had worked as officials or consultants to the old regime—was guilty of 'Communist conceit', meaning an ignorant and childish belief that Communists could solve all the problems for themselves. It would be a long time before the party could hope to train a sufficient number of Communist experts. Until then, Communists had to learn to work with the bourgeois experts and, at the same time, keep them under firm control.

Lenin's views on the experts were generally accepted by other party leaders, but they were less popular with the Communist rank-and-file. Most Communists had very little concept of the kind of expertise required at the higher levels of government. But they had a clear idea of what it meant at local level if minor officials from the old regime had managed to work their way into similar jobs with the soviet, or if a chief accountant happened to disapprove of the local Communist activists at his plant, or even if the village schoolteacher was a religious believer who made trouble for the Komsomol and taught catechism in school.

To most Communists it seemed obvious that if something important had to be done, it was best to do it through the party. Of course,
the party's central apparat could not compete with the huge government bureaucracy on a day-to-day administrative level—it was far
too small. But at local level, where the party committees and the
soviets were both building from scratch, the situation was different.
The party committee began to emerge as the dominant local authority
after the Civil War, with the soviet falling into a secondary role not
unlike that of the old zemstvo. Policy transmitted through the party
chain of command (from the Politburo, Orgburo, or Central Committee to the local party committees) had a much better chance of
being implemented than the mass of decrees and instructions that
came down from the central government to the uncooperative and
often chaotic soviets. The government had no hiring and firing
powers over soviet personnel, and it did not have much effective
budgetary control either. The party committees, on the other hand,
were staffed by Communists who were obliged by party discipline to
obey instructions from higher party organs. The party secretaries
who headed the committees, though formally elected by their local
party organizations, could in practice be removed and replaced by
the Secretariat of the party's Central Committee.

But there was one problem. The party's apparat—a hierarchy of
committees and 'cadres' (who were really appointed officials), topped
by the Central Committee's Secretariat—was to all intents and
purposes a bureaucracy; and bureaucracy was something that Communists disliked on principle. In the succession struggle of the mid-
1920s (see below, pp. 108–10), Trotsky tried to discredit Stalin, the
party's General Secretary, by pointing out that he had built a party
bureaucracy and was manipulating it for his own political ends.
However, this criticism seemed to make little impact on the party as
a whole. One reason was that the appointment (rather than election)
of party secretaries was much less of a departure from Bolshevik
tradition than Trotsky claimed: in the old days of the pre-1917
underground party, the committees had always relied heavily on the
leadership of professional revolutionaries sent out by the Bolshevik
Centre; and, even when the committees came above ground in 1917,
it was more common for them to forward urgent requests for 'cadres
from the Centre' than to insist on their democratic right to choose
their own local leadership.

In more general terms, however, it seems that most Communists simply did not regard the party apparat as a bureaucracy in the pejorative sense. To them (as to Max Weber), a bureaucracy operated by applying a clearly defined body of law and precedent, and was also characterized by a high degree of specialization and deference to professional expertise. But the party apparat of the 1920s was not specialized to any significant degree, and (except on security and military matters) it did not defer to professional experts. Its officials were not encouraged to 'go by the book': in the early years, there were no compilations of party decrees to fall back on, and later, any secretary who stuck to the letter of an old Central Committee instruction rather than responding to the spirit of the current party line was likely to be rebuked for 'bureaucratic tendencies'.

When Communists said that they did not want a bureaucracy, they meant that they did not want an administrative structure that would not or could not respond to revolutionary commands. But, by the same token, they wanted very much to have an administrative structure that *would* respond to revolutionary commands—one whose officials were willing to accept orders from the revolution's leaders and eager to carry out policies of radical social change. That was the revolutionary function that the party apparat (or bureaucracy) could perform, and most Communists instinctively recognized it.

Most Communists also believed that the organs of the 'proletarian dictatorship' ought to be proletarian, meaning by this that former workers should hold the responsible administrative jobs. This may not have been quite what Marx meant by proletarian dictatorship, and it was not quite what Lenin intended either. (The workers 'would like to build a better apparatus for us,' Lenin wrote in 1923, 'but they do not know how. They cannot build one. They have not yet developed the culture required for this; and it is culture that is required.'[11]) Nevertheless, it was taken for granted in all the party's debates that an institution's political soundness, revolutionary fervour, and freedom from 'bureaucratic degeneration' were directly correlated with the percentage of its cadres that came from the working class. The class criterion was applied to all the bureaucracies, including the party apparat. It was also applied in the party's own recruitment of members, which would necessarily affect the composition of the Soviet administrative elite in the future.

In 1921, the industrial working class was in a shambles and the regime's relationship with it was in a state of crisis. But by 1924, economic revival had eased some of the difficulties, and the working class was beginning to recover and grow. It was in that year that the party reaffirmed its commitment to a proletarian identity by announcing the Lenin Levy, a campaign to recruit hundreds of thousands of workers as party members. Implicit in this decision was a commitment to continue creating a 'proletarian dictatorship' by encouraging workers to move into administrative jobs.

By 1927, after three years of heavy working-class recruitment, the Communist Party had a total of over a million full members and candidates, of whom 39 per cent were currently workers by occupation and 56 per cent had been workers by occupation when they joined the party.[12] The difference between these two percentages indicates the approximate size of the group of worker-Communists who had moved permanently into administrative and other white-collar jobs. For workers who joined the party in the first decade of Soviet power, the odds on subsequent promotion into administrative work (even excluding promotions after 1927) were at least 50:50.

The party apparat was a more popular destination for rising working-class Communists than the government bureaucracy, partly because the workers felt more at home in a party environment and partly because educational deficiencies were less of a problem for a local party secretary than, say, a department head in the government's Commissariat of Finance. In 1927, 49 per cent of the Communists in responsible positions in the party apparat were former workers, whereas the corresponding figure for Communists in the government and soviet bureaucracy was 35 per cent. The discrepancy was even more marked at the highest levels of the administrative hierarchy. Very few of the Communists in the top government jobs were working-class, while almost half the regional party secretaries (heads of *oblast'*, *guberniya* and *krai* organizations) were former workers.[13]

The leadership struggle

While Lenin lived, the Bolsheviks acknowledged him as the party's leader. Nevertheless, the party did not formally have a leader, and it offended Bolsheviks to think that it necessarily required one. In moments of political turbulence, it was not unheard of for party comrades to rebuke Lenin for trading too much on his personal authority; and, while Lenin usually insisted on having his way, he did not require flattery or any particular show of respect. The Bolsheviks had nothing but contempt for Mussolini and his Italian Fascists, regarding them as political primitives for dressing up in comic-opera uniforms and swearing loyalty to *Il Duce*. Furthermore, they had learned the lessons of history, and had no intention of letting the Russian Revolution degenerate as the French Revolution had done when Napoleon Bonaparte declared himself Emperor. Bonapartism—the transformation of a revolutionary war leader into a dictator—was a danger that was often discussed in the Bolshevik Party, usually with implicit reference to Trotsky, the creator of the Red Army and hero of Communist youth during the Civil War. It was assumed that any potential Bonaparte would be a charismatic figure, capable of stirring oratory and grandiose visions, and probably wearing military uniform.

Lenin died in January 1924. But his health had been in serious decline since the middle of 1921, and thereafter he was only intermittently active in political life. A stroke in May 1922 left him partially paralysed, and a second stroke in March 1923 caused further paralysis and loss of speech. His political death, therefore, was a gradual process, and Lenin himself was able to observe its first results. His responsibilities as head of the government were taken over by three deputies, of whom Aleksei Rykov, who became Lenin's successor as Chairman of the Council of People's Commissars in 1924, was the most important. But it was clear that the main locus of power was not in the government but in the party's Politburo, which had seven full members including Lenin. The other Politburo members were Trotsky (Commissar for War), Stalin (General Secretary of the party), Zinoviev (head of the Leningrad party organization and also head of the Comintern), Kamenev (head of the Moscow party organization), Rykov (first deputy Chairman of the Council of People's Commissars), and Mikhail Tomsky (head of the Central Council of Trade Unions).

During Lenin's illness—and indeed after his death—the Politburo pledged itself to act as a collective leadership, and all its members vehemently denied that any one of them could replace Lenin or aspire to a similar position of authority. Nevertheless, a fierce though rather furtive succession struggle was in progress in 1923, with the triumvirate of Zinoviev, Kamenev, and Stalin pitted against Trotsky. Trotsky—the odd man out in the leadership, both because of his late entry into the Bolshevik Party and his spectacular performance since—was perceived as an ambitious contender for the top position, though he strongly denied it. In *The New Course*, written late in 1923, Trotsky retaliated with the warning that the old guard of the Bolshevik Party was losing its revolutionary spirit, succumbing to 'conservative, bureaucratic factionalism', and behaving more and more like a small ruling elite whose only concern was to stay in power.

Lenin, removed from active leadership by his illness but still able to observe the manœuvring of his would-be successors, was developing a similarly jaundiced view of the Politburo, which he began to describe as an 'oligarchy'. In the so-called 'Testament' of December 1922, Lenin surveyed the qualities of various party leaders—including the two he identified as outstanding, Stalin and Trotsky—and, in effect, damned them all with faint praise. His comment on Stalin was that he had accumulated enormous powers as General Secretary of the party, but might not always use those powers with sufficient caution. A week later, after a clash between Stalin and Lenin's wife, Nadezhda Krupskaya, over Lenin's sickbed regime, Lenin added a postscript to the Testament saying that Stalin was 'too rude' and should be removed from his position as General Secretary.[14]

At the time, many Bolsheviks would have been surprised to find Stalin ranked as Trotsky's equal in political stature. Stalin had none of the attributes that the Bolsheviks normally associated with outstanding leadership. He was not a charismatic figure, a fine orator, or a distinguished Marxist theoretician like Lenin or Trotsky. He was not a war hero, an upstanding son of the working class, or even much of an intellectual. He was a 'grey blur', in Nikolai Sukhanov's words—a good backroom politician, an expert on the internal working of the party, but a man without personal distinction. It was generally assumed that Zinoviev rather than Stalin was the dominant member of the Politburo triumvirate. Lenin, however, was in a better position than most to appreciate Stalin's capacities, for Stalin had been his right-hand man in the internal party struggle of 1920–1.

The triumvirate's battle with Trotsky came to a head in the winter of 1923–4. Despite the existence of a formal ban on party factions, the situation was in many ways comparable with that of 1920–1, and Stalin followed much the same strategy as Lenin had done. In the party discussions and election of delegates preceding the Thirteenth Party Conference, Trotsky's supporters campaigned as an opposition, while the party apparat was mobilized in support of 'the Central

Committee majority', that is, the triumvirate. The 'Central Committee majority' won, though there were pockets of support for Trotsky in the party cells of the central government bureaucracy, the universities, and the Red Army.[15] After the initial voting, an intensive assault on the pro-Trotsky cells induced many of them to defect to the majority. Only a few months later, when delegates were elected in the spring of 1924 for the forthcoming Party Congress, Trotsky's support seemed to have evaporated almost completely.

This was essentially a victory for the party machine—that is, a victory for Stalin, the General Secretary. The General Secretary was in a position to manipulate what one scholar has labelled a 'circular flow of power'.[16] The Secretariat appointed the secretaries who headed local party organizations, and could also dismiss them if they showed undesirable factional leanings. The local party organizations elected delegates to the national party conferences and congresses, and it was increasingly common for the secretaries to be routinely elected at the top of the local delegate list. The national party congresses, in turn, elected the members of the party's Central Committee, Politburo, and Orgburo—and, of course, the Secretariat. In short, the General Secretary could not only punish political opponents but also stack the congresses which confirmed his tenure in office.

With the crucial battle of 1923–4 behind him, Stalin proceeded systematically to consolidate his gains. In 1925, he broke with Zinoviev and Kamenev, forcing them into a defensive opposition in which they looked like the aggressors. Later, Zinoviev and Kamenev joined Trotsky in a united opposition, which Stalin defeated with ease: their supporters found themselves appointed to jobs in distant provinces; and, while the opposition leaders could still take the floor at party congresses, there were so few oppositionist delegates present that the leaders seemed irresponsible *frondeurs* who had totally lost touch with the mood of the party. In 1927, the opposition leaders and many of their supporters were finally expelled from the party for breaking the rule against factionalism. Trotsky and a number of other oppositionists were then sent off to administative exile in distant provinces.

Issues were argued in the conflict between Stalin and Trotsky, particularly with relation to industrialization strategy and policy towards the peasants. But Stalin and Trotsky were not deeply divided on these substantive issues (see below, pp. 114–16): both were industrializers without any special tenderness towards the peasantry, though Stalin's public stance in the mid-1920s was more moderate than Trotsky's; and a few years later, Stalin was to be accused of stealing Trotsky's policies in the First Five-Year Plan drive for rapid industrialization. For rank-and-file party members, the contenders' disagreements on issues were much less clearly perceived than some of their personal characteristics. Trotsky was widely (though not necessarily favourably) known to be a Jewish intellectual who had shown ruthlessness and a flamboyant, charismatic style of leadership during the Civil War; Stalin, a more neutral and shadowy figure, was known to be not charismatic, intellectual, or Jewish.

In a sense, the real issue in a conflict between a party machine and its challengers is the machine itself. Thus, whatever their original disagreements with the dominant faction, all the oppositions of the 1920s ended up with the same central grievance: the party had become 'bureaucratized', and Stalin had killed the tradition of internal party democracy.[17] This 'oppositionist' viewpoint has even been attributed to Lenin in his last years[18]—and perhaps with some justice, since Lenin too had been forced out of the inner circle of leaders, though in his case the cause was illness rather than political defeat. But it would be hard to see Lenin, Stalin's political mentor in so many ways, as a real convert on principle to the cause of party democracy against the party machine. In the past, it had not been concentration of power *per se* that worried Lenin, but the question in whose hands power was concentrated. Similarly, in the Testament of December 1922, Lenin did not propose reducing the powers of the party Secretariat. He simply said that someone other than Stalin should be appointed General Secretary.

Still, whatever the elements of continuity between Lenin and the Stalin of the 1920s, Lenin's death and the succession struggle constituted a political turning-point. In seeking power, Stalin used Leninist methods against his opponents, but used them with a thoroughness and ruthlessness that Lenin—whose personal authority in the party was long established—never approached. Once in power, Stalin began by taking Lenin's old role: first among equals in the Politburo. But Lenin, meanwhile, had been transformed by death into the Leader, endowed with almost godlike qualities, beyond error or reproach, his body embalmed and reverently placed in the Lenin Mausoleum for the inspiration of the people.[19] The posthumous Lenin cult had destroyed the old Bolshevik myth of a leaderless party. If the new leader wished to become more than first among equals, he had a foundation on which to build.

Building socialism in one country

The Bolsheviks summarized their objectives in power as 'the building of socialism'. However vague their concept of socialism may have been, they had a clear idea that the key to 'building socialism' was economic development and modernization. As prerequisites of socialism, Russia needed more factories, railways, machinery, and technology. It needed urbanization, a shift of population from the countryside to the towns, and a much larger, permanent urban working class. It needed greater popular literacy, more schools, more skilled workers and engineers. Building socialism meant transforming Russia into a modern industrial society.

The Bolsheviks had a clear image of this transformation because it was essentially the transformation wrought by capitalism in the more advanced countries of the West. But the Bolsheviks had taken power 'prematurely'—that is, they had undertaken to do the capitalists' work for them in Russia. The Mensheviks thought this risky in practice and highly dubious in theory. The Bolsheviks themselves did not really know how it was going to be accomplished. In the first years after the October Revolution, they often implied that Russia would need the help of industrialized Western Europe (once Europe had followed Russia's revolutionary example) in order to move forward to socialism. But the revolutionary movement in Europe collapsed, leaving the Bolsheviks still uncertain how to proceed, but determined to make their way somehow. Looking back at the old argument about premature revolution in 1923, Lenin continued to find the Mensheviks' objections 'infinitely commonplace'. In a revolutionary situation, as Napoleon said of war, *'on s'engage et puis on voit'*. The Bolsheviks had taken the risk and, Lenin concluded, there could now—six years later—be no doubt that 'on the whole' they had been successful.[20]

This was perhaps putting a brave face on it, for even the most optimistic Bolsheviks had been shaken by the economic situation that confronted them at the end of the Civil War. It was as if, in mockery of all the Bolsheviks' aspirations, Russia had shrugged off the twentieth century and regressed from comparative to total backwardness. Towns had withered, machinery was rusting in deserted factories, mines were flooded, and half the industrial working class had apparently been reabsorbed into the peasantry. As the 1926 census would reveal, European Russia was actually *less* urbanized in the years immediately after the Civil War than it had been in 1897. The peasants had reverted to traditional subsistence agriculture, seemingly intent on recapturing that golden age in the past before the advent of serfdom.

The introduction of NEP in 1921 was an admission that the Bolsheviks could perhaps do the work of the big capitalists, but for the time being could not get along without the small ones. In the towns, private trade and small-scale private industry were allowed to revive. In the countryside, the Bolsheviks had already let the peasants have their way over the land, and were now anxious to ensure that they played their role as reliable 'petty-bourgeois' producers for the urban market, as well as consumers of urban manufactured goods. The policy of assisting peasants to consolidate their holdings (begun under Stolypin) was continued by Soviet authorities in the 1920s, though without any frontal attack on the authority of the *mir*. From the Bolshevik standpoint, small-capitalist peasant farming was preferable to the traditional communal and near-subsistence cultivation of the village, and they did their best to encourage it.

But the Bolsheviks' attitude to the private sector during NEP was always ambivalent. They needed it to restore the shattered economy after the Civil War, and they assumed that they would probably need it for the early stages of subsequent economic development. However, even a partial revival of capitalism was offensive and frightening to most party members. When 'concessions' for manufacturing and mining were granted to foreign companies, Soviet authorities hovered anxiously, waiting for the moment when the enterprise looked solid enough for them to withdraw the concession and buy the foreign company out. Local private entrepreneurs ('Nepmen') were treated with great suspicion, and the restrictions on their activities became so onerous by the second half of the 1920s that many businesses went into liquidation, and the remaining Nepmen acquired the shady look of profiteers operating on the fringes of the law.

The Bolsheviks' approach to the peasantry during NEP was even more contradictory. Collective and large-scale farming was their long-term objective, but the conventional wisdom of the mid-1920s held that this was a prospect only for the distant future. In the meantime, the peasantry must be conciliated and allowed to follow its own petty-bourgeois path; and it was in the state's economic interest to encourage the peasants to improve their agricultural methods and increase production. This implied that the regime tolerated and even approved of peasants who worked hard and made a success of their individual farming.

In practice, however, the Bolsheviks were extremely suspicious of peasants who became more prosperous than their neighbours. They regarded such peasants as potential exploiters and rural capitalists, often classifying them as 'kulaks', which meant that they suffered various forms of discrimination including loss of voting rights. For all their talk of forging an alliance with the 'middle' peasant (the category between 'prosperous' and 'poor', into which the great majority of all peasants fell), the Bolsheviks were continually on the watch for signs of class differentiation within the peasantry, hoping for a chance to throw themselves into a class struggle and support the poor peasants against the richer ones.

But it was the town, not the village, that the Bolsheviks saw as the key to economic development. When they spoke of building socialism, the main process that they had in mind was industrialization, which would ultimately transform not only the urban economy but also the rural one. In the immediate aftermath of the Civil War, it seemed a gigantic task just to restore industrial production to the levels of 1913: Lenin's electrification plan was virtually the only long-range development scheme of the first half of the 1920s, and, for all the publicity given to it, the original goals were quite modest. But in 1924-5, an unexpectedly rapid industrial and general economic recovery caused an upsurge of optimism among the Bolshevik leaders, and a reassessment of the possibilities of major industrial development in the near future. Feliks Dzerzhinsky, head of the Cheka during the Civil War and one of the party's best organizers, took over the chairmanship of the Supreme Economic Council (Vesenkha) in 1924 and began to mould it into a powerful ministry of industry which, like its Tsarist predecessors, focused largely on the development of the metallurgical, metalworking, and machine-building industries. The new optimism about rapid industrial development was reflected in Dzerzhinsky's confident statement at the end of 1925:

These new tasks [of industrialization] are not just tasks of the kind we were considering in abstract terms ten, fifteen or even twenty years ago, when we said that it is impossible to build socialism without setting a course for the industrialization of the country. Now we are not posing the question on a general theoretical level, but as a definite, concrete objective of all our present economic activity.[21]

There was no real disagreement among the party leaders on the desirability of rapid industrialization, although inevitably the issue was bandied around in the factional struggles of the mid-1920s. Trotsky, one of the few Bolsheviks who had actively supported state economic planning even in the dismal early years of NEP, would have been happy to champion the cause of industrialization against his political opponents. But in 1925 Stalin made it clear that industrialization was now *his* issue and one of his highest priorities. On the eighth anniversary of the October Revolution, Stalin compared the party's recent decision to press forward with industrialization on the basis of a Five-Year Plan with Lenin's momentous decision to seize political power in 1917.[22] This was a bold comparison, suggesting not only the stature Stalin hoped for himself but also the importance he attached to the industrialization policy. Already, it appeared, he was staking out his place in history as Lenin's successor: he was to be Stalin the Industrializer.

The party's new orientation was expressed in Stalin's slogan 'Socialism in One Country'. What this meant was that Russia was preparing to industrialize, to become strong and powerful, and to create the preconditions of socialism by its own unaided efforts. National modernization, not international revolution, was the primary objective of the Soviet Communist Party. The Bolsheviks did not need revolutions in Europe as a prop for their own proletarian revolution. They did not need the goodwill of foreigners—whether revolutionaries or capitalists—to build Soviet power. Their own forces were sufficient, as they had been in October 1917, to win the fight.

Given the undeniable fact of Soviet isolation in the world and Stalin's intention to industrialize no matter what the cost, 'Socialism in One Country' was a useful rallying cry and good political strategy. But it was the kind of strategy that Old Bolsheviks, trained in a strict school of Marxist theory, often felt compelled to dispute even when they had no major practical objections. There were, after all, *theoretical* problems to be ironed out, disturbing undertones of national chauvinism, as if the party were pandering to the politically backward masses of the Soviet population. First Zinoviev (leader of the Comintern until 1926) and then Trotsky took the bait, raising objections to 'Socialism in One Country' that were ideologically impeccable and politically disastrous. The objections enabled Stalin to smear his opponents, while at the same time underlining the politically advantageous fact that Stalin had taken a stand for nation-building and Russian national strength.[23]

When Trotsky, a Jewish intellectual, pointed out that the Bolsheviks had always been internationalists, Stalin's supporters portrayed him as a cosmopolitan who cared less about Russia than about Europe. When Trotsky correctly asserted that he was no less an industrializer than Stalin, Stalin's men recalled that he had advocated labour conscription in 1920 and thus, unlike Stalin, was probably an industrializer who was prepared to sacrifice the interests of the Russian working class. Yet, when the financing of industrialization became an issue and Trotsky argued that foreign trade and credits were essential if the Russian population were not to be squeezed beyond endurance, this was only further proof of Trotsky's 'internationalism'—not to mention his lack of realism, since it appeared increasingly unlikely that large-scale foreign trade and credits would be obtainable. Stalin, by contrast, took the position that was simultaneously patriotic and practical: the Soviet Union had no need or desire to beg favours from the capitalist West.

However, the financing of the industrialization drive was a serious issue, not to be dismissed by rhetorical flourishes. The Bolsheviks knew that capital accumulation had been a prerequisite for bourgeois industrial revolution, and that, as Marx had vividly described, this process had meant suffering for the population. The Soviet regime must also accumulate capital in order to industrialize. The old Russian bourgeoisie had already been expropriated, and the new bourgeoisie of Nepmen and kulaks had not had time or opportunity to accumulate much. If, being politically isolated as a result of the revolution, Russia could no longer follow Witte's example and obtain capital from the West, the regime must draw on its own resources and those of the population, still predominantly peasant. Did Soviet industrialization therefore mean 'squeezing the peasantry'? If it did, could the regime survive the political confrontation that was likely to follow?

In the mid-1920s, this issue was the subject of a debate between

Preobrazhensky, an Oppositionist, and Bukharin, then a Stalinist. These two, who had earlier co-authored *The ABC of Communism*, were both noted Marxist theoreticians, specializing respectively in economic and political theory. In their debate, Preobrazhensky—arguing as an economist—said that it would be necessary to exact 'tribute' from the peasantry to pay for industrialization, largely by turning the terms of trade against the rural sector. Bukharin found this unacceptable in political terms, objecting that it was likely to alienate the peasants, and that the regime could not afford to risk breaking the worker–peasant alliance that Lenin had described as the political basis of NEP. The result of the debate was inconclusive, since Bukharin agreed that it was necessary to industrialize and therefore to accumulate capital somehow, and Preobrazhensky agreed that coercion and violent confrontation with the peasantry were undesirable.[24]

Stalin did not participate in the debate, which led many to assume that he shared the position of his ally, Bukharin. However, there were already some indications that Stalin's attitude to the peasantry was less conciliatory than Bukharin's: he had taken a tougher line on the kulak threat, and in 1925 he explicitly dissociated himself from Bukharin's cheerful exhortation to the peasantry to 'Get rich' with the blessing of the regime. Moreover, Stalin had committed himself very firmly to an industrialization drive; and the conclusion to be drawn from the Preobrazhensky–Bukharin debate was that Russia should either postpone its industrialization or risk a major confrontation with the peasantry. Stalin was not a man to announce unpopular policies in advance, but with hindsight it is not hard to guess which conclusion he preferred. As he noted in 1927, the economic recovery of NEP, which had brought industrial output and the size of the industrial proletariat almost up to prewar levels, had changed the balance of power between town and countryside in favour of the town. Stalin intended to industrialize, and if this meant a political confrontation with the countryside, Stalin thought that 'the town'—that is, the urban proletariat and the Soviet regime—would win.

In introducing NEP in 1921, Lenin described it as a strategic retreat, a time for the Bolsheviks to rally their forces and gather strength before renewing the revolutionary assault. Less than a decade later, Stalin abandoned most of the NEP policies and initiated a new phase of revolutionary change with the First Five-Year Plan industrialization drive and the collectivization of peasant agriculture. Stalin said, and no doubt believed, that this was the true Leninist course, the path that Lenin himself would have followed had he lived. Other party leaders including Bukharin and Rykov disagreed, as will be discussed in the next chapter, pointing out that Lenin had said that the moderate and conciliatory policies of NEP must be followed 'seriously and for a long time' before the regime could hope to take further decisive steps towards socialism.

Historians are divided on Lenin's political legacy. Some accept Stalin as Lenin's true heir, whether for good or ill, while others see Stalin as essentially the betrayer of Lenin's revolution. Trotsky, of course, took the latter view and saw himself as the rival heir, but he had no real disagreements in principle with Stalin's abandonment of NEP and his drive for economic and social transformation during the First Five-Year Plan. In the 1970s, and then briefly in the era of Gorbachev's *perestroika* in the Soviet Union, it was the 'Bukharin alternative' to Stalin that attracted scholars who saw a fundamental divergence between Leninism (or 'original Bolshevism') and Stalinism.[25] The Bukharin alternative was, in effect, a continuation of NEP for the foreseeable future, implying at least the possibility that, having gained power, the Bolsheviks could achieve their revolutionary economic and social goals by evolutionary means.

Whether Lenin would have abandoned NEP at the end of the 1920s had he lived is one of the 'if' questions of history that can never be definitively answered. In his last years, 1921–3, he was pessimistic about the prospects for radical change—as were all the Bolshevik leaders at that time—and anxious to discourage any lingering regrets in the party for the policies of War Communism that had just been jettisoned. But he was an exceptionally volatile thinker and politician, whose mood—like that of other Bolshevik leaders—might have changed sharply in response to the unexpectedly rapid economic recovery of 1924–5. In January 1917, after all, Lenin had thought it possible that 'the decisive battles of this revolution' would not come in his lifetime, but by September of the same year he was insisting on the absolute necessity of seizing power in the name of the proletariat. Lenin in general did not care to be a passive victim of circumstance, which was essentially the Bolsheviks' understanding of their position under NEP. He was a revolutionary by temperament, and NEP was by no means a realization of his revolutionary objectives in economic and social terms.

Beyond the debate about Lenin, however, lies the broader question of whether the Bolshevik Party as a whole was ready to accept NEP as the end and outcome of the October Revolution. After Khrushchev's denunciation of the abuses of the Stalin era at the Twentieth Party Congress in 1956, many Soviet intellectuals of the older generation wrote memoirs of their youth in the 1920s in which NEP seemed almost like a golden age; and Western historians have often taken a similar view. But the virtues of NEP in retrospect— relative relaxation and diversity within the society, a comparatively *laissez-faire* attitude on the part of the regime—were not qualities that were much appreciated by Communist revolutionaries at the time. Communists of the 1920s were afraid of class enemies, intolerant of cultural pluralism and uneasy about the lack of unity in the party leadership and the loss of a sense of direction and purpose. They wanted their revolution to transform the world, but it was very clear during NEP how much of the old world had survived.

To Communists, NEP had the smell of Thermidor, the period of degeneration of the great French Revolution. In 1926–7, the struggle between the party leadership and the Opposition reached new heights of bitterness. Each side accused the other of conspiracy and betrayal of the revolution. Analogies from the French Revolution were cited frequently, sometimes in connection with the threat of 'Thermidorian degeneration', sometimes—ominously—by reference to the salutary effects of the guillotine. (In the past, Bolshevik intellectuals had prided themselves on the knowledge of revolutionary history that taught them that the downfall of revolutions come when they start to devour their own.)[26]

There were signs, too, that the sense of malaise was not limited to the party's elite. Many rank-and-file Communists and sympathizers, especially among the young, were becoming disillusioned, inclined to believe that the revolution had reached an impasse. Workers (including Communist workers) were resentful of the privileges of 'bourgeois experts' and Soviet officials, the profits of sharp-dealing Nepmen, high unemployment, and the perpetuation of inequality of opportunity and living standards. Party agitators and propagandists frequently had to respond to the angry question 'What did we fight for?' The mood in the party was not one of satisfaction that finally the young Soviet Republic had entered a quiet harbour. It was a mood of restlessness, dissatisfaction, and barely subdued belligerence and, especially among party youth, nostalgia for the old heroic days of the Civil War. For the Communist Party—a young party in the 1920s, moulded by the experiences of revolution and Civil War, still perceiving itself as (in Lenin's phrase in 1917) 'the working class in arms'—peace had perhaps come too soon.

5 Stalin's Revolution

THE industrialization drive of the First Five-Year Plan (1929–32) and the forced collectivization of agriculture that accompanied it have often been described as a 'revolution from above'. But the imagery of war was equally appropriate, and at the time—'in the heat of the battle', as Soviet commentators liked to put it—war metaphors were even more common than revolutionary ones. Communists were 'fighters'; Soviet forces had to be 'mobilized' to the 'fronts' of industrialization and collectivization; 'counter-attacks' and 'ambushes' were to be expected from the bourgeois and kulak class enemy. It was a war against Russia's backwardness, and at the same time a war against the proletariat's class enemies inside and outside the country. In the view of some later historians, indeed, this was the period of Stalin's 'war against the nation'.[1]

The war imagery was clearly meant to symbolize a return to the spirit of the Civil War and War Communism, and a repudiation of unheroic compromises of NEP. But Stalin was not simply playing with symbols, for in many ways the Soviet Union during the First Five-Year Plan did resemble a country at war. Political opposition and resistance to the regime's policies were denounced as treachery and often punished with almost wartime severity. The need for vigilance against spies and saboteurs became a constant theme in the Soviet press. The population was exhorted to patriotic solidarity and had to make many sacrifices for the 'war effort' of industrialization: as a further (if unintentional) re-creation of wartime conditions, rationing was reintroduced in the towns.

Although the wartime crisis atmosphere is sometimes seen purely as a response to the strains of crash industrialization and collectivization, it actually predated them. The psychological state of war emergency began with the great war scare of 1927, when it was widely believed in the party and the country as a whole that a renewed military intervention by the capitalist powers was imminent. The Soviet Union had recently suffered a series of rebuffs in its foreign and Comintern policy—a British raid on the Soviet trade mission (ARCOS) in London, the nationalist Kuomintang's attack on its Communist allies in China, the assassination of a Soviet diplomatic plenipotentiary in Poland. Trotsky and other Opposition-ists blamed Stalin for the foreign policy disasters, especially China. A number of Soviet and Comintern leaders publicly interpreted these rebuffs as evidence of an active anti-Soviet conspiracy, led by Britain, which was likely to end in a concerted military onslaught on the Soviet Union. Domestic tension was increased when the GPU (successor to the Cheka) began rounding up suspected enemies of the regime, and the press reported incidents of anti-Soviet terrorism and the discovery of internal conspiracies against the regime. In expectation of a war, peasants began to withhold grain from the market; and there was panic buying of basic consumer goods by both the rural and urban population.

Most Western historians conclude that there was no actual, immediate danger of intervention; and this was also the view of the Soviet Commissariat of Foreign Affairs and, almost certainly, of Politburo members like Aleksei Rykov who were not conspiracy-minded. But others in the party leadership were more easily alarmed. They included the excitable Bukharin, currently head of the Comin-tern, where alarmist rumours flourished and hard information on the intentions of foreign governments was scarce.

Stalin's attitude is harder to gauge. He remained silent during some months of anxious discussion of the war danger. Then, in the middle of 1927, he very skilfully turned the issue back on the Opposition. Denying that war was immediately imminent, he never-theless pilloried Trotsky for his statement that, like Clemenceau during the First World War, he would continue active opposition to the country's leadership even with the enemy at the gates of the capital. To loyal Communists and Soviet patriots, this sounded close to treason; and it was probably decisive in enabling Stalin to deliver the final blow against the Opposition a few months later, when Trotsky and other Opposition leaders were expelled from the party.

Stalin's struggle with Trotsky in 1927 was the occasion for an ominous raising of the political temperature. Breaking a previous taboo in the Bolshevik Party, the leadership sanctioned arrest and administrative exile of political opponents and other forms of GPU harassment of the Opposition. (Trotsky himself was sent into exile in Alma-Ata after his expulsion from the party; in January 1929 he was deported by Politburo order from the Soviet Union.) At the end of 1927, responding to GPU reports of the danger of an Opposition *coup*, Stalin presented the Politburo with a set of proposals that can only be compared with the infamous Law of Suspects in the French Revolution.[2] His proposals, which were accepted but not made public, were that

persons propagating opposition views be regarded as dangerous accomplices of the external and internal enemies of the Soviet Union and that such persons be sentenced as 'spies' by administrative decree of the GPU; that a widely ramified network of agents be organized by the GPU with the task of seeking out hostile elements within the government apparatus, all the way to its top, and within the party, including the leading bodies of the party. 'Everyone who arouses the slightest suspicion should be removed,' Stalin concluded . . .[3]

The crisis atmosphere generated by the show-down with the Opposition and the war scare was exacerbated in the early months of 1928 by the onset of a major confrontation with the peasantry (see below, pp. 124–6), and charges of disloyalty directed against the old 'bourgeois' intelligentsia. In March 1928, the State Prosecutor announced that a group of engineers in the Shakhty region of the Donbass was to be tried for deliberate sabotage of the mining industry and conspiracy with foreign powers.[4] This was the first in a series of show trials of bourgeois experts, in which the prosecution linked the internal threat from class enemies with the threat of intervention by foreign capitalist powers, and the accused confessed their guilt and offered circumstantial accounts of their cloak-and-dagger activities.

The trials, large portions of which were reported verbatim in the daily newspapers, conveyed the overt message that, despite its claims of loyalty to Soviet power, the bourgeois intelligentsia remained a class enemy, untrustworthy by definition. Less overt, but clearly audible to the Communist managers and administrators who worked with bourgeois experts, was the message that party cadres, too, were at fault—guilty of stupidity and credulousness, if not worse, for having been hoodwinked by the experts.[5]

The new policy tapped into feelings of suspicion and hostility to experts from the old privileged classes that were endemic in the Russian working class and among rank-and-file Communists. It was in part, no doubt, a response to the scepticism of many experts and engineers that the high targets set by the First Five-Year Plan could be reached. Nevertheless, it was a policy that had enormous costs for a regime that was preparing to embark on a crash programme of industrialization, just as the 1928–9 campaign against 'kulak' enemies did in the agricultural realm. The country lacked experts of all kinds, especially engineers, whose skills were crucial to the industrialization drive (the great majority of qualified Russian engineers in 1928 were 'bourgeois' and non-Communist).

Stalin's motives for launching the anti-expert campaign have puzzled historians. Because the charges of conspiracy and sabotage were so implausible, and the confessions of the accused coerced and fraudulent, it is often assumed that Stalin and his colleagues could not possibly have believed them. As new data emerge from the archives, however, it looks increasingly as if Stalin (though not necessarily his Politburo colleagues) did believe in these conspiracies—or at least half believed, realizing at the same time that belief could be turned to political advantage.

When Vyacheslav Menzhinskii, head of the OGPU (previously the GPU), sent Stalin material from the interrogation of experts accused of membership in the 'Industrial Party', whose leaders had allegedly planned a *coup* backed by émigré capitalists and co-ordinated with plans for foreign military intervention, Stalin replied in terms that suggest that he both accepted the confessions at face value and took the danger of imminent war very seriously. The most interesting evidence, Stalin told Menzhinskii, concerned the timing of the planned military intervention:

It turns out they had intended the intervention for 1930, but then postponed it to 1931, or even 1932. That's quite probable and important. It is even more important because this information came from a primary source, i.e. from the group of Riabushinskii, Gukasov, Denisov, and Nobel' [capitalists with major prerevolutionary Russian interests], which represents the most powerful socio-economic group of all existing groups in the USSR and in emigration, the most powerful in terms of capital and in terms of its connections with the French and English governments.

Now that this evidence was in hand, Stalin concluded, the Soviet regime would be able to give it intense publicity at home and abroad, 'and thus paralyse and stop all attempts at intervention in the next one or two years, which is of the utmost importance to us'.[6]

Regardless of whether, or in what way, Stalin and other leaders believed in anti-Soviet plots and immediate military threats, these ideas became widely disseminated in the Soviet Union. This was not only because of the regime's propaganda efforts but also because such notions, reinforcing existing prejudices and fears, were credible to large segments of the Soviet public. Beginning in the late 1920s, internal and external conspiracies were regularly invoked to explain economic problems such as food shortages and industrial, transport, and power breakdowns. The war danger became equally embedded in Soviet *mentalité* in this period, with recurrent war scares regularly occupying the attention of the Politburo and the newspaper-reading public right up to the actual outbreak of war in 1941.

Stalin versus the Right

In the winter of 1927–8, the party leadership found itself divided on policy towards the peasantry, with Stalin on one side and a group later known as the Right Opposition on the other. The immediate problem was grain procurement. Despite a good harvest in the autumn of 1927, peasant marketing and state procurement of grain fell far below expectations. The war scare was a factor, but so also was the low price that the state was offering for grain. With the industrialization drive already in prospect, the question was whether the regime should run the political risk of squeezing the peasants harder, or take the economic consequences of buying them off.

During NEP, it was part of the regime's economic philosophy to further state capital accumulation by paying relatively low prices for the peasants' agricultural produce, while at the same time charging relatively high prices for the manufactured goods produced by nationalized industry. But in practice this had always been mitigated by the existence of a free market in grain, which kept state prices close to the market level. The state had not wanted confrontation with the peasantry, and had therefore made concessions when, as happened in the 'scissors crisis' of 1923–4, the discrepancy between agricultural and industrial prices became too great.

In 1927, however, the impending industrialization drive changed the equation in a number of ways. Unreliable grain procurements jeopardized plans for large-scale grain export to balance the import of foreign machinery. Higher grain prices would reduce the funds available for industrial expansion, and perhaps make it impossible to fulfil the First Five-Year Plan. Moreover, since it was surmised that a very large proportion of all marketed grain came from only a small proportion of Russia's peasant farmers, it seemed likely that the benefit from higher grain prices would go to 'kulaks'—the regime's enemies—rather than the peasantry as a whole.

At the Fifteenth Party Congress, which met in December 1927, the main topics on the public agenda were the First Five-Year Plan and the excommunication of the Left (Trotskyite–Zinovievite) Opposition. But behind the scenes, the grain procurements issue was very much on the leaders' minds, and anxious discussions were held with delegates from the main grain-producing regions of the country. Shortly after the Congress, a number of Politburo and Central Committee members departed on urgent investigative missions to these regions. Stalin himself, in one of his few trips to the provinces since the Civil War, went to investigate the situation in Siberia. The Siberian party committee, led by one of the party's rising stars, the well-educated and efficient Sergei Syrtsov, had been attempting to avoid confrontation with the peasantry over procurements, and had recently been assured by Rykov (head of the Soviet government and a Politburo member) that this was the correct line to follow. Stalin, however, thought otherwise. On his return from Siberia early in 1928, he made his views known to the Politburo and the Central Committee.[7]

The basic problem, Stalin concluded, was that kulaks were hoarding grain and attempting to hold the Soviet state to ransom. Conciliatory measures like raising grain prices or increasing the supply of manufactured goods to the countryside were pointless, since the kulaks' demands would only escalate. In any case, the state could not afford to meet their demands, because industrial investment had priority. The short-term solution (sometimes referred to as the 'Urals-Siberian method' of dealing with the peasantry) was coercion: peasant 'hoarders' should be prosecuted under Article 107 of the Criminal Code, originally designed to deal with urban speculators.

The long-term solution, Stalin suggested, was to press forward with agricultural collectivization, which would ensure a reliable source of grain for the needs of the towns, the Red Army, and export, and would also break the kulaks' dominance in the grain market. Stalin denied that this policy implied radical measures against the kulaks' ('dekulakization') or a return to the Civil War practice of forced requisitioning of grain. But the denial itself had a sinister ring: for Communists looking for guidelines, the reference to Civil War policies coupled with the absence of any catchwords associated with NEP amounted to a signal to attack.

Stalin's policy—confrontation rather than conciliation, prosecutions, barn searches, road-blocks to prevent peasants taking their grain to traders offering a higher price than the state's—was put into effect in the spring of 1928, and produced a temporary improvement in the level of grain procurements, together with a sharp increase in tension in the countryside. But there was also a great deal of tension within the party about the new policy. In January, local party organizations had received a variety of often contradictory instructions from the Politburo's and Central Committee's visiting firemen. While Stalin was telling the Siberian Communists to be tough, Moshe Frumkin (deputy Commissar of Finance) was touring the neighbouring region of the southern Urals and advising conciliation and the offer of manufactured goods in direct exchange for grain; and Nikolai Uglanov (head of the Moscow party organization and a candidate member of the Politburo) was giving similar advice in the lower Volga area, and moreover noting that excessive pressure from the centre had led some local party officials to use undesirable 'War Communist methods' to get in the grain.[8] Whether by accident or design, Stalin had made the Uglanovs and Frumkins look foolish. Within the Politburo, he had departed from his earlier practice of building a consensus and, in the most arbitrary and provocative manner, simply forced his policy through.

A Right Opposition to Stalin began to coalesce in the party leadership early in 1928, only a few months after the final defeat of the Left Opposition. The essence of the Right's position was that the political framework and basic social policies of NEP should remain unchanged, and that they represented the true Leninist approach to the building of socialism. The Right opposed coercion of the peasantry, undue emphasis on the kulak danger, and policies intended to stimulate class war in the countryside by playing the poor peasants against the more prosperous ones. To the argument that coercion of the peasantry was necessary to guarantee grain deliveries (and hence grain exports and the financing of the industrialization drive), the Right responded with the suggestion that the First Five-Year Plan targets for industrial output and development should be kept 'realistic', that is, relatively low. The Right also opposed the new policy of aggressive class war against the old intelligentsia exemplified by the Shakhty trial, and attempted to defuse the crisis atmosphere engendered by constant discussion of the imminence of war and the danger from spies and saboteurs.

The Politburo's two major Rightists were Rykov, head of the Soviet government, and Bukharin, chief editor of *Pravda*, head of the Comintern, and distinguished Marxist theoretician. Behind their specific policy disagreements with Stalin lay the sense that Stalin had unilaterally changed the rules of the political game as it had been played since Lenin's death, brusquely discarding the conventions of collective leadership at the same time as he seemed to be abandoning many of the basic policy assumptions of NEP. Bukharin, a fiery polemicist for Stalin in the battles with the Trotskyite and Zinoviev-ite Oppositions, had a particular sense of personal betrayal. Stalin had treated him as a political equal and assured him that they were the two 'Himalayas' of the party, but his actions now suggested that he had little genuine political or personal respect for Bukharin. Reacting impetuously to his disappointment, Bukharin took the politically disastrous step of opening secret discussions with some of the defeated Left Opposition leaders in the summer of 1928. His private characterization of Stalin as a 'Genghis Khan' who would destroy the Revolution quickly became known to Stalin, but did not increase his credibility with those whom he had so recently attacked on Stalin's behalf.

Despite this private initiative of Bukharin's, the Politburo Right-ists made no real attempt to organize an opposition faction (having observed the penalties for 'factionalism' that the Left had incurred), and conducted their arguments with Stalin and his Politburo sup-porters behind closed doors. However, this tactic also turned out to have severe disadvantages, since the Politburo's closet Rightists were forced to participate in public attacks on a vague and anonymous 'rightist danger'—meaning a tendency to faintheartedness, indecisive leadership, and lack of revolutionary confidence—within the party. It was clear to those outside the closed circle of the party leadership that some sort of power struggle was going on, but neither the issues nor the identity of those under attack for rightism were clearly defined for many months. The Politburo Rightists could not seek broad support in the party, and their platform was publicized only in distorted paraphrase by their opponents, and in occasional hints and Aesopian references by the Rightists themselves.

The Right's two main power bases were the Moscow Party

organization, headed by Uglanov, and the Central Council of Trade Unions, headed by a Rightist member of the Politburo, Mikhail Tomsky. The first fell to the Stalinists in the autumn of 1928, and subsequently underwent a thorough purge directed by Stalin's old associate, Vyacheslav Molotov. The second fell a few months later, the guiding hand in this case being that of a rising Stalinist supporter, Lazar Kaganovich, still only a candidate member of the Politburo but already renowned for his toughness and political skill on a previous assignment to the notoriously troublesome Ukrainian party organization. Isolated and outmanœuvred, the Politburo Rightists were finally identified by name and brought to judgement early in 1929. Tomsky lost the leadership of the trade unions, and Bukharin was removed from his positions in the Comintern and *Pravda* editorial board. Rykov—the senior member of the Politburo Right, a more cautious and pragmatic politician than Bukharin but perhaps also more of a force to be reckoned with in the party leadership— remained head of the Soviet government for almost two years after the collapse of the Right, but was replaced by Molotov at the end of 1930.

The Right's real strength in the party and the administrative elite is difficult to assess, given the absence of an open conflict or an organized faction. Since an intensive purge of the party and government bureaucracy followed the defeat of the Right, it might seem that the Right had (or was believed to have) substantial support.[9] However, the officials demoted for rightism were not necessarily ideological Rightists. The label of rightism was applied both to ideological deviationists and bureaucratic deadwood—that is, officials who were judged too incompetent, apathetic, or corrupt to rise to the challenge of implementing Stalin's aggressive policies of revolution from above. These categories were clearly not identical: the common label was simply one of the Stalinists' ways of discrediting the ideological Right.

Like previous oppositions to Stalin, the Right was defeated by the party machine which Stalin controlled. But, in contrast to the earlier leadership struggles, this one involved clear-cut issues of principle and policy. Since these issues were not put to a vote, we can only speculate on the attitude of the party as a whole. The Right's platform involved less danger of social and political upheaval, and did not require party cadres to change the habits and orientation of NEP. On the debit side, the Right was promising much less in the way of achievement than Stalin; and the party in the late 1920s was hungry for achievement, and did not have our retrospective knowledge of what it was going to cost. The Right, after all, was proposing a moderate, small-gains, low-conflict programme to a party that was belligerently revolutionary, felt itself threatened by an array of foreign and domestic enemies, and continued to believe that society could and should be transformed. Lenin had won acceptance for such a programme in 1921. But the Right in 1928–9 had no Lenin to lead it; and the NEP policies of retreat could no longer be justified (as in 1921) by the imminence of total economic collapse and popular revolt.

If the leaders of the Right did not seek to publicize their platform or force a broad party debate on the issues, they may have had good reasons that went beyond their expressed scruples about party unity. The Right's platform was rational and perhaps also (as they claimed) Leninist, but it was not a good platform to campaign on within the Communist Party. In political terms, the Rightists had the kind of problem that would, for example, confront British Conservative leaders who had decided to offer major concessions to the trade unions, or US Republicans who planned to extend Federal controls and increase government regulation of business. Such policies may, for pragmatic reasons, prevail in the closed councils of government (which was the hope and basic strategy of the Right in 1928). But they do not provide good slogans for rallying the party stalwarts.

While the Right, like earlier oppositions, also took up the cause of greater democracy within the party, this had dubious value as a way of winning Communist votes. Local party officials complained that it undermined their authority. In a particularly sharp exchange in the Urals, Rykov was told that the Right seemed to be out to 'get the [regional party] secretaries'[10]—that is, blame them for anything that went wrong and, on top of that, pretend they had no right to their jobs because they were not properly elected. From the standpoint of a middle-level provincial official, the Rightists were elitists rather than democrats, men who had perhaps served too long in Moscow and lost touch with the party's grass roots.

The industrialization drive

To Stalin, as to the foremost modernizer of the late Tsarist period, Count Witte, rapid development of Russia's heavy industry was a prerequisite of national strength and military might. 'In the past,' Stalin said in February 1931,

we had no fatherland, nor could we have had one. But now that we have overthrown capitalism and power is in our hands, in the hands of the people, we have a fatherland, and we must uphold its independence. Do you want our socialist fatherland to be beaten and to lose its independ-ence? If you do not want this, you must put an end to its backwardness in the shortest possible time and develop a genuine Bolshevik tempo in building up its socialist economy.

This was a matter of absolute urgency, for the pace of Soviet industrialization would determine whether the socialist fatherland survived or crumbled before its enemies.

To slacken the tempo would mean falling behind. And those who fall behind get beaten. But we do not want to be beaten. No, we refuse to be beaten! One feature of the history of old Russia was the continual beatings she suffered because of her backwardness. She was beaten by the Mongol khans. She was beaten by the Turkish beys. She was beaten by the Swedish feudal rulers. She was beaten by the Polish and Lithuanian gentry. She was beaten by British and French capitalists. She was beaten by Japanese barons. All beat her—because of her backwardness, because of her military backwardness, cultural backward-ness, political backwardness, industrial backwardness, agricultural back-wardness . . . We are fifty or a hundred years behind the advanced countries. We must make good this distance in ten years. Either we do it or we shall go under.[11]

With the adoption of the First Five-Year Plan in 1929, industrial-ization became the top priority of the Soviet regime. The state agency heading the industrialization drive, the Commissariat of Heavy Industry (successor to the Supreme Economic Council), was led from 1930 to 1937 by Sergo Ordzhonikidze, one of the most powerful and dynamic members of the Stalinist leadership. The First Five-Year Plan focused on iron and steel, pushing the established metal-lurgical plants of Ukraine to maximum output and constructing massive new complexes like Magnitogorsk in the southern Urals from scratch. Tractor plants also had high priority, not only because of the immediate requirements of collectivized agriculture (made more urgent by the peasants' slaughter of draught animals during the collectivization process) but also because they could be relatively easily converted to tank production in the future. The machine-tool industry was rapidly expanded in order to free the country from dependence on machinery imports from abroad. The textile industry languished, despite the fact that the state had invested quite heavily in its development during NEP and it possessed a large and experienced workforce. As Stalin is said to have remarked, the Red Army would not fight with leather and textiles but with metal.[12]

The metal priority was inextricably linked with national security and defence considerations but, as far as Stalin was concerned, it seemed to have a significance that went beyond this. Stalin, after all, was the Bolshevik revolutionary who had taken his party name from the Russian word for steel (*stal'*); and in the early 1930s the cult of steel and pig-iron production exceeded even the emerging cult of Stalin. Everything was sacrificed for metal in the First Five-Year Plan. Indeed, investment in coal, electric power, and railways was so inadequate that fuel and power shortages and transport breakdowns often threatened to bring the metallurgical plants to a standstill. In the view of Gleb Krzhizhanovsky, the Old Bolshevik who headed the State Planning Commission until 1930, Stalin and Molotov were so obsessed with metal production that they tended to forget that the plants were dependent on rail shipments of raw materials and reliable supplies of fuel, water, and electricity.

Yet the organization of supply and distribution was possibly the most formidable task assumed by the state during the First Five-Year Plan. As it had done (unsuccessfully and temporarily) under War Communism a decade earlier, the state took over almost total control of the urban economy, distribution, and trade; and this time the takeover was to be permanent. Curtailment of private manufacturing and trading began in the latter years of NEP, and the process gathered speed with a drive against Nepmen—combining vilification in the press, legal and financial harassment, and numerous arrests of private entrepreneurs for 'speculation'—in 1928–9. By the early 1930s, even the artisans and small shopkeepers had been put out of business or forced into state-supervised co-operatives. With the simultaneous collectivization of a substantial part of peasant agriculture, the old mixed economy of NEP was fast disappearing.

To the Bolsheviks, the principle of centralized planning and state control of the economy had great significance, and the introduction of the First Five-Year Plan in 1929 was a milestone on the road to socialism. Certainly it was in these years that the institutional foundations of the Soviet planned economy were laid, although it was a period of transition and experimentation in which the 'planning' component of economic growth cannot always be taken too literally. The First Five-Year Plan had a much more tenuous relationship to the actual functioning of the economy than later Five-Year Plans: in fact, it was a hybrid of genuine economic planning and political exhortation. One of the paradoxes of the time was that at the height of the Plan, in the years 1929–31, the state planning agencies were being so ruthlessly purged of Rightists, ex-Mensheviks and bourgeois economists that they were scarcely able to function at all.

Both before and after its introduction in 1929, the First Five-Year Plan went through many versions and revisions, with competing sets of planners responding in different degrees to pressure from the politicians.[13] The basic version adopted in 1929 failed to anticipate mass collectivization of agriculture, vastly underestimated industry's need for labour, and dealt extremely fuzzily with issues like artisan production and trade, where the regime's policy remained ambiguous or unarticulated. The Plan set out production targets—though in key areas like metal these were repeatedly raised after the Plan had gone into operation—but gave only the vaguest indication of where the resources for increased production were to come from. Neither the successive versions of the Plan nor the final statement of the Plan's achievements bore much relation to reality. Even the title of the Plan turned out to be inaccurate, since it was ultimately decided to complete (or conclude) the First Five-Year Plan in its fourth year.

Industry was exhorted to 'overfulfil' the Plan rather than simply to carry it out. This Plan, in other words, was not meant to allocate resources or balance demands but to drive the economy forward pell-mell. The Stalingrad Tractor plant, for example, could best carry out the Plan by producing *more* tractors than planned, even if this threw the schedules of plants supplying Stalingrad with metal, electrical parts, and tyres into total disarray. Supply priorities were not determined by the written Plan but by a series of *ad hoc* decisions from the Commissariat of Heavy Industry, the government's Council of Labour and Defence, and even the party's Politburo. Fierce competition surrounded the official list of top-priority (*udarnye*) enterprises and construction projects, since inclusion meant that suppliers were required to ignore all previous contracts and obligations until the top-priority orders were filled.

But the top priorities were constantly changing in response to crisis, impending disaster, or a new raising of targets in one of the key industrial sectors. 'Breaks in the industrialization front', requiring that fresh reserves of men and materials be rushed in, provided an element of drama to the coverage in the Soviet press, and indeed to the everyday life of Soviet industrialists. The successful Soviet manager during the First Five-Year Plan was less like an obedient functionary than a wheeling-and-dealing entrepreneur, ready to cut corners and seize any opportunity to outdo his competitors. The end—fulfilling and overfulfilling the Plan—was more important than the means; and there were cases when plants desperate for supplies ambushed freight trains and commandeered their contents, suffering no worse consequences than an aggrieved note of complaint from the authorities in charge of transport.

However, despite the emphasis on immediate increase in industrial output, the real purpose of the First Five-Year Plan was to build. The giant new construction projects—Nizhny Novgorod (Gorky) Auto, Stalingrad and Kharkov Tractor, Kuznetsk and Magnitogorsk Metallurgical, Dnieper (Zaporozhe) Steel, and many others—swallowed up enormous resources during the First Five-Year Plan, but came into full production only after 1932, under the Second Five-Year Plan (1933–7). They were an investment for the future. Because of the magnitude of the investment, decisions made during the First Five-Year Plan on the location of the new industrial giants were in effect redrawing the economic map of the Soviet Union.[14]

As early as 1925, during Stalin's conflict with the Zinovievite Opposition, the investment issue had played some part in internal party politics, as Stalin's campaigners had made sure that regional party leaders understood the benefits that his industrialization plans would bring to their particular regions. But it was in the last years of the 1920s, with the final First Five-Year Plan decisions imminent, that the Bolsheviks' eyes were really opened to a whole new dimension of politics—regional competition for development allocations. At the Sixteenth Party Conference in 1929, speakers had difficulty keeping their minds on the ideological struggle with the Right because of their intense concern with more practical questions: as one Old Bolshevik wryly noted, 'Every speech ends . . . "Give us a factory in the Urals, and to hell with the Rights! Give us a power station, and to hell with the Rights!"'[15]

The party organizations of Ukraine and the Urals were at daggers drawn over the distribution of investment monies for mining and metallurgical complexes and machine-building plants; and their rivalry—which drew in major national politicians like Lazar Kaganovich, formerly party secretary in Ukraine, and Nikolai Shvernik, who headed the Urals party organization before taking over national leadership of the trade unions—was to continue throughout the 1930s. Intense rivalries also sprang up over the location of specific plants scheduled for construction during the First Five-Year Plan. Half a dozen Russian and Ukrainian cities put in bids for the tractor plant ultimately built in Kharkov. A similar battle, probably the first of its kind, had raged from 1926 over the site of the Urals Machine-Building Plant (Uralmash): Sverdlovsk, the ultimate victor, began construction on local funds and without central authorization in order to force Moscow's hand on the location decision.[16]

Strong regional competition (for example, that between Ukraine and the Urals) often resulted in a double victory—the authorization of two separate plants, one in each region, where the planners' original intention had been to build only a single plant. This was one factor behind the soaring targets and ever-increasing costs that were characteristic of the First Five-Year Plan. But it was not the only factor, for Moscow's central politicians and planners were clearly in the grip of 'gigantomania', the obsession with hugeness. The Soviet Union must build more and produce more than any other country. Its plants must be the newest and the biggest in the world. It must not only catch up with the West in economic development, but surpass it.

Modern technology, as Stalin never tired of pointing out, was essential to the process of catching up and surpassing. The new auto and tractor factories were built for assembly-line production, although many experts had advised against it, because the legendary capitalist Ford must be beaten at his own game. In practice, the new conveyor belts often stood idle during the First Five-Year Plan, while workers painstakingly assembled a single tractor by traditional methods on the shop floor. But even an idle conveyor-belt had a function. In substantive terms, it was part of the First Five-Year Plan investment in future production. In symbolic terms, photographed by the Soviet press and admired by official and foreign visitors, it passed on the message that Stalin wanted the Soviet people and the world to receive: backward Russia would soon become 'Soviet America'; its great breakthrough in economic development was under way.

Collectivization

The Bolsheviks had always believed that collectivized agriculture was superior to individual peasant small-farming, but it was assumed during NEP that converting the peasants to this point of view would be a long and arduous process. In 1928, collective farms (*kolkhozy*) accounted for only 1.2 per cent of the total sown area, with 1.5 per cent in state farms, and the remaining 97.3 per cent under individual peasant cultivation.[17] The First Five-Year Plan did not anticipate any large-scale transition to collectivized agriculture during its term; and indeed the formidable problems of rapid industrialization seemed quite enough for the regime to handle for the next few years, without adding a basic reorganization of agriculture.

However, as Stalin recognized—and as both Preobrazhensky and Bukharin had done in their debates a few years earlier (see above, pp. 115–16)—the question of industrialization was closely linked to the question of peasant agriculture. For the industrialization drive to succeed, the state needed reliable grain deliveries and low grain prices. The procurements crisis of 1927–8 underlined the fact that the peasants—or the small minority of relatively prosperous peasants who provided most of the marketed grain—could 'hold the state to ransom' as long as a free market existed and the state's grain prices were effectively negotiable, as they had been during NEP.

As early as January 1928, Stalin had indicated that he saw the kulak hoarder as the villain in the procurements crisis, and believed that collectivization of peasant agriculture would provide the lever of control that the state needed to guarantee adequate deliveries at the state's time and price. But encouragement of voluntary collectivization in 1928 and the first half of 1929 produced only modest results; and procurements remained an acute problem, preoccupying the regime not only because of the food shortages in the towns but also because of the commitment to grain export as a means of financing industrial purchases abroad. With the coercive procurement methods favoured by Stalin generally in the ascendant, hostility mounted between the regime and the peasantry: despite intensive efforts to discredit kulaks and stimulate class antagonism within the peasantry, village unity seemed rather to have been reinforced by outside pressure than to be crumbling from within.

In the summer of 1929, having largely eliminated the free market in grain, the regime imposed procurement quotas with penalties for non-delivery. In the autumn, attacks on the kulaks became more strident, and the party leaders began to speak of an irresistible peasant movement towards mass collectivization. This no doubt reflected their sense that the regime's confrontation with the peasantry had gone so far that there was no drawing back, since few can have deceived themselves that the process could be accomplished without a bitter struggle. In the words of Yurii Pyatakov, a former Trotskyite who had become an enthusiastic supporter of the First Five-Year Plan:

There is no solution to the problem of agriculture within the framework of individual farming, and therefore *we are obliged to adopt extreme rates of collectivisation of agriculture* . . . In our work we must adopt the rates of the Civil War. Of course I am not saying we must adopt the methods of the Civil War, but that each of us . . . is obliged to work with the same tension with which we worked in the time of armed struggle with our class enemy. *The heroic period of our socialist construction has arrived.*[18]

By the end of 1929, the party had committed itself to an all-out drive to collectivize peasant agriculture. But the kulaks, class enemies of the soviet regime, were not to be admitted to the new collectives. Their exploitative tendencies could no longer be tolerated, Stalin announced in December. The kulaks must be 'liquidated as a class'.

The winter of 1929–30 was a time of frenzy, when the party's apocalyptic mood and wildly revolutionary rhetoric did indeed recall that of an earlier 'heroic period'—the desperate climax of the Civil War and War Communism in 1920. But in 1930 it was not just rhetorical revolution that the Communists were bringing to the countryside, and they were not simply raiding the villages for food and departing, as they had done during the Civil War. Collectivization was an attempt to reorganize peasant life, and at the same time establish administrative controls that would reach down to village level. The exact nature of the required reorganization must have been unclear to many Communists in the provinces, since instructions from the centre were both fervent and imprecise. But it was clear that control was one of the objectives, and that the method of reorganization was belligerent confrontation.

In practical terms, the new policy required officials in the countryside to force an immediate showdown with the kulaks. That meant that local Communists went into the villages, collected a small band of poor or greedy peasants, and proceeded to intimidate a handful of 'kulak' families (usually the richest peasants, but sometimes peasants who were simply unpopular in the village, or disliked by the local authorities for some other reason), drive them from their homes, and confiscate their property.

At the same time, local officials were supposed to be encouraging the rest of the peasants to organize themselves voluntarily into collectives—and it was clear from the tone of central instructions in the winter of 1929–30 that this 'voluntary' movement had to produce quick and impressive results. What this usually meant in practice was that the officials called a village meeting, announced the organization of a kolkhoz, and lectured and browbeat the villagers until a sufficient number agreed to inscribe their names as voluntary kolkhoz members. Once this had been achieved, the initiators of the new kolkhoz would attempt to take possession of the villagers' animals—the main movable item of peasant property—and declare them the property of the collective. For good measure, Communist (and particularly Komsomol) collectivizers were likely to desecrate the church or insult local 'class enemies' like the priest and the schoolteacher.

These actions produced immediate outrage and chaos in the countryside. Rather than hand over their animals, many peasants slaughtered them on the spot or rushed to the nearest town to sell them. Some expropriated kulaks fled to the towns, but others hid in the woods by day and returned to terrorize the village by night. Wailing peasant women, often in the company of the priest, hurled insults at the collectivizers. Officials were often beaten, stoned, or shot at by unseen assailants as they approached or departed from the villages. Many new kolkhoz members hastily left the villages to find work in the towns or on the new construction projects.

To this manifest disaster, the regime reacted in two ways. In the first place, the OGPU came in to arrest the expropriated kulaks and other troublemakers, and subsequently organized mass deportations to Siberia, the Urals, and the north. In the second place the party leadership backed a few steps away from extreme confrontation with the peasantry as the time for spring sowing approached. In March, Stalin published the famous article entitled 'Dizzy with Success', in which he blamed local authorities for exceeding their instructions and ordered that most of the collectivized animals (except those of kulaks) be returned to their original owners.[19] Seizing the moment, peasants hastened to withdraw their names from the lists of kolkhoz members, causing the proportion of peasant households officially collectivized throughout the USSR to drop from over half to under a quarter between 1 March and 1 June 1930.

Some Communist collectivizers, betrayed and humiliated by 'Dizzy with Success', were reported to have turned Stalin's portrait to the wall and succumbed to melancholy thoughts. Nevertheless, the collapse of the collectivization drive was only temporary. Tens of thousands of Communists and urban workers (including the well-known '25,000-ers', mainly recruited from the big plants of Moscow, Leningrad, and Ukraine) were urgently mobilized to work in the countryside as kolkhoz organizers and chairmen. Villagers were steadily persuaded or coerced to sign up for the kolkhoz once again, this time keeping their cows and chickens. By 1932, according to official Soviet figures, 62 per cent of peasant households had been collectivized. By 1937, the figure had risen to 93 per cent.[20]

Collectivization was undoubtedly a real 'revolution from above' in the countryside. But it was not quite the kind of revolution described in the contemporary Soviet press, which greatly exaggerated the scope of the changes that had taken place; and in some respects it was actually a less radical reorganization of peasant life than that attempted in the Stolypin reforms of the late Tsarist period (see above, p. 36). As portrayed in the Soviet press, the kolkhoz was a much larger unit than the old village, and its agricultural methods had been transformed by mechanization and the introduction of tractors. In fact, the tractors were largely imaginary in the early 1930s; and the highly publicized 'kolkhoz giants' of 1930–1 quickly collapsed, or were simply eliminated by the same kind of paper transaction that had created them. The typical kolkhoz was the old village, with the peasants—actually somewhat fewer peasants than before, as a result of migration and deportations, and considerably fewer draught animals—living in the same wooden huts and tilling the same village fields as they had done before. The main things that had changed in the village were its management and its marketing procedures.

The village *mir* was abolished in 1930, and the kolkhoz administration that took its place was headed by an appointed chairman (in the early years, usually a worker or Communist from the towns). Within the village/kolkhoz, the peasants' traditional leadership had been intimidated, and in part removed by the deportation of the kulaks. According to the Russian historian V. P. Danilov, 381,000 peasant households—at least 1.5 million people—were dekulakized and deported in 1930–1, not counting those who suffered a similar fate in 1932 and the early months of 1933.[21] (More than half the deported kulaks were put to work in industry and construction; and, while most of them were working as free rather than convict labourers within a few years, they were still forbidden to move out of the region to which they had been deported and could not return to their native villages.)

The collective farms had to deliver set amounts of grain and technical crops to the state, with payment divided among the kolkhoz members according to their work contribution. Only the produce of the peasants' small private plots was still individually marketed, and this concession was not formalized until a few years after the original collectivization drive. For the general kolkhoz produce, delivery quotas were very high—up to 40 per cent of the crops, or two to three times the percentage that the peasants had previously marketed—and prices were low. The peasants used all their repertoire of passive resistance and evasion, but the regime stuck to its guns and took everything it could find, including food and seed grain. The result was that the major grain-producing areas of the country—Ukraine, Central Volga, Kazakhstan, and Northern Caucasus—were plunged into famine in the winter of 1932–3. The famine left a legacy of enormous bitterness: according to rumours collected in the Central Volga region, peasants saw it as a punishment intentionally visited on them by the regime because of their resistance to collectivization. Recent calculations based on Soviet archival data put famine deaths in 1933 at three to four million.[22]

One of the immediate consequences of the famine was that in December 1932 the regime reintroduced internal passports, issuing them automatically to the urban population but not to the rural one: for the duration of the crisis, every effort was made to keep starving peasants from leaving the countryside and seeking refuge and rations in the towns. This undoubtedly reinforced peasants' belief that collectivization was a second serfdom; and it also left some Western observers with the impression that one of the purposes of collectivization was to keep peasants locked up on the farm. The regime had no such intention (except under the special circumstances created by the famine), since its main objective during the 1930s was rapid industrialization, which meant a rapidly expanding urban labour force. It had long been an accepted truth that Russia's countryside was greatly overpopulated, and the Soviet leaders expected that collectivization and mechanization would rationalize agricultural production and thus further reduce the number of working hands that agriculture required. In functional terms, the relationship between collectivization and the Soviet industrialization drive had much in common with that between the enclosure movement and Britain's industrial revolution more than a century earlier.

Of course this was not an analogy that Soviet leaders were likely to draw: Marx, after all, had emphasized the suffering caused by enclosures and peasant uprooting in Britain, even though the same process rescued peasants from 'the idiocy of rural life' and raised them to a higher level of social existence in the long term by transforming them into urban proletarians. Soviet Communists may have felt some similar ambivalence about collectivization and the accompanying peasant out-migration, which was a bewildering mixture of voluntary departure to the newly created jobs in industry, flight from the kolkhoz and involuntary departure via deportation. But they also clearly felt defensive and embarrassed about the disasters associated with collectivization, and tried to hide the whole subject in a smokescreen of evasions, implausible assertions, and false optimism. Thus in 1931, a year in which two and a half million peasants migrated permanently to the towns, Stalin made the incredible statement that the kolkhoz had proved so attractive to peasants that they no longer felt the traditional urge to flee from the miseries of rural life.[23] But this was only by way of preamble to his main point—that organized recruitment of labour from the kolkhoz should replace spontaneous and unpredictable peasant departures.

In the period 1928–32, urban population in the Soviet Union increased by almost twelve million, and at least ten million persons left peasant agriculture and became wage-earners.[24] These were enormous figures, a demographic upheaval unprecedented in Russia's experience and, it has been claimed, in that of any other country over so short a period. Young and able-bodied peasants were disproportionately represented in the migration, and this surely contributed to the subsequent weakness of collectivized agriculture and demoralization of the peasantry. But, by the same token, the migration was part of the dynamics of Russia's industrialization. For every three peasants joining collective farms during the First Five-Year Plan, one peasant left the village to become a blue- or white-collar wage-earner elsewhere. The departures were as much a part of Stalin's revolution in the countryside as collectivization itself.

Cultural Revolution

The struggle against class enemies was a major preoccupation of Communists during the First Five-Year Plan, as it had been during the Civil War. In the collectivization campaign, 'liquidation of the kulaks as a class' was a focal point of Communist activity. In the reorganization of the urban economy, private entrepreneurs (Nepmen) were the class enemies that had to be eliminated. At the same period, the international communist movement adopted a new belligerent policy of 'class against class'. These policies—all involving repudiation of a more conciliatory approach that had prevailed during NEP—had their counterpart in the cultural and intellectual sphere, where the class enemy was the bourgeois intelligentsia. Struggle against the old intelligentsia, bourgeois cultural values, elitism, privilege, and bureaucratic routine constituted the phenomenon which contemporaries labelled 'Cultural Revolution'.[25] The purpose of Cultural Revolution was to establish Communist and proletarian 'hegemony', which in practical terms meant both asserting party control over cultural life and opening up the administrative and professional elite to a new cohort of young Communists and workers.

The Cultural Revolution was initiated by the party leadership—or, more precisely, Stalin's faction of the leadership—in the spring of 1928, when the announcement of the forthcoming Shakhty trial (see above, p. 122) was coupled with a call for Communist vigilance in the cultural sphere, re-examination of the role of bourgeois experts, and rejection of the old intelligentsia's pretensions to cultural superiority and leadership. This campaign was closely linked with Stalin's struggle against the Right. The Rightists were depicted as protectors of the bourgeois intelligentsia, over-reliant on the advice of non-party experts, complacent about the influence of experts and former Tsarist officials within the government bureaucracy, and prone to infection by 'rotten liberalism' and bourgeois values. They were likely to choose bureaucratic methods rather than revolutionary ones, and favour the government apparat over that of the party. Moreover, they were probably Europeanized intellectuals who had lost touch with the party's proletarian rank-and-file.

But there was more to the Cultural Revolution than a factional struggle within the leadership. The fight against bourgeois cultural dominance appealed very much to Communist youth, as well as to a number of militant Communist organizations whose drive had been thwarted by the party leadership during NEP, and even to groups of non-Communist intellectuals in various fields who were at odds with the established leadership of their professions. Groups like the Russian Association of Proletarian Writers (RAPP) and the League of Militant Atheists had been agitating throughout the 1920s for more aggressive policies of cultural confrontation. Young scholars in the Communist Academy and the Institute of Red Professors had been itching for a fight with the entrenched senior scholars, mainly non-Communist, who still dominated many academic fields. The Komsomol Central Committee and its secretariat, always tending towards revolutionary 'avantgardism' and aspiring to a larger policy-making role, had long suspected that the numerous institutions with which the Komsomol had policy disagreements had succumbed to bureaucratic degeneration. For the young radicals, Cultural Revolution was a vindication and, as one observer put it, an unleashing.

Seen from this perspective, Cultural Revolution was an iconoclastic and belligerent youth movement, whose activists, like the Red Guards of the Chinese Cultural Revolution in the 1960s, were by no means a docile tool of the party leadership. They were intensely party-minded, asserting their own right as Communists to lead and dictate to others, but at the same time they were instinctively hostile to most existing authorities and institutions, which they suspected of bureaucratic and 'objectively counter-revolutionary' tendencies. They were self-consciously proletarian (although most of the activists were white-collar by social origin as well as by occupation), scornful of the bourgeoisie and, in particular, of middle-aged, respectable 'bourgeois Philistines'. The Civil War was their revolutionary touchstone and the source of much of their rhetorical imagery. Sworn enemies of capitalism, they nevertheless tended to admire America because its capitalism was modern and on the grand scale. Radical innovation in any field had an enormous appeal to them.

Because many of the initiatives taken in the name of Cultural Revolution were spontaneous, they produced some unexpected results. Militants carried their anti-religious campaign to the villages at the height of collectivization, confirming peasant suspicions that the kolkhoz was the work of Antichrist. Raids by the Komsomol

'Light Cavalry' disrupted work in government offices; and the Komsomol's 'Cultural Army' (created primarily to fight illiteracy) almost succeeded in abolishing local education departments—which was certainly not an objective of the party leadership—on the grounds that they were bureaucratic.

Young enthusiasts broke up performances of 'bourgeois' plays in state theatres by whistling and booing. In literature, the militants of RAPP launched a campaign against the respected (though not strictly proletarian) writer Maxim Gorky just at the time when Stalin and other party leaders were trying to persuade him to return from his exile in Italy. Even in the realm of political theory, the radicals followed their own path. They believed, as many Communist enthusiasts had done during the Civil War, that apocalyptic change was imminent: the state would wither away, taking with it familiar institutions like law and the school. In mid-1930, Stalin stated quite clearly that this belief was mistaken. But his pronouncement was almost ignored until, more than a year later, the party leadership began a serious attempt to discipline the activists of Cultural Revolution and put an end to their 'hare-brained scheming'.

In fields like social science and philosophy, young Cultural Revolutionaries were sometimes used by Stalin and the party leadership to discredit theories associated with Trotsky or Bukharin, attack former Mensheviks, or facilitate the subordination of respected 'bourgeois' cultural institutions to party control.[26] But this aspect of Cultural Revolution coexisted with a brief flowering of visionary utopianism which was far from the world of practical politics and factional intrigue. The visionaries—often outsiders in their own professions, whose ideas had previously seemed eccentric and unrealizable—were busy with plans for new 'socialist cities', projects for communal living, speculations on the transformation of nature, and the image of the 'new Soviet man'. They took seriously the First Five-Year Plan slogan 'We are building a new world'; and for a few years at the end of the 1920s and the beginning of the 1930s, their ideas were also taken seriously, receiving wide publicity and also, in many cases, substantial funding from various government agencies and other official bodies.

Although the Cultural Revolution was described as proletarian, this should not be taken literally in the realm of high culture and scholarship. In literature, for example, the young activists of RAPP used 'proletarian' as a synonym for 'Communist': when they spoke of establishing 'proletarian hegemony', they were expressing their own desire to dominate the literary field and to be acknowledged as the Communist Party's only accredited representative among literary organizations. To be sure, the RAPPists were not totally cynical in invoking the name of the proletariat, for they did their best to encourage cultural activities in the factories and open channels of communication between professional writers and the working class. But this was all very much in the spirit of the Populists' 'going to the people' in the 1870s[27] (see above, pp. 24–5). RAPP's intelligentsia leaders were for the proletariat rather than of it.

Where the proletarian aspect of Cultural Revolution had substance was in the policy of proletarian 'promotion' vigorously pursued by the regime at this period. The treachery of the bourgeois intelligentsia, Stalin said apropos of the Shakhty trial, made it imperative to train proletarian replacements with all possible speed. The old dichotomy of Reds and experts must be abolished. It was time that the Soviet regime acquired its own intelligentsia (a term which in Stalin's usage covered both the administrative and specialist elite), and this new intelligentsia must be recruited from the lower classes, especially the urban working class.[28]

The policy of 'promoting' workers into administrative jobs and sending young workers to higher education was not new, but it had never been implemented with such urgency or on such a massive scale as during the Cultural Revolution. Enormous numbers of workers were promoted directly into industrial management, became soviet or party officials, or were appointed as replacements for the 'class enemies' purged from the central government and trade-union bureaucracy. Of the 861,000 persons classified as 'leading cadres and specialists' in the Soviet Union at the end of 1933, over 140,000—more than one in six—had been blue-collar workers only five years earlier. But this was only the tip of the iceberg. The total number of workers moving into white-collar jobs during the First Five-Year Plan was probably at least one and a half million.

At the same time, Stalin launched an intensive campaign to send young workers and Communists to higher education, producing a major upheaval in the universities and technical schools, outraging the 'bourgeois' professors and, for the duration of the First Five-Year Plan, making it extremely difficult for high-school graduates from white-collar families to obtain a higher education. About 150,000 workers and Communists entered higher education during the First Five-Year Plan, most of them studying engineering, since technical expertise rather than Marxist social science was now regarded as the best qualification for leadership in an industrializing society. The group, which included Nikita Khrushchev, Leonid Brezhnev, Aleksei Kosygin, and a host of future party and government leaders, was to become the core of the Stalinist political elite after the Great Purges of 1937–8.

For members of this favoured group—'sons of the working class', as they liked to call themselves in later years—the Revolution had indeed fulfilled its promises to give power to the proletariat and turn workers into masters of the state. For other members of the working class, however, the balance-sheet on Stalin's Revolution was much less favourable. Living standards and real wages dropped sharply for most workers during the First Five-Year Plan. Trade unions were reined-in after Tomsky's removal, losing any real ability to press for workers' interests in negotiations with management. As new peasant recruits (including former kulaks) flooded into industrial jobs, the party leaders' sense of a special relationship and special obligations towards the working class weakened.[29]

The demographic and social upheaval during the period of the First Five-Year Plan had been enormous. Millions of peasants had left the villages, driven out by collectivization, dekulakization, or famine, or drawn to the towns by the new availability of jobs. But this was only one of many kinds of uprooting that had shattered the settled pattern of life for individuals and families. Urban wives had gone to work because one pay-cheque was no longer enough; rural wives had been deserted by husbands who disappeared to the towns; children who had been lost or abandoned by their parents had drifted into gangs of homeless youth (*besprizornye*). 'Bourgeois' high-school students who had expected to go to college found their path blocked, while young workers who had only seven years' general education were drafted to study engineering. Expropriated Nepmen and kulaks fled to towns where they were not known to start a new life. Priests' children left home to avoid being stigmatized along with their parents. Trains carried loads of deportees and convicts to unknown and unwanted destinations. Skilled workers were 'promoted' into management, or 'mobilized' to distant construction sites like Magnitogorsk; Communists were sent to the countryside to run collective farms; office-workers were fired in the 'cleansing' of government agencies. A society that had scarcely had time to settle down after the upheavals of war, revolution, and civil war a decade earlier was mercilessly shaken up once again in Stalin's Revolution.

The decline in living standards and quality of life affected almost all classes of the population, urban and rural. Peasants suffered most, as a result of collectivization. But life in the towns was made miserable by food rationing, queues, constant shortages of consumer goods including shoes and clothing, acute overcrowding of housing, the endless inconveniences associated with the elimination of private trade, and deterioration of urban services of all kinds. The urban population of the Soviet Union soared, rising from 29 million at the beginning of 1929 to almost 40 million at the beginning of 1933—an increase of 38 per cent in four years. The population of Moscow jumped from just over 2 million at the end of 1926 to 3.7 million at the beginning of 1933; over the same period, the population of Sverdlovsk (Ekaterinburg), an industrial city in the Urals, rose by 346 per cent.[30]

In the political sphere, too, there had been changes, though of a more subtle and incremental kind. The cult of Stalin began in earnest at the end of 1929 with the celebration of his fiftieth birthday. At party conferences and other large gatherings, it became customary for Communists to greet Stalin's entrance with wild applause. But Stalin, mindful of Lenin's example, appeared to deprecate such enthusiasm; and his position as General Secretary of the party remained formally unchanged.

With the ruthless onslaught on the Left Opposition fresh in the minds, the 'Rightist' leaders trod carefully; and the punishment after their defeat was correspondingly mild. But this was the last open (or quasi-open) party opposition in the party. The ban on factions that had existed in theory since 1921 now existed in practice, with the result that potential factions automatically became conspiracies. Overt disagreements on policy were now a rarity in party congresses. The party leadership was increasingly secretive about its deliberations, and the minutes of Central Committee meetings were no longer routinely circulated and accessible to rank-and-file party members. The leaders—particularly the supreme Leader—began to cultivate the godlike attributes of mystery and inscrutability.

The Soviet press had also changed, becoming far less lively and informative about internal affairs than it had been in the 1920s. Economic achievements were trumpeted, often in a way that involved blatant distortion of reality and manipulation of statistics; setbacks and failures were ignored; and news of the 1932–3 famine was kept out of the papers altogether. Exhortations for higher productivity and greater vigilance against 'wreckers' were the order of the day; frivolity was suspect. The newspapers no longer carried Western-style advertisements for the latest Mary Pickford film nor reported trivia like street accidents, rapes, and robberies.

Contact with the West became much more restricted and dangerous during the First Five-Year Plan. Russia's isolation from the outside world had begun with the 1917 Revolution, but there was a fair volume of traffic and communication in the 1920s. Intellectuals could still publish abroad; foreign journals could still be ordered. But suspicion of foreigners was a strong motif in the show trials of the Cultural Revolution, and this reflected a growing xenophobia in the leadership, and no doubt in the population as well. The First Five-Year Plan goal of 'economic autarchy' also implied withdrawal from the outside world. This was the time in which the closed frontiers, siege mentality, and cultural isolation that were to be characteristic of the Soviet Union in the Stalin (and post-Stalin) period were firmly established.[31]

As in Peter the Great's time, the people grew thinner as the state grew strong. Stalin's Revolution had extended direct state control over the whole urban economy and greatly increased the state's ability to exploit peasant agriculture. It had also greatly strengthened the state's police arm, and created Gulag, the labour-camp empire that became intimately involved in the industrialization drive (primarily as a supplier of convict labour in areas where free labour was in short supply) and would grow rapidly in the coming decades. The persecution of 'class enemies' in collectivization and the Cultural Revolution had left a complex legacy of bitterness, fear, and suspicion, as well as encouraging such practices as denunciation, purging, and 'self-criticism'. Every resource and every nerve had been strained in the course of Stalin's Revolution. It remained to be seen how far the aim of dragging Russia out of backwardness had been achieved.

6 Ending the Revolution

IN Crane Brinton's terms, a revolution is like a fever which grips the patient, rises to a climax, and finally subsides, leaving the patient to resume his normal life—'perhaps in some respects actually strengthened by the experience, immunized at least for a while from a similar attack, but certainly not wholly made over into a new man'.[1] Using Brinton's metaphor, the Russian Revolution went through several bouts of fever. The 1917 revolutions and the Civil War constituted the first bout, 'Stalin's Revolution' of the First Five-Year Plan period was the second, and the Great Purges was the third. In this scheme, the NEP interlude was a time of convalescence followed by a relapse or, some might argue, a new injection of the virus into the hapless patient. A second period of convalescence began in the mid-1930s, with the stabilization policies that Trotsky labelled the 'Soviet Thermidor' and Timasheff called 'the great retreat'.[2] After another relapse during the Great Purges of 1937–8, the fever appeared to be cured and the patient rose shakily from his bed to try to resume normal life.

But was the patient really the same man as before his bouts of revolutionary fever? Was his old life there to resume? Certainly the 'convalescence' of NEP meant in many respects a resumption of the kind of life that had been interrupted by the outbreak of war in 1914, the revolutionary upheavals of 1917, and the Civil War. But the 'convalescence' of the 1930s had a different character, for by this time many of the links with the old life had been broken. It was less a matter of resuming the old life than of starting a new one.

The structures of everyday life in Russia had been changed by the First Five-Year Plan upheavals in a way that had not been true of the earlier revolutionary experience of 1917–20. In 1924, during the NEP interlude, a Muscovite returning after ten years' absence could have picked up his city directory (immediately recognizable, because its old design and format had scarcely changed since the prewar years) and still have had a good chance of finding listings for his old doctor, lawyer, and even stockbroker, his favourite confectioner (still discreetly advertising the best imported chocolate), the local tavern and the parish priest, and the firms which had formerly repaired his clocks and supplied him with building materials or cash registers. Ten years later, in the mid-1930s, almost all these listings would have disappeared, and the returning traveller would have been further disoriented by the renaming of many Moscow streets and squares, and the destruction of churches and other familiar landmarks. Another few years, and the city directory itself would be gone, not to resume publication for half a century.

Since revolutions involve an abnormal concentration of human energy, idealism, and anger, it is in the nature of things that their intensity will at some point subside. But how does one end the revolution without repudiating it? This is a tricky problem for revolutionaries who last long enough in power to see the revolutionary impulse wane. The erstwhile revolutionary can scarcely follow Brinton's metaphor and announce that he has now recovered from his revolutionary fever. But Stalin was fully equal to this challenge. His way of ending the Revolution was to declare victory.

The rhetoric of victory filled the air in the first half of the 1930s. A new journal entitled *Our Achievements*, founded by the writer Maxim Gorky, epitomized this spirit. The battles of industrialization and collectivization had been won, Soviet propagandists trumpeted. The enemy classes had been liquidated. Unemployment had vanished. Primary education had become universal and compulsory, and (it was claimed) adult literacy in the Soviet Union had risen to 90 per cent.[3] With its Plan, the Soviet Union had taken a giant step forward in human mastery of the world: men were no longer the helpless victims of economic forces over which they had no control. A 'new Soviet man' was emerging in the process of building socialism. Even the physical environment was being transformed, as factories rose in the empty steppe and Soviet scientists and engineers applied themselves to 'the conquest of nature'.[4]

To say that the Revolution had been won was implicitly to say that the Revolution was over. It was time to enjoy the fruits of victory, if any could be found, or at any rate to rest from the strenuous exertions of revolution. In the mid-1930s, Stalin spoke of life having become more light-hearted, and promised 'a holiday on our street'. The virtues of order, moderation, predictability, and stability came back into official favour. In the economic sphere, the Second Five-Year Plan (1933–7) was more sober and realistic than its wildly ambitious predecessor, though the emphasis on building a heavy industrial base was unchanged. In the countryside, the regime made conciliatory overtures towards the peasantry within the framework of collectivization, trying to make the kolkhoz work. A non-Marxist commentator, Nicholas Timasheff, approvingly described what was happening as a 'great retreat' from revolutionary values and methods. Trotsky, disapproving, categorized it as 'Soviet Thermidor', a betrayal of the revolution.

In this final Chapter, I will examine three aspects of the transition from revolution to post-revolution. The first section deals with the nature of the revolutionary victory proclaimed by the regime in the 1930s ('*Revolution accomplished*'). The second section examines the Thermidorian policies and tendencies of the same period ('*Revolution betrayed*'). The subject of the third section, *The Terror*, is the Great Purges of 1937–8. This throws a new light on the 'return to normalcy' of the second section, reminding us that normalcy can be almost as elusive as victory. Just as there was hollowness in the regime's declaration of revolutionary victory, so there was also a good deal of phoniness and make-believe in its assurances that life was returning to normal, much as the population wished to accept them. It is no easy matter to end a revolution. The revolutionary virus stays in the system, liable to flare up again under stress. This happened in the Great Purges, a final bout of revolutionary fever that burned up almost everything that remained of the Revolution— energy, idealism, commitment, language and, finally, the revolutionaries themselves.

'*Revolution accomplished*'

When the Seventeenth Party Congress met early in 1934, it was called 'The Congress of Victors'. Their victory was the economic transformation that had occurred during the period of the First Five-Year Plan. The urban economy had been completely nationalized except for a small co-operative sector; agriculture had been collectivized. Thus the Revolution had succeeded in changing the modes of production; and as every Marxist knows, the mode of production is the economic base on which the entire superstructure of society, politics, and culture rests. Now that the Soviet Union had a socialist base, how could the superstructures fail to adjust themselves accordingly? By changing the base, the Communists had done all that needed to be done—and probably all that could be done in Marxist terms—to create a socialist society. The rest was just a matter of time. A socialist economy would automatically produce socialism, just as capitalism had produced bourgeois democracy.

This was the theoretical formulation. In practice, most Communists understood the revolutionary task and the victory in simpler terms. The task had been industrialization and economic modernization, epitomized in the First Five-Year Plan. Every new smokestack and every new tractor was a token of victory. If the Revolution had succeeded in laying the foundations of a powerful modern industrialized state in the Soviet Union, capable of defending itself against external enemies, it had accomplished its mission. In these terms, what had been achieved?

Nobody could miss the visible signs of the Soviet industrialization drive. Construction sites were everywhere. There had been headlong urban growth during the First Five-Year Plan: old industrial centres had expanded vastly, quiet provincial towns had been transformed by the advent of a big factory, and new industrial and mining settlements were springing up all over the Soviet Union. Massive new metallurgical and machine-building plants were under construction or already in operation. The Turksib railway and the giant Dnieper hydroelectric dam had been built.

The First Five-Year Plan was declared to have been successfully completed in 1932, after four and a half years. The official results, which were the subject of a Soviet propaganda barrage at home and abroad, must be treated with great caution. Nevertheless, Western economists have generally accepted that there was real growth, amounting to what Walt Rostow later labelled industrial 'take-off'. Summarizing the results of the First Five-Year Plan, a British economic historian notes that 'though the claims in their totality are dubious, there is no doubt at all that a mighty engineering industry was in the making, and output of machine-tools, turbines, tractors, metallurgical equipment, etc. rose by genuinely impressive percentages'. Although steel production fell far short of its target, it still rose (according to Soviet figures) by almost 50 per cent. Output of iron ore more than doubled, though the planned increase was even greater, and hard coal and pig iron came close to doubling in the period 1927/8 to 1932.[5]

This is not to deny that there were problems with an industrialization drive that emphasized speed and output with such ruthless singlemindedness. Industrial accidents were common; there was massive waste of materials; quality was low, and the percentage of defective output high. The Soviet strategy was expensive in financial and human terms, and not necessarily optimal even in terms of growth rates: one Western economist has calculated that the Soviet Union could have achieved similar levels of growth by the mid-1930s without any basic departure from the NEP framework.[6] All too often, 'fulfilling and over-fulfilling the Plan' meant throwing rational planning to the winds and focusing narrowly on a few high-priority output targets at the expense of all else. New factories might be producing glamorous goods like tractors and turbines, but there was a dire shortage of nails and packing materials all through the First Five-Year Plan, and all branches of industry were affected by the collapse of peasant haulage and cartage which was an unplanned consequence of collectivization. The Donbass coal industry was in crisis in 1932, and a number of other key industrial sectors had acute construction and production problems.[7]

Despite the problems, industry was the sphere in which the Soviet leaders genuinely believed they were in the process of achieving something remarkable. Virtually all Communists felt this way, even those who had earlier sympathized with the Left or Right Oppositions; and something of the same pride and excitement was apparent in the younger generation, regardless of party affiliation, and to some extent in the urban population as a whole. Many former Trotskyites had left the Opposition because of their enthusiasm for the First Five-Year Plan, and even Trotsky himself basically approved of it. Those Communists who had leaned to the Right in 1928–9 had recanted and fully associated themselves with the industrialization drive. In the internal calculus of many former doubters, Magnitogorsk, the Stalingrad Tractor Plant, and the other great industrial projects outweighed the negative aspects of Stalin's course like the heavy-handed repression and the collectivization excesses.

Collectivization was the Achilles' heel of the First Five-Year Plan, a regular source of crises, confrontations, and improvised solutions. On the positive side, it provided the desired mechanism for state grain procurements at low, non-negotiable prices and in larger volume than the peasants wanted to sell. On the debit side, it left the peasantry resentful and unwilling to work, caused massive slaughter of livestock, led to famine in 1932–3 (provoking crises throughout the economy and administrative system), and forced the state to invest much more heavily in the agricultural sector than was compatible with the original strategy of 'squeezing the peasantry'.[8] In theory, collectivization could have meant many things. As practised in the Soviet Union in the 1930s, it was an extreme form of state economic exploitation which the peasantry understandably regarded as 'a second serfdom'. This was demoralizing not only to peasants but also to the Communist cadres who experienced it at first hand.

Nobody was really happy about collectivization; it was seen by Communists as a battle won, but at great cost. Furthermore, the kolkhoz that actually came into being was very different from the kolkhoz of Communist dreams or the one that was depicted in Soviet propaganda. The real kolkhoz was small, village-based, and primitive, whereas the dream kolkhoz was a showplace of large-scale, modern, mechanized agriculture. Not only was the real kolkhoz lacking in tractors, which were removed to regional Machine-Tractor Stations, it was also acutely short of traditional draught power because of the slaughter of horses during collectivization. Living standards in the village had dropped sharply with collectivization, going down to the barest subsistence level in many places. Electricity had become even less common in the countryside than it had been in the 1920s because of the disappearance of the 'kulak' millers whose water-powered turbines had generated it. To the chagrin of many rural Communist officials, collectivized agriculture was not even fully socialized because peasants were allowed small private plots, even though this encouraged them to skimp on work in the collective fields. As Stalin admitted in 1935, the private plot was essential to the peasant family's survival, since it provided most of the peasants' (and the nation's) milk, eggs, and vegetables. For much of the 1930s, the only payment that most peasants received from the kolkhoz for their work was a small share of the grain harvest.[9]

As to the Revolution's political goals, it would scarcely be an exaggeration to say that the regime's survival through the anxious months of 1931, 1932, and 1933 seemed in itself a victory—perhaps even a miracle—to many Communists. Still, this was not a victory to celebrate in public. Something more was needed, preferably something about socialism. In the early 1930s, it had become fashionable to talk about 'the building of socialism' and 'socialist construction'. But these phrases, never precisely defined, suggested process rather than completion. In 1936, with the introduction of the new Soviet Constitution, Stalin indicated that the 'construction' phase was essentially finished. This meant that socialism was an accomplished fact in the Soviet Union.

Theoretically, it was quite a leap. Exactly what 'socialism' meant was always vague, but if Lenin's *State and Revolution* (written in September 1917) was a guide, it involved local ('soviet') democracy, the disappearance of class antagonism and class exploitation, and the withering away of the state. The last requirement was a stumbling block, for even the most optimistic Soviet Marxist could hardly maintain that the Soviet state had withered away, or was likely to do so in the near future. The solution was found by introducing a new, or at least hitherto neglected, theoretical distinction between social-ism and communism. It was only under *communism*, it transpired, that the state would wither away. Socialism, though not the final end of the Revolution, was the best that could be achieved in a world of mutually antagonistic nation-states in which the Soviet Union existed in the midst of capitalist encirclement. With the advent of world revolution, the state could wither. Until then, it must remain strong and powerful to protect the world's only socialist society from its enemies.

What were the characteristics of the socialism that now existed in the Soviet Union? The answer to this question was given in the new Soviet Constitution, the first since the revolutionary Constitution of the Russian Republic in 1918. To understand it, we need to recall that according to Marxist–Leninist theory a transitional phase of proletarian dictatorship lay between the revolution and socialism. That phase, which began in Russia in October 1917, was character-ized by intense class war, as the old possessing classes resisted their expropriation and destruction by the proletarian state. It was the cessation of class war, Stalin explained in introducing the new Constitution, that marked the transition from the dictatorship of the proletariat to socialism.

According to the new Constitution, all Soviet citizens possessed the equal rights and guaranteed civil liberties appropriate to social-ism. Now that the capitalist bourgeoisie and kulaks had been eliminated, class struggle had disappeared. There were still classes in Soviet society—the working class, the peasantry, and the intelli-gentsia (strictly defined as a stratum rather than a class)—but their relations were free of antagonism and exploitation. They were equal in status, and equal also in their devotion to socialism and the Soviet state.[10]

These assertions have infuriated many non-Soviet commentators over the years. Socialists have denied that the Stalinist system was true socialism; others have pointed out that the Constitution's promises of freedom and equality were a sham. While there is room for argument about the degree of fraudulence, or the degree of intention to defraud,[11] such reactions are understandable because the Constitution had only the most tenuous relationship to Soviet reality. In the context of our present discussion, however, the Constitution need not be taken too seriously: as far as claims of revolutionary victory are concerned, this was an afterthought that had little emotional charge in the Communist party or the society as a whole. Most people were indifferent, some were confused. A poignant response to the news that socialism already existed in the Soviet Union came from a young journalist, a true believer in the socialist future, who knew how primitive and miserable life was in his native village. Was *this* then socialism? 'Never, neither before or after, have I experienced such disappointment, such grief.'[12]

The new Constitution's guarantee of equal rights represented a real change from the 1918 Constitution of the Russian Republic. The 1918 Constitution had explicitly *not* given equal rights: members of the old exploiting classes had been deprived of the right to vote in soviet elections, and urban workers' votes were heavily weighted as against peasants' votes. Associated with this was an elaborate structure of class-discriminatory laws and regulations designed to put workers in a privileged position and disadvantage the bourgeoisie that had been in place since the Revolution. Now, under the 1936 Constitution, everyone had the right to vote, regardless of class. The stigmatized category of 'disenfranchised persons' (*lishentsy*) disappeared. Class-discriminatory policies and practices were being phased out even before the new Constitution. In university admissions, for example, discrimination in favour of workers had been dropped a few years before.

Thus, the shift away from class discrimination was real, although it was by no means as complete as the Constitution implied, and met considerable resistance from Communists who were used to doing things the old way.[13] The significance of the change could be interpreted in two ways. On the one hand, the dropping of class discrimination could be seen as a prerequisite for socialist equality ('Revolution accomplished'). On the other hand, it could be taken as the regime's definitive abandonment of the proletariat ('Revolution betrayed'). The status of the working class and its relationship to Soviet power under the new order remained unclear. There never was any straightforward official statement that the era of proletarian dictatorship had ended (though this was the logical inference to be drawn if the Soviet Union had already entered the era of socialism), but usage shifted away from terms like 'proletarian hegemony' towards blander formulations like 'the leading role of the working class'.

Marxist critics like Trotsky might say that the party had lost its moorings by allowing the bureaucracy to replace the working class as its main source of social support. But Stalin had a different view. From Stalin's standpoint, one of the great achievements of the Revolution had been the creation of a 'new Soviet intelligentsia' (which in essence meant a new managerial and professional elite), recruited from the working class and peasantry. The Soviet regime no longer had to depend on holdovers from the old elites, whose loyalty would always be dubious, but could now rely on its own elite of home-grown 'leading cadres and specialists', men who owed their promotion and careers to the Revolution and could be relied on to be completely loyal to it (and to Stalin). Once the regime had this 'new class'—'yesterday's workers and peasants, promoted to command positions'—as a social base, the whole issue of the proletariat and its special relationship to the regime became unimportant in Stalin's eyes. After all, as he implied in his comments to the Eighteenth Party Congress in 1939, the flower of the old revolutionary working class had in fact been transplanted into the new Soviet intelligentsia, and if workers who had failed to rise were envious, so much the worse for them. There is little doubt that this point of view made perfect sense to the 'sons of the working class' in the new elite, who, in the manner of the upwardly mobile everywhere, were both proud of their disadvantaged background and happy to have left it far behind.

'Revolution betrayed'

The pledge of *liberté, égalité, fraternité* is a part of almost all revolutions, but it is a pledge that the victorious revolutionaries almost inevitably dishonour. The Bolsheviks knew this in advance because they had read Marx. They did their best, even in the euphoria of October, to be hard-headed scientific revolutionaries and not utopian dreamers. They hedged their promises of *liberté*, *égalité*, and *fraternité* with references to class war and the dictatorship of the proletariat. But it was as difficult to repudiate the classic revolutionary slogans as it would have been to conduct a successful revolution without enthusiasm. Emotionally, the Old Bolshevik leaders could not help being somewhat egalitarian and libertarian; and they were somewhat utopian too, for all their Marxist theory. The new Bolsheviks of 1917- and Civil-War vintage had the same emotional response without the intellectual inhibitions. While the Bolsheviks did not exactly set out to make an egalitarian, libertarian, and utopian revolution, the Revolution made the Bolsheviks at least intermittently egalitarian, libertarian, and utopian.

The ultra-revolutionary strain in post-October Bolshevism came to the fore during the Civil War, and again during the First Five-Year Plan Cultural Revolution. It was manifested in class-war militancy, aggressive rejection of social privilege, anti-elitism, wage egalitarianism, cultural iconoclasm, hostility to the family, and experimentation in everything from organizational methods to education. In Lenin's time, such tendencies were often pejoratively labelled 'leftist' or 'avant-gardist'; but the leaders also viewed them with a certain indulgence, as products of youthful revolutionary exuberance or untutored proletarian instinct. The paradox of Stalin's retreat from revolutionary enthusiasm was that it was so well grounded in Leninist tradition and Bolshevik ideology.

With the 'great retreat' of the 1930s, the Stalinist party shed the iconoclasm and anti-bourgeois fervour of the Cultural Revolution and became, as it were, respectable. Respectability meant new cultural and moral values, reflecting the metaphorical transition from proletarian youth to middle-class middle age; a striving for order and manageable routine; and acceptance of a social hierarchy based on education, occupation, and status. Authority was to be obeyed rather than challenged. Tradition was to be respected rather than flouted. The regime was still described as 'revolutionary', but that increasingly meant revolutionary in origin and legitimacy rather than revolutionary in practice. These were the changes that Trotsky excoriated in his *Revolution Betrayed*. Many of them, of course, could also be seen in quite a different light, namely that of necessary and pragmatic adjustments to the postrevolutionary condition, if one accepted Stalin's premise that revolutionary aims had been accomplished, not abandoned.

In industry, with the Second Five-Year Plan marking a transition to sober planning with less sloganeering about unreachable targets and more rationality, the watchwords of the 1930s were raising productivity and acquiring skills. The principle of material incentives became firmly established, with increased piecework and differentiation of workers' wages according to skill, and bonuses for output above the norm. Specialists' salaries were raised, and in 1932 the average salary of engineers and technicians stood higher in relation to the average worker's wage than at any time in the Soviet period before or after. These were logical policies, given the state's priority of rapid industrial growth, but they accentuated the regime's movement away from the original revolutionary identification with the working class. Stalin's denunciation of vulgar egalitarianism (*uravnilovka*) in wages policy in his famous 'Six Conditions' speech of 23 June 1931[15] was less remarkable for its substantive content (since the levelling tendencies of the First Five-Year Plan were largely spontaneous, not the product of any earlier official endorsement of the principle of wage egalitarianism) than for its casual disrespect for one of the sacred cows of workers' revolution.

The Stakhanovite Movement (named for a record-breaking coal-miner from the Donbass) was perhaps the most curious example of the Soviet postrevolutionary ethos and the regime's ambivalent attitude towards workers. The Stakhanovite was a norm-buster, lavishly rewarded for his achievements and fêted by the media, but in the real world almost inevitably resented and shunned by his fellow workers. He was also an innovator and rationalizer of production, encouraged to challenge the conservative wisdom of the experts and expose the unspoken agreement between factory management, engineers, and trade-union branches to resist the constant pressure from above to raise norms. The Stakhanovite movement glorified individual workers, while being at the same time essentially anti-labour and in some respects also anti-management.[16]

The manners and style of leadership also changed. In the 1920s, proletarian manners were cultivated even by Bolshevik intellectuals: when Stalin told a party audience that he was a 'crude' man, it sounded more like self-promotion than self-deprecation. But in the 1930s, Stalin began to present himself to Soviet Communists and foreign interviewers as a man of culture, like Lenin. Among his colleagues in the party leadership, the newly risen Khrushchevs, confident of their proletarian origins but afraid of behaving like peasants, were beginning to outnumber the Bukharins, who were confident of their culture but afraid of behaving like bourgeois intellectuals. At a lower level of officialdom, Communists tried to learn the rules of polite behaviour and put away their Army boots and cloth caps, not wanting to be mistaken for members of the non-upwardly-mobile proletariat. A new schoolmistressly tone of rather smug didacticism, later familiar to generations of Intourist visitors, could be detected in the pages of *Pravda*.

In education, the policy reorientation of the 1930s was in dramatic contrast to what had gone before. The progressive educational tendencies of the 1920s had run wild during Cultural Revolution, with formal classroom teaching often abandoned in favour of 'socially useful labour' outside the school and lectures, textbooks, homework, and individual testing of academic achievement almost totally discredited. Between 1931 and 1934, these tendencies were abruptly reversed. Later in the 1930s, school uniforms reappeared, making boys and girls in Soviet high schools look very like their predecessors in Tsarist gymnasia. The reorganization of higher education was also in many respects a return to traditional, prerevolutionary norms. The old professors recovered their authority; entrance requirements were once again based on academic rather than social and political criteria; and examinations, degrees, and academic titles were reinstated.[17]

History, a subject banished soon after the Revolution on the grounds that it was irrelevant to contemporary life and had traditionally been used to inculcate patriotism and the ideology of the ruling class, reappeared in the curricula of schools and universities. Mikhail Pokrovsky, an Old Bolshevik and distinguished Marxist historian whose disciples had been very active in the scholarly branch of Cultural Revolution, was posthumously criticized for reducing history to an abstract record of class conflict without names, dates, heroes, or stirring emotions. Stalin ordered new history textbooks, many of which were written by Pokrovsky's old enemies, the conventional 'bourgeois' historians who paid only lip-service to Marxism. Heroes returned to history: Tarlé's *Napoleon* was an early success, but the rehabilitation extended to great Russian leaders of the past like Ivan the Terrible (purger of the Russian boyars in the sixteenth century) and Peter the Great (the 'Tsar-Transformer', architect of Russia's first modernization at the beginning of the eighteenth century).[18]

Motherhood and the virtues of family life were also extolled from the mid-1930s. Despite their reservations about sexual liberation, the Bolsheviks had legalized abortion and divorce shortly after the Revolution and were popularly regarded as enemies of the family and traditional moral values. In the 1920s, the leaders had held to the principle that state intervention in matters of private sexual morality was undesirable, although it had always been assumed that all aspects of a *Communist*'s personal conduct should be open to the scrutiny of his party comrades. In the 1930s, Stalin's 'great retreat' involved not only an assertion of traditional family values, but also an extension of the principle of legitimate scrutiny of personal conduct from Communists alone to the population as a whole.

In the Stalin era, divorce became more difficult to obtain, free marriage lost its legal status, and persons taking their family responsibilities lightly were harshly criticized ('A poor husband and father cannot be a good citizen'). Male homosexuality was criminalized; and in 1936, after a public discussion showing support for both the pro- and anti-abortion viewpoints, abortion was also outlawed. Gold wedding-rings reappeared in the shops, and the traditional New Year trees (*elki*, the Russian equivalent of Christmas trees) were revived 'to bring joy to Soviet children'.[19] To Communists who had assimilated the more emancipated attitudes of an earlier period, this all came very close to the dreaded Philistinism of the petty bourgeoisie, especially given the sentimental and sanctimonious tones in which children and the family were now discussed. Of course, the policies that were most jarring to Communist intellectuals were often those that were most enthusiastically welcomed by the 'Philistine, petty-bourgeois' majority of the Soviet population.[20]

There was a retreat from the support for the cause of women's emancipation in this period, at least as far as educated, middle-class Russian women were concerned.[21] The old-style liberated Communist woman, assertively independent and ideologically committed on issues like abortion, was no longer in favour. The new message was that the family came first, despite the growing numbers of women who were receiving education and entering paid employment. No achievement could be greater than that of a successful wife and mother. In a campaign inconceivable in the 1920s, wives of members of the new Soviet elite were directed into voluntary community activities that bore a strong resemblance to the upper-class charitable work that Russian socialist and even liberal feminists had always despised. At a national 'meeting of wives' in 1936, the wives of industrial managers and engineers described the successes of the volunteer movement at a meeting in the Kremlin attended by Stalin and the army leader Klim Voroshilov, to whom the wives presented traditional Russian shirts embroidered with their own hands. Later, the proceedings were published in a handsome volume with roses decorating the endpapers.[22]

Embourgeoisement was not restricted to women. In the 1930s, privileges and a high standard of living became a normal and almost obligatory concomitant of elite status, in contrast to the situation in the 1920s, where Communists' incomes were constrained, at least in theory, by a 'party maximum' that kept their salaries from rising above the average wages of a skilled worker. The elite—which included professionals (Communist and non-party) as well as Communist officials—was set apart from the masses of the population not only by high salaries but also by privileged access to services and goods and a variety of material and honorific rewards. Elite members could use shops that were not open to the general public, buy goods that were not available to other consumers, and take their holidays at special resorts and well-appointed dachas. They often lived in special apartment blocks and went to work in chauffeur-driven cars. Many of these provisions arose out of the closed distribution systems that developed during the First Five-Year Plan in response to acute shortages, but remained to become a permanent feature of the landscape.

The party leaders were still somewhat sensitive on the question of elite privilege; conspicuous flaunting or greed could earn reprimands, or even cost lives during the Great Purges. Up to a point, at any rate, the privileges of the elite were hidden. There were many Old Bolsheviks around who still favoured the ascetic life and criticized those who succumbed to luxury: Trotsky's thrusts on this question in *The Revolution Betrayed* were not so different from comments made by the orthodox Stalinist, Molotov, in his memoirs;[23] and conspicuous consumption and acquisitiveness were among the abuses for which disgraced Communist officials elite members were routinely criticized during the Great Purges. Needless to say, there were conceptual problems for Marxists about the emergence of a privi-

leged bureaucratic class, the 'new class' (to use the term popular-
ized by the Yugoslav Marxist Milovan Djilas), or 'new service nobility' (in Robert Tucker's term).[24] Stalin's way of dealing with these
problems was to call the new privileged class an 'intelligentsia', thus
switching the focus from socio-economic to cultural superiority. In
Stalinist representation, this intelligentsia (new elite) was given a
vanguard role comparable to that of the Communist Party in politics;
as a cultural vanguard, it necessarily had access to a wider range of
cultural values (including consumer goods) than was available, for
the time being, to the rest of the population.[25]

Cultural life was very much affected by the regime's new orientation. In the first place, cultural interests and cultured behaviour
(*kul'turnost'*) were among the visible marks of elite status that
Communist officials were expected to display. In the second place,
non-Communist professionals—that is, the old 'bourgeois intelligentsia'—belonged to the new elite, mixed socially with Communist
officials and shared the same privileges. This constituted a real
repudiation of the party's old anti-expert bias that had made the
Cultural Revolution possible (in his 'Six Conditions' speech in 1931,
Stalin had reversed course on the question of 'wrecking' by the
bourgeois intelligentsia, saying baldly that the old technical intelligentsia had abandoned its attempt to sabotage the Soviet economy,
realizing that the penalties were too great and that the success of the
industrialization drive was already assured). With the old intelligentsia's return to favour, the Communist intelligentsia—especially the
activists of Cultural Revolution—fell out of favour with the party
leadership. One of the basic assumptions of Cultural Revolution had
been that the revolutionary age demanded a different culture from
that of Pushkin and *Swan Lake*. But in the Stalin era, with the old
bourgeois intelligentsia staunchly defending the cultural heritage and
a newly middle-class audience looking for an accessible culture to
master, Pushkin and *Swan Lake* came out the winners.

It was early days, however, to talk of a true return to normalcy.
There were external tensions, which increased steadily throughout
the 1930s. At the 'Congress of Victors' in 1934, one of the topics of
discussion was Hitler's recent accession to power in Germany—an
event that gave concrete meaning to the previously inchoate fears of
military intervention by the Western capitalist powers. There were
internal strains of many kinds. Talk of family values was all very
well, but the cities and railway stations were once again, as in the

Civil War, flooded by abandoned and orphaned children. Embourgeoisement was available only for a tiny minority of urban-dwellers; the rest were crammed into 'communal apartments', with several families each occupying a room, sharing a kitchen and bathroom in what had formerly been a one-family residence, and rationing of all basic goods was still in force. Stalin might tell kolkhozniks that 'Life is becoming better, comrades', but at the time—early 1935—only two harvests separated them from the 1932–3 famine.

The precariousness of postrevolutionary 'normalcy' was demonstrated in the winter of 1934–5. Bread rationing was to be lifted on 1 January 1935, and the regime planned a propaganda blitz on the 'Life is becoming better' theme. The newspapers celebrated the abundance of goods that would shortly be available (admittedly, only in few high-priced commercial stores) and enthusiastically described the merriment and elegance of the masked balls with which Muscovites greeted the New Year. In February, a congress of kolkhozniks was to be held to endorse the new Kolkhoz Charter, which guaranteed the private plot and made other concessions to the peasants. All this duly took place in the first months of 1935—but in an atmosphere of tension and foreboding, overshadowed by the assassination of Sergei Kirov, the Leningrad party leader, in December. The party and its leadership were thrown into spasm by this event; mass arrests followed in Leningrad. For all the signs and symbols of a postrevolutionary 'return to normalcy', normalcy was still far away.

Terror

Imagine, we say, O Reader, that the Millennium were struggling on the threshold, and yet not so much as groceries could be had,—owing to traitors. With what impetus would a man strike traitors, in that case! . . . As to the temper there was in men and women, does not this one fact say enough: the height SUSPICION had risen to? Preternatural we often called it; seemingly in the language of exaggeration: but listen to the cold deposition of witnesses. Not a music patriot can blow himself a snatch of melody from the French Horn, sitting mildly pensive on the housetop, but Mercier will recognize it to be a signal which one Plotting Committee is making to another . . . Louvet, who can see as deep into a millstone as the most, discerns that we shall be invited back to our old Hall of the Manege, by a Deputation; and then the Anarchists will massacre Twenty-two of us, as we walk over. It is Pitt and Cobourg; the gold of Pitt. . . . Behind, around, before, it is one huge Preternatural Puppet-play of Plots; Pitt pulling the wires.[26]

On 29 July 1936, the Central Committee sent a secret letter to all local party organizations 'On the terrorist activity of the Trotskyite–Zinovievite counter-revolutionary bloc' stating that former Oppositionist groups, which had become magnets for 'spies, provocateurs, diversionists, White guards, [and] kulaks' who hated Soviet power, had been responsible for the murder of Sergei Kirov, the Leningrad party leader. Vigilance—'the ability to recognize an enemy of the party, no matter how well he might be disguised'—was an essential attribute of every Communist.[27] This letter was a prelude to the first show trial of the Great Purges, held in August, in which Lev Kamenev and Grigorii Zinoviev, two former Opposition leaders, were convicted of complicity in Kirov's murder, and sentenced to death.

In a second show trial, held early in 1937, the emphasis was on wrecking and sabotage in industry. The chief defendant was Yurii Pyatakov, a former Trotskyite who had been Ordzhonikidze's right-hand man at the Commissariat of Heavy Industry since the beginning of the 1930s. In June of the same year, Marshal Tukhachevsky and other military leaders were accused of being German spies and immediately executed after a secret court martial. In the last of the show trials, held in March 1938, the defendants included Bukharin and Rykov, the former Rightist leaders, and Genrikh Yagoda, former head of the secret police. In all these trials, Old Bolshevik defendants publicly confessed to a variety of extraordinary crimes, which they described in court in great circumstantial detail. Almost all of them were sentenced to death.[28]

Apart from their more flamboyant crimes, such as the murder of Kirov and the writer Maxim Gorky, the conspirators confessed to many acts of economic sabotage designed to provoke popular discontent against the regime and facilitate its overthrow. These included organizing accidents in mines and factories in which many workers were killed, causing delays in the payment of wages, and holding up distribution of goods so that rural stores were deprived of sugar and tobacco and urban bread shops ran out of bread. The conspirators also confessed that they had habitually practised deception, pretending to have renounced their Oppositionist views and proclaiming their devotion to the party line, but all the while privately dissenting, doubting, and criticizing.[29]

Foreign intelligence agencies—German, Japanese, British, French, Polish—were said to be behind all the conspiracies, whose ultimate objective was to launch a military attack on the Soviet Union, overthrow the Communist regime, and restore capitalism. But the linchpin of conspiracy was Trotsky, allegedly an agent not only of the Gestapo but also (since 1926!) of the British Intelligence Service, who acted as intermediary between foreign powers and his conspiratorial network in the Soviet Union.[30]

The Great Purges were not the first episode of terror in the Russian Revolution. Terror against 'class enemies' had been part of the Civil War, and it was also part of collectivization and Cultural Revolution. Indeed, Molotov stated in 1937 that a direct line of continuity ran from the Shakhty and 'Industrial Party' trials of the Cultural Revolution to the present—with the important difference that this time the conspirators against Soviet power wreckers were not 'bourgeois specialists' but Communists, or at least people who 'masked themselves' as such and managed to worm their way into top positions in the party and government.[31]

Mass arrests in the upper echelons began in the latter part of 1936, particularly in industry. But it was at the February–March plenum of the Central Committee in 1937 that Stalin, Molotov, and Nikolai Ezhov (new head of the NKVD, as the secret police was renamed in 1934) gave the signal that really started the witch-hunts.[32] For two full years in 1937 and 1938, top Communist officials in every branch of the bureaucracy—government, party, industrial, military, and finally even police—were denounced and arrested as 'enemies of the people'. Some were shot; others disappeared into Gulag. Khrushchev disclosed in his Secret Speech to the Twentieth Party Congress that out of 139 full and candidate members of the Central Committee elected at the party's 'Congress of Victors' in 1934, all but 41 fell victim to the Great Purges. Continuity of leadership was almost completely broken: the Purges destroyed not only most surviving members of the Old Bolshevik cohort, but also a large part of the party cohorts formed in the Civil War and the period of collectivization. Only twenty-four members of the Central Committee elected at the Eighteenth Party Congress in 1939 had been members of the previous Central Committee, elected five years earlier.[33]

Communists in high positions were not the only victims of the Purges. The intelligentsia (both the old 'bourgeois' intelligentsia and the Communist intelligentsia of the 1920s, especially the activists of Cultural Revolution) was hard hit. So were former 'class enemies'— the usual suspects in any Russian revolutionary terror, even when, as in 1937, they were not specifically designated—and anybody else who had ever been put on an official blacklist for any reason. Persons with relatives abroad or foreign connections were particularly at risk. Stalin even issued a special secret order to arrest tens of thousands of 'former kulaks and criminals', including recidivists, horsethieves, and religious sectarians with prison records, and shoot them or send them to Gulag; in addition, 10,000 habitual criminals who were currently serving sentences in Gulag were to be shot.[34] The total dimensions of the Purges, for many years a matter of speculation in the West, are beginning to emerge more clearly as scholars investigate previously inaccessible Soviet archives. According to NKVD archives, the number of convicts in Gulag labour camps rose by half a million in the two years beginning 1 January 1937, reaching 1.3 million on 1 January 1939. In the latter year, 42 per cent of Gulag prisoners had been convicted of 'political' crimes (counter-revolution, spying, and so on), 24 per cent were classified as 'socially harmful or socially dangerous elements', and the rest were ordinary criminals. But many Purge victims were executed in prison, never reaching Gulag. The NKVD recorded 681,692 such executions in 1937–8.[35]

What was the point of the Great Purges? Explanations in terms of *raison d'état* (rooting out a potential wartime Fifth Column) are unconvincing; explanations in terms of totalitarian imperatives only beg the question of what totalitarian imperatives are. If we view the phenomenon of the Great Purges in the context of revolution, the question becomes less puzzling. Suspicion of enemies—in the pay of foreign powers, often masked, involved in constant conspiracies to destroy the revolution and inflict misery on the people—is a standard feature of revolutionary mentality that Thomas Carlyle captured vividly in the passage on the Jacobin Terror of 1794 quoted at the beginning of this section. In normal circumstances, people reject the idea that it is better that ten innocent men perish than that one guilty man go free; in the abnormal circumstances of revolution, they often accept it. Prominence is no guarantee of security in revolutions; rather the contrary. That the Great Purges uncovered so many 'enemies' in the guise of revolutionary leaders should come as no surprise to students of the French Revolution.

It is not hard to trace a revolutionary genesis for the Great Purges. As already noted, Lenin had no scruples about revolutionary terror and was intolerant of opposition, inside the party and out. Nevertheless, in Lenin's time a sharp distinction was drawn between the methods that were permissible for handling opposition outside the party and those that could be used on dissidents within. The Old Bolsheviks held to the principle that internal party disagreements were outside the scope of the secret police, since the Bolsheviks must never follow the Jacobins' example of turning terror on their own comrades. Admirable as that principle was, however, the fact that the Bolshevik leaders needed to affirm it says something about the atmosphere of internal party politics.

In the early 1920s, when organized opposition outside the Bolshevik Party disappeared and internal party factions were formally banned, dissident groups within the party in effect inherited the position of the old opposition parties outside it, and it was hardly surprising if they began to receive similar treatment. At any rate, there was no great outcry within the Communist Party when, in the late 1920s, Stalin used the secret police against the Trotskyites and then (following the model of Lenin's treatment of Cadet and Menshevik leaders in 1922–3) deported Trotsky from the country. During the Cultural Revolution, Communists who had worked closely with disgraced 'bourgeois experts' seemed in danger of being charged with something worse than stupidity. Stalin drew back, and even allowed the Rightist leaders to remain in positions of authority. Yet this went against the grain: it was manifestly difficult for Stalin— and for many rank-and-file Communists—to tolerate persons who had once been Oppositionists.

A revolutionary practice that is important in understanding the genesis of the Great Purges is the periodic 'cleansing' of membership (*chistki*, or purges with a small 'p') that the party conducted from the early 1920s. The frequency of party purges increased from the end of the 1920s: they were held in 1929, 1933–4, 1935, and 1936. In a party purge, every party member had to stand up and justify himself before a purge commission, rebutting criticism made openly from the floor or secretly via denunciation. The effect of repeated purges was that old offences were raised time after time and became virtually impossible to slough off. Undesirable relatives, prerevolutionary connections with other political parties, membership of party Oppositions, past scandals and official rebukes, even past bureaucratic mistakes and confusions of identity—all these hung round the neck of party members, getting heavier by the year. The party leaders' suspicion that the party was full of undeserving and unreliable members seemed to be exacerbated rather than mollified by each successive purge.[36]

Moreover, each purge created more potential enemies for the regime, since those expelled from the party were likely to be aggrieved by this blow to their status in society and prospects of advancement. In 1937, one Central Committee member suggested in camera that there were probably more *former* Communists in the country than current members of the party, and this was clearly a thought that he and others found deeply disturbing.[37] For the party already had so many enemies—and so many of them were hidden! There were the old enemies, those who had lost their privileges during the Revolution, priests, and so on. And now there were the *new* enemies, those who had fallen victim to the recent policies of liquidating kulaks and Nepmen as classes. Whether or not a particular kulak had been a sworn enemy of Soviet power before his dekulakization, he surely became one at that moment. The worst thing about this was that so many of the expropriated kulaks fled to the cities, started new lives, hid their past (as they must, to hold a job), masqueraded as honest workers—became, in short, hidden enemies of the revolution. How many apparently dedicated young Komsomols were out there concealing the fact that their fathers had once been kulaks or priests! No wonder, as Stalin warned, that individual class enemies became *even more dangerous* once the enemy classes had been destroyed. Of course they did, because that act of destruction had personally injured them; they had been given a real, concrete cause for grievance against the Soviet regime.

The volume of denunciations in the dossiers of all Communist administrators increased steadily year by year. It was one of the populist aspects of Stalin's revolution to encourage ordinary citizens to write in if they had cause to complain against 'abuses of power' by local officials; and the investigations that followed often led to the officials' dismissal. But many complaints were motivated as much by malice as by a quest for justice. A generalized sense of grievance, rather than the specific offences cited, seems to have inspired many of the denunciations of kolkhoz chairmen and other rural officials that angry kolkhozniks wrote in great quantity in the 1930s.[38]

The Great Purges could not have snowballed as they did without popular participation. Self-interested denunciations played a part, as did complaints against bosses that were based on real grievances. Spy-mania flared up, as it had done many times in the past twenty years: a young Pioneer, Lena Petrenko, caught a spy on the train on her way back from summer camp when she heard him speaking German; another vigilant citizen pulled at the beard of a religious mendicant and it came off in his hand, disclosing a spy who had just come over the frontier. At 'self-criticism' meetings in offices and party cells, fear and suspicion combined to produce scapegoating, hysterical accusations, and bullying.[39]

This was something different from popular terror, however. Like the Jacobin Terror of the French Revolution, it was state terror in which erstwhile revolutionary leaders were the most visible victims. In contrast to earlier episodes of revolutionary terror, spontaneous popular violence played only a minor role. Moreover, the focus of terror had shifted from the original 'class encuries' (nobles, priests, and other real opponents of the Revolution) to 'enemies of the people' in the Revolution's own ranks.

Yet the differences between the two cases are as intriguing as the similarities. In the French Revolution, Robespierre, the instigator of the Terror, ended up as its victim. In the Great Terror of the Russian Revolution, by contrast, the chief terrorist, Stalin, survived unscathed. Though Stalin eventually sacrificed his obedient instrument (Ezhov, head of the NKVD from September 1936 to December 1938, who was arrested in the spring of 1939 and later shot), there is no indication that he felt events had gone seriously out of control, or that he ever felt himself in danger, or that he got rid of Ezhov for any reason but Machiavellian prudence.[40] The repudiation of 'mass purging' and the disclosure of 'excesses' of vigilance at the Eighteenth Party Congress in March 1939 was carried out calmly; in his own speech, Stalin paid little attention to the subject, though he did spend a minute refuting comments in the foreign press that the Purges had weakened the Soviet Union.[41]

Reading the transcripts of the Moscow show trials, and of Stalin's and Molotov's speeches at the February–March plenum, one is struck not just by the theatricality of proceedings but also by their staginess, the sense of contrivance and calculation, the lack of any raw emotional response on the leaders' part to the news of their colleagues' treachery. This is revolutionary terror with a difference; one feels the hand of a director, if not an *auteur*.

In *The 18th Brumaire of Louis Bonaparte*, Marx made his famous comment that all great events are played twice, the first time as tragedy, the second time as farce. While the Great Terror of the

Russian Revolution was not farce, it had some of the characteristics of a replay, something staged with an earlier model in mind. It is possible, as Stalin's Russian biographer suggests, that the Jacobin Terror actually served Stalin as a model: Certainly the term 'enemies of the people', which Stalin seems to have introduced into Soviet discourse in connection with the Great Purges, had French Revolutionary antecedents.[42] In that light, it becomes easier to understand why the baroque setting of snowballing denunciations and rampant popular suspicion was required to achieve the relatively straightforward purpose of killing political enemies. Indeed, it is tempting to go further and suggest that, in enacting a terror (which must precede Thermidor, according to the classic revolutionary sequence, not follow it), Stalin may even have felt that he was definitively rebutting Trotsky's charge that his rule had led to 'a Soviet Thermidor'.[43] Who could say that Stalin was a Thermidorian reactionary, a betrayer of revolution, after this demonstration of revolutionary terror that dwarfed even that of the French Revolution?

What was the legacy of the Russian Revolution? Until the end of 1991, the Soviet system itself could be so described. The red flags and the banners proclaiming 'Lenin lives! Lenin is with us!' were there right up to the end. The ruling Communist party was a legacy of the Revolution; so were the collective farms, the Five- and Seven-Year Plans, chronic shortages of consumer goods, cultural isolation, Gulag, the division of the world into 'socialist' and 'capitalist' camps, and the assertion that the Soviet Union was 'leader of the progressive forces of mankind'. Though the regime and the society were no longer revolutionary, the Revolution remained as the keystone in Soviet national tradition, a focus of patriotism, a subject to be learnt by children in school and celebrated in Soviet public art.

The Russian Revolution also left a complex international legacy. This was the great revolution of the twentieth century, the symbol of socialism, anti-imperialism, and rejection of the old order in Europe. For good or ill, the international socialist and communist movements of the twentieth century have lived under its shadow, as have the Third-World liberation movements in the postwar era. The Cold War was part of the legacy of the Russian Revolution, as well as a back-handed tribute to its continuing symbolic power. It was the Russian Revolution that represented hope of freedom from oppression to some, and provoked nightmares of a worldwide triumph of atheistic communism in others. It was the Russian Revolution that established a definition of socialism that hinged on the seizure of state power and its use as an instrument of economic and social transformation.

Revolutions have two lives. In the first life, they are considered part of the present, inseparable from contemporary politics. In the second life, they cease to be part of the present and move into history and national legend. Being part of history does not mean total removal from politics, as is shown by the example of the French Revolution, still a touchstone of French political debate two centuries later. But it imposes a distance; and as far as historians are concerned, it permits more latitude and detachment in interpretation. By the 1990s, the Russian Revolution was long overdue to be moved out of the present into history, but the expected transfer kept being delayed. In the West, despite the persistence of Cold-War hangovers, historians, if not politicians, had more or less decided that the Russian Revolution was history. In the Soviet Union, however, interpretation of the Russian Revolution remained politically charged and linked with contemporary politics right up to the Gorbachev era, and even in a sense beyond. With the collapse of the Soviet Union, the Russian Revolution did not sink gracefully into history. It was flung there—'on to the dust-heap of history', to borrow Trotsky's phrase—in a spirit of vehement national rejection.

This repudiation, which amounted to a wish to forget not only the Russian Revolution but the whole Soviet era, left a strange emptiness in Russian historical consciousness. Soon, in the vein of Peter Chaadaev's jeremiad on the nonentity of Russia a century and a half earlier, a chorus of laments arose about Russia's fatal historical inferiority, backwardness, and exclusion from civilization. For late twentieth-century Russians, former Soviet citizens, it seemed that what had been lost with the discrediting of the myth of the Revolution was not so much belief in socialism as confidence in Russia's significance in the world. The Revolution gave Russia a meaning, a historical destiny. Through the Revolution, Russia became a trailblazer, an international leader, a model and inspiration for 'the progressive forces of the whole world'. Now, overnight as it seemed, all that was gone. The party was over; after seventy-four years, Russia had fallen out of 'the vanguard of history' into its old posture of recumbent backwardness. In a poignant moment for Russia and the Russian Revolution, it turned out that the 'future of progressive humanity' was really its past.

Notes

Details of titles included in the Select Bibliography are given only at the first citation.

Introduction (*pages 1–14*)

1. The term 'the Russian Revolution' has never been used in Russia. In Soviet usage, it was 'the October Revolution', or simply 'October'. The favoured post-Soviet term seems to be 'the Bolshevik Revolution' or sometimes 'the Bolshevik *putsch*'.
2. Dates before the calendar change in 1918 are given in the old style, which in 1917 was thirteen days behind the Western calendar which Russia adopted in 1918.
3. Crane Brinton, *The Anatomy of Revolution* (rev. edn.; New York, 1965). In the French Revolution, 9 Thermidor (27 July 1794) was the date in the revolutionary calendar on which Robespierre fell. The word 'Thermidor' is used as a shorthand both for the end of revolutionary terror and the end of the heroic phase of revolution.
4. See below, Ch. 6, p. 166.
5. My thinking about state terror owes a considerable debt to Colin Lucas's article, 'Revolutionary Violence, the People and the Terror,' forthcoming in K. Baker (ed.), *The Political Culture of the Terror* (Oxford, 1994).
6. The party's name was changed from Russian Social-Democratic Labour Party (Bolshevik) to Russian (later, All-Union) Communist Party (Bolshevik) in 1918. The terms 'Bolshevik' and 'Communist' were used interchangeably in the 1920s, but 'Communist' became the normal usage in the 1930s.
7. Adam B. Ulam, 'The Historical Role of Marxism', in his *The New Face of Soviet Totalitarianism* (Cambridge, Mass., 1963), 35.
8. 'The Great Purges' is a Western term, not a Soviet one. For many years, there was no acceptable public way to refer to the episode in Russian because it had not officially happened; in private conversation, it was usually referred to obliquely as '1937'. The confusion of nomenclature between 'purges' and 'the Great Purges' comes from the Soviet use of a euphemism: when the Terror was brought to an end with a quasi-repudiation at the Eighteenth Party Congress in 1939, what was nominally repudiated were 'mass purges' (*massovye chistki*), though in fact no party purge in the strict sense had

occurred since 1936. The euphemism was used briefly in Russian but soon disappeared, whereas in English it caught on permanently.

9. *The Great Terror* is the title of Robert Conquest's classic work on the subject.

Chapter 1 (pages 15–39)

1. Frank Lorimer, *The Population of the Soviet Union* (Geneva, 1946), 10, 12.
2. A. G. Rashin, *Formirovanie rabochego klassa Rossii* (Moscow, 1958), 328.
3. Barbara A. Anderson, *Internal Migration during Modernization in Late Nineteenth-Century Russia* (Princeton, NJ, 1980), 32–8.
4. A. Gerschenkron, *Economic Backwardness in Historical Perspective* (Cambridge, Mass., 1962), 5–30.
5. On peasant rebelliousness and working-class revolution, see Leopold Haimson, 'The Problem of Social Stability in Urban Russia, 1905–1917', *Slavic Review*, 23, no. 4 (1964) 633–7.
6. See Marc Raeff, *Origins of the Russian Intelligentsia. The Eighteenth-Century Nobility* (New York, 1966).
7. This is discussed in Richard S. Wortman, *The Development of a Russian Legal Consciousness* (Chicago, 1976), 286–9 and *passim*.
8. See the argument in Richard Pipes, *Russia under the Old Regime* (New York, 1974), ch. 10.
9. On the Populists' prescience on this question, see Gerschenkron, *Economic Backwardness* 167–73.
10. For a negative view, see Richard Pipes, *Social Democracy and the St Petersburg Labor Movement, 1885–1897* (Cambridge, Mass., 1963); for a more positive one, see Allan K. Wildman, *The Making of a Workers' Revolution. Russian Social Democracy, 1891–1903* (Chicago, 1967).
11. Quoted from Sidney Harcave, *First Blood. The Russian Revolution of 1905* (New York, 1964), 23.
12. For an analysis of Bolshevik and Menshevik membership to 1907, see David Lane, *The Roots of Russian Communism* (Assen, The Netherlands, 1969), 22–3, 26.
13. For a lucid discussion of the split, see Jerry F. Hough and Merle Fainsod, *How the Soviet Union is Governed* (Cambridge, Mass., 1979), 21–6.
14. Quoted from Trotsky, 'Our Political Tasks' (1904) in Isaac Deutscher, *The Prophet Armed* (London, 1970), 91–2.
15. Haimson, 'The Problem of Social Stability', 624–33.
16. See Roberta Thompson Manning, 'Zemstvo and Revolution: The Onset of the Gentry Reaction, 1905–1907', in Leopold Haimson,

ed., *The Politics of Rural Russia, 1905–1914* (Bloomington, Ind., 1979).

17. Mary Schaeffer Conroy, *Petr Arkad'evich Stolypin. Practical Politics in Late Tsarist Russia* (Boulder, Colo., 1976), 98.

18. See Dorothy Atkinson, 'The Statistics on the Russian Land Commune, 1905–1917', *Slavic Review*, 32, no. 4 (1973).

19. For a vivid fictional representation of what this meant in psychological terms, see Alexander Solzhenitsyn, *Lenin in Zurich* (New York, 1976).

20. The family tragedy is portrayed with sympathy and understanding in Robert K. Massie, *Nicholas and Alexandra* (New York, 1967).

Chapter 2 (*pages 40–67*)

1. For a critical historiographical survey of this argument, see Stephen F. Cohen, 'Bolshevism and Stalinism', in Robert C. Tucker, ed., *Stalinism* (New York, 1977).

2. Quoted from W. G. Rosenberg, *Liberals in the Russian Revolution* (Princeton, NJ, 1974), 209.

3. George Katkov, *Russia, 1917: The February Revolution* (London, 1967), 444.

4. A. Tyrkova-Williams, *From Liberty to Brest-Litovsk* (London, 1919), 25.

5. Quoted from Allan K. Wildman, *The End of the Russian Imperial Army* (Princeton, NJ, 1980), 260.

6. Sukhanov, *The Russian Revolution, 1917*, i. 104–5.

7. Quoted from Leonard Schapiro, *The Origin of the Communist Autocracy* (Cambridge, Mass., 1955), 42 (n. 20).

8. V. I. Lenin, *Collected Works* (Moscow, 1964), xxiv. 21–6. The critic quoted by Lenin was Goldenberg.

9. For a careful analysis of membership data for 1917, see T. H. Rigby, *Communist Party Membership in the USSR, 1917–1967* (Princeton, NJ, 1968), ch. 1.

10. Wildman, *The End of the Russian Imperial Army*. In addition to its central theme, the Army in the period Feb.–Apr. 1917, this book offers one of the best analyses available of the February transfer of power.

11. Marc Ferro, *The Russian Revolution of February 1917*, trans. by J. L. Richards (London, 1972), 112–21.

12. Ibid. 121–30.

13. On the July Days, see A. Rabinowitch, *Prelude to Revolution: The Petrograd Bolsheviks and the July 1917 Uprising* (Bloomington, Ind., 1968).

14. Quoted from A. Rabinowitch, *The Bolsheviks Come to Power* (New York, 1976), 115.

15. Newspaper interview with General Alekseev (*Rech'*, 13 Sept. 1917, p. 3), in Robert Paul Browder and Alexander F. Kerensky, ed., *The Russian Provisional Government 1917. Documents* (Stanford, 1961), iii. 1622.

16. Quoted from Robert V. Daniels, *Red October* (New York, 1967), 82.

17. The actions and intentions of major Bolshevik participants in the October Revolution were later subject to a great deal of self-serving revision and political myth-making—not only in official Stalinist histories, but also in Trotsky's classic history-*cum*-memoir, *The History of the Russian Revolution*. See the discussion in Daniels, *Red October*, ch. 11.

18. Leon Trotsky, *The History of the Russian Revolution*, trans. by Max Eastman (Ann Arbor, Mich., 1960), iii. chs. 4–6.

19. See, for example, Roy A. Medvedev, *Let History Judge. The Origins and Consequences of Stalinism* (1st edn.; New York, 1973), 381–4.

20. For one interpretation, see John Keep, *The Russian Revolution. A Study in Mass Mobilization* (New York, 1976), 306–81, 464–71.

21. The following analysis is based on O. Radkey, *Russia Goes to the Polls. The Election to the All-Russian Constituent Assembly 1917* (Ithaca, NY, 1989).

Chapter 3 (*pages 68–92*)

1. For a valuable discussion of these issues, see Ronald G. Suny, 'Nationalism and Class in the Russian Revolution: A Comparative Discussion,' in E. Frankel, J. Frankel, and B. Knei-Paz (eds.), *Russia in Revolution: Reassessments of 1917* (Cambridge, 1992).

2. On the impact of the Civil War, see D. Koenker, W. Rosenberg, and R. Suny (eds.), *Party, State, and Society in the Russian Civil War* (Bloomington, Ind., 1989).

3. T. H. Rigby, *Communist Party Membership in the USSR, 1917–1967* (Princeton, NJ, 1968), 242; *Vsesoyuznaya partiinaya perepis' 1927 goda. Osnovnye itogi perepisi* (Moscow, 1927), 52.

4. Robert C. Tucker, 'Stalinism as Revolution from Above,' in Tucker, *Stalinism*, 91–2.

5. This argument is elaborated in Sheila Fitzpatrick, 'The Civil War as a Formative Experience', in A. Gleason, P. Kenez, and R. Stites (eds.), *Bolshevik Culture* (Bloomington, Ind., 1985).

6. Quoted from John W. Wheeler-Bennett, *Brest-Litovsk. The Forgotten Peace, March 1918* (New York, 1971), 243–4.

7. Figures cited from Aleksandr I. Solzhenitsyn, *The Gulag Archipelago* (New York, 1973), 300. On the Cheka's activity in Petrograd, see Mary McAuley, *Bread and Justice. State and Society in Petrograd, 1917–1922* (Oxford, 1991), 375–93.

8. For a sample of Lenin's statements on terror, see W. Bruce Lincoln, *Red Victory. A History of the Russian Civil War* (New York, 1989), 134–9; for Trotsky's views, see his *Terrorism and Communism. A Reply to Comrade Kautsky* (1920).

9. On peasant attitudes, see Orlando Figes, *Peasant Russia, Civil War. The Volga Countryside in Revolution, 1917–1921* (Oxford, 1989).

10. On the economy, see Silvana Malle, *The Economic Organization of War Communism, 1918–1921* (Cambridge, 1985).

11. See Alec Nove, *An Economic History of the USSR* (London, 1969), ch. 3. A detailed historiographical discussion is in E. Gimpelson, '*Voennyi kommunizm*' (Moscow, 1973), 239–82.

12. For the argument that there was no 'second revolution', see T. Shanin, *The Awkward Class. Political Sociology of Peasantry in a Developing Society: Russia 1910–1925* (Oxford, 1972), 145–61.

13. N. Bukharin and E. Preobrazhensky, *The ABC of Communism*, trans. by E. and C. Paul (London, 1969), 355.

14. On continuity between the period of the Stolypin reforms and the 1920s, especially through the presence in the countryside of agricultural specialists working on land consolidation, see George L. Yaney, 'Agricultural Administration in Russia from the Stolypin Land Reform to Forced Collectivization: An Interpretive Study,' in James R. Millar (ed.), *The Soviet Rural Community* (Urbana, Ill., 1971), 3–35.

15. See Richard Stites, *Revolutionary Dreams. Utopian Vision and Experimental Life in the Russian Revolution* (Oxford, 1989) and William G. Rosenberg (ed.), *Bolshevik Visions. First Phase of the Cultural Revolution in Soviet Russia* (2nd edn., Ann Arbor, Mich., 1990).

16. Bukharin and Preobrazhensky, *The ABC of Communism*, 118.

17. Quoted from Sheila Fitzpatrick, *The Commissariat of Enlightenment* (London, 1970), 20.

18. T. H. Rigby, *Lenin's Government. Sovnarkom, 1917–1922* (Cambridge, 1979).

19. *Sto sorok besed s Molotovym. Iz dnevnikov F. I. Chueva* (Moscow, 1991), 184.

20. Bukharin and Preobrazhensky, *The ABC of Communism*, 272.

21. See Sheila Fitzpatrick, *Education and Mobility in the Soviet Union, 1921–1934* (Cambridge, 1979), ch. 1.

Chapter 4 (pages 93–119)

1. On the vanishing working class, see D. Koenker, 'Urbanization and Deurbanization in the Russian Revolution and Civil War,' in D. Koenker, W. Rosenberg, and R. Suny (eds.), *Party, State, and Society in the Russian Civil War* (Bloomington, Ind., 1989), and

Sheila Fitzpatrick, 'The Bolsheviks' Dilemma: The Class Issue in Party Politics and Culture,' in Sheila Fitzpatrick, *The Cultural Front* (Ithaca, NY, 1992).

2. Oliver H. Radkey, *The Unknown Civil War in Soviet Russia* (Stanford, Calif., 1976), 263.

3. See Paul A. Avrich, *Kronstadt, 1921* (Princeton, NJ, 1970), and Israel Getzler, *Kronstadt, 1917–1921* (Cambridge, 1983).

4. On NEP, see Lewis H. Siegelbaum, *Soviet State and Society between Revolutions, 1918–1929* (Cambridge, 1992), and S. Fitzpatrick, A. Rabinowitch, and R. Stites (eds.), *Russia in the Era of NEP* (Bloomington, Ind., 1991).

5. Lenin, 'Political Report of the Central Committee to the Eleventh Party Congress' (Mar. 1922), in V. I. Lenin, *Collected Works* (Moscow, 1966), xxxiii. 282.

6. Published from the formerly secret section of the Central Party Archives in *Izvestiia TsK KPSS*, 1990 no. 4, 191–3.

7. A. I. Mikoyan, *Mysli i vospominaniya o Lenine* (Moscow, 1970), 139. See also *Sto sorok besed s Molotovym*, 181.

8. *Sto sorok besed s Molotovym*, 176.

9. Rigby, *Communist Party Membership*, 96–100, 98. For a lively recreation of the 1921 purge at local level, see F. Gladkov, *Cement*, trans. by A. S. Arthur and C. Ashleigh (New York, 1989), ch. 16.

10. Lenin, *Collected Works*, xxxiii. 288.

11. 'Better Fewer, But Better' (2 Mar. 1923), in Lenin, *Collected Works*, xxxiii. 488.

12. I. N. Yudin, *Sotsial'naya baza rosta KPSS* (Moscow, 1973), 128.

13. *Kommunisty v sostave apparata gosuchrezhdenii i obshchestvennykh organizatsii. Itogi vsesoyuznoi partiinoi perepisi 1927 goda* (Moscow, 1929), 25; *Bol'shevik*, 1928 no. 15, 20.

14. The 'Testament' (not included in the English *Collected Works*, which is a translation of the Russian 4th edn.) is in V. I. Lenin, *Polnoe sobranie sochinenii* (5th edn.; Moscow, 1964), xlv. 435–6.

15. See Robert V. Daniels, *The Conscience of the Revolution* (Cambridge, Mass., 1960), 225–30.

16. The phrase is Robert V. Daniels's. For a clear and concise discussion, see Hough and Fainsod, *How the Soviet Union is Governed*, 124–33, 144.

17. This is the unifying theme of Robert V. Daniels's study of the Communist Oppositions of the 1920s, *The Conscience of the Revolution*—although, as his title indicates, Daniels sees the pleas for internal party democracy as an expression of revolutionary idealism rather than as an inherent function of opposition.

18. See Moshe Lewin, *Lenin's Last Struggle* (New York, 1968), for the argument that Lenin's political thinking changed radically in his last years.
19. On the emergence of the Lenin cult, see Nina Tumarkin, *Lenin Lives!* (Cambridge, 1983).
20. Lenin, 'Our Revolution (A Propos of the Notes of N. Sukhanov)', in his *Collected Works*, xxxiii. 480.
21. Quoted from Yu. V. Voskresenskii, *Perekhod Kommunisticheskoi Partii k osushchestvleniyu politiki sotsialisticheskoi industrializatsii SSSR (1925–1927)* (Moscow, 1969), 162.
22. J. V. Stalin, 'October, Lenin and the Prospects of Our Development', in his *Works* (Moscow, 1954), vii. 258.
23. For these discussions, see E. H. Carr, *Socialism in One Country*, ii. 36–51.
24. For a detailed examination of the debate, see A. Erlich, *The Soviet Industrialization Debate, 1924–1926* (Cambridge, Mass., 1960).
25. See Stephen F. Cohen, 'Bolshevism and Stalinism', in Tucker (ed.), *Stalinism*, and *Bukharin and the Bolshevik Revolution* (New York, 1973); and Moshe Lewin, *Political Undercurrents in Soviet Economic Debates: From Bukharin to the Modern Reformers* (Princeton, NJ, 1974).
26. On the party debates on Thermidor, see Deutscher, *The Prophet Unarmed* (London, 1970), 312–32, and Michal Reiman, *The Birth of Stalinism*, trans. by George Saunders (Bloomington, Ind., 1987), 22–3.

Chapter 5 (pages 120–47)

1. See e.g. Adam B. Ulam, *Stalin* (New York, 1973), ch. 8.
2. With the Law of Suspects (17 Sept. 1793), the Jacobin Convention ordered the immediate arrest of all persons who might be deemed a threat to the revolution by virtue of their actions, connections, writings, or general demeanour. On Stalin's admiration of this measure, see Dimitri Volkogonov, *Triumf i tragediia. Politicheskii portret Stalina* (Moscow, 1989), bk. 1, pt. 2, 201.
3. Quoted from document in the Political Archive of the German Foreign Ministry by Reiman, *Birth of Stalinism*, 35–6.
4. On the Shakhty trial and the later 'Industrial Party' trial, see Kendall E. Bailes, *Technology and Society under Lenin and Stalin* (Princeton, NJ, 1978), chs. 3–5.
5. See Sheila Fitzpatrick, 'Stalin and the Making of a New Elite,' in Fitzpatrick, *The Cultural Front*, 153–4, 162–5.
6. Document from the former Central Party Archives (*RTsKhIDNI*,

f. 558n, op. 1, d. 5276, ll. 1–5) cited from Library of Congress exhibit, 'Revelations from the Russian Archives' (Washington, DC, 17 June–16 July 1992).

7. Stalin's statements on the procurements crisis (Jan.–Feb. 1928) are in J. V. Stalin, *Works* (Moscow, 1954), xi. 3–22. See also Moshe Lewin, *Russian Peasants and Soviet Power* (London, 1968), 214–40.

8. Frumkin's advice is reported in *Za chetkuyu klassovuyu liniyu* (Novosibirsk, 1929) 73–4; Uglanov's recommendations were outlined by him in a speech in Moscow at the end of January, published in *Vtoroi plenum MK RKP(b), 31 yanv.–2 fev. 1928. Doklady i rezoliutsii* (Moscow, 1928), 9–11, 38–40.

9. See Cohen, *Bukharin and the Bolshevik Revolution*, 322–3.

10. This comment was made by the Urals party secretary Ivan Kabakov, in response to a belated 'Rightist' speech that Rykov made in Sverdlovsk in the summer of 1930. *X Ural'skaya konferentsiya Vsesoyuznoi Kommunisticheskoi Partii (bol'shevikov)* (Sverdlovsk, 1930), Bull. 6, 14.

11. J. V. Stalin, *Works* (Moscow, 1955), xiii. 40–1.

12. Stalin's remark is quoted in *Puti industrializatsii*, 1928 no. 4, 64–5.

13. See E. H. Carr and R. W. Davies, *Foundations of a Planned Economy, 1926–1929* (London, 1969), i. 843–97.

14. On major construction projects of the First Five-Year Plan, see Anne Rassweiler, *The Generation of Power: The History of Dneprostroi* (Oxford, 1988) and John Scott, *Behind the Urals* (Boston, 1942) (on Magnitogorsk).

15. David Ryazanov, in *XVI konferentsiya VKP(b), aprel' 1929 g. Stenograficheskii otchet* (Moscow, 1962), 214.

16. On the politics of the First Five-Year Plan industrialization, see Sheila Fitzpatrick, 'Ordzhonikidze's Takeover of Vesenkha: A Case Study in Soviet Bureaucratic Politics,' *Soviet Studies* 37: 2 (Apr., 1985).

17. Alec Nove, *An Economic History of the USSR* (London, 1969), 150.

18. Quoted from R. W. Davies, *The Socialist Offensive* (Cambridge, Mass., 1980), 148.

19. J. V. Stalin, *Works* (Moscow, 1955), xii. 197–205.

20. Figures cited from Nove, *Economic History of the USSR*, 197 and 238. On the 25,000-ers, see Lynne Viola, *The Best Sons of the Fatherland* (New York, 1987).

21. *Slavic Review*, 50: 1 (1991), 152.

22. Estimates of deaths from V. Tsaplin in *Voprosy istorii*, 1989 no. 4, 175–81, and E. Osokina in *Istoriya SSSR*, 1991 no. 5, 18–26. For two different approaches to the famine, see Robert Conquest, *Harvest of Sorrow. Soviet Collectivization and the Terror-Famine* (New

York, 1986), and Sheila Fitzpatrick, *Stalin's Peasants* (New York, 1994), 69–76.

23. Stalin, *Works*, xiii. 54–5.
24. See Sheila Fitzpatrick, 'The Great Departure. Rural-Urban Migration in the Soviet Union, 1929–1933', in William R. Rosenberg and Lewis H. Siegelbaum (eds.), *Social Dimensions of Soviet Industrialization* (Bloomington, Ind., 1993), 21–2.
25. The discussion that follows is drawn from Sheila Fitzpatrick (ed.), *Cultural Revolution in Russia, 1928–1931* (Bloomington, Ind., 1978).
26. For examples, see E. J. Brown, *The Proletarian Episode in Russian Literature, 1928–1932* (New York, 1953); David Joravsky, *Soviet Marxism and Natural Science, 1917–1932* (London, 1961); Loren R. Graham, *The Soviet Academy of Sciences and the Communist Party, 1927–1932* (Princeton, NJ, 1967).
27. Katerina Clark, in Fitzpatrick (ed.), *Cultural Revolution*, 198.
28. The following discussion is drawn from Fitzpatrick, 'Stalin and the Making of a New Elite,' in Fitzpatrick, *The Cultural Front*, and Fitzpatrick, *Education and Social Mobility*, 184–205.
29. On the changing situation of workers during the First Five-Year Plan, see Hiroaki Kuromiya, *Stalin's Industrial Revolution* (Cambridge, 1988). On subsequent developments, see Donald Filtzer, *Soviet Workers and Stalinist Industrialization* (New York, 1986).
30. *Izmeneniia sotsial'noi struktury sovetskogo obshchestva 1921-seredina 30-kh godov* (Moscow, 1979), 194; *Sotsialisticheskoe stroitel'stvo SSSR. Statisticheskii ezhegodnik* (Moscow, 1934), 356–7.
31. On Soviet isolation, see Jerry F. Hough, *Russia and the West: Gorbachev and the Politics of Reform* (2nd edn.; New York, 1990), 44–66.

Chapter 6 (*pages 148–72*)

1. Crane Brinton, *The Anatomy of Revolution* (rev. edn., New York, 1965), 17.
2. L. Trotsky, *The Revolution Betrayed* (London, 1937); Nicholas S. Timasheff, *The Great Retreat: The Growth and Decline of Communism in Russia* (New York, 1946).
3. On the literacy claims, see Fitzpatrick, *Education and Social Mobility*, 168–76. The suppressed national population census of 1937 found that 75 per cent of the population aged 9 to 49 were literate (*Sotsiologicheskie issledovaniya*, 1990 no. 7, 65–6). Inclusion of the 50-plus age group would obviously have lowered the figure.
4. Douglas R. Weiner, *Models of Nature: Ecology, Conservation and Cultural Revolution in Soviet Russia* (Bloomington, Ind., 1988).
5. Alec Nove, *An Economic History of the USSR* (new edn.; London,

1992), 195–6. For a *glasnost'*-era critique of the official statistics, see V. Selyunin and G. Khanin, 'Lukavaya tsifra,' *Novyi mir*, 1987 no. 2.

6. Holland Hunter, 'The Overambitious First Soviet Five-Year Plan', *Slavic Review*, 32: 2 (1973), 237–57.

7. On the crisis in the Donbass coal industry in 1932, see Hiroaki Kuromiya, 'The Commander and the Rank and File. Managing the Soviet Coal-Mining Industry, 1928–33,' in W. Rosenberg and L. Siegelbaum (eds.), *Social Dimensions of Soviet Industrialization* (Bloomington, Ind., 1993), 154–8.

8. See James R. Millar, 'What's Wrong with the "Standard Story"?', from James Millar and Alec Nove, 'A Debate on Collectivization', *Problems of Communism*, July–Aug. 1976, 53–5.

9. For a more detailed discussion of the actual kolkhoz of the 1930s, see Fitzpatrick, *Stalin's Peasants*, chs. 4–5.

10. Stalin, 'On the Draft of the Constitution of the USSR' (25 Nov. 1936), Russian text in I. Stalin, *Sochineniya*, i. (14), edited by Robert H. McNeal (Stanford, Calif., 1967), 135–83. For the text of the Constitution, accepted by the Eighth Extraordinary Congress of Soviets of the USSR on 5 Dec. 1936, see *Istoriya sovetskoi konstitutsii (v dokumentakh) 1917–1956* (Moscow, 1957), 345–59.

11. For an argument that the regime's genuine intention to democratize soviet elections was frustrated by the social tensions associated with the Great Purges, see J. Arch Getty, 'State and Society under Stalin: Constitutions and Elections in the 1930s', *Slavic Review*, 50: 1 (Spring 1991).

12. Quoted in N. L. Rogalina, *Kollektivizatsiya: uroki proidennogo puti* (Moscow, 1989), 198.

13. See Sheila Fitzpatrick, 'Ascribing Class. The Construction of Social Identity in Soviet Russia', *Journal of Modern History*, 4 (1993), 745–70. Note that although the old forms of discrimination were disappearing, there were new forms. Kolkhozniks did not enjoy equal rights with other citizens, not to mention deported kulaks and other administrative exiles.

14. See Fitzpatrick, 'Stalin and the Making of a New Elite', in Fitzpatrick, *The Cultural Front*, 177–8.

15. 'New Conditions—New Tasks in Economic Construction' (23 June 1931), in Stalin, *Works*, xiii. 53–82.

16. Lewis H. Siegelbaum, *Stakhanovism and the Politics of Productivity in the USSR, 1935–1941* (Cambridge, 1988).

17. Fitzpatrick, *Education and Social Mobility*, 212–33; Timasheff, *The Great Retreat*, 211–25.

18. See John Barber, *Soviet Historians in Crisis: 1928–1932* (New York, 1981), 126–41.

19. Timasheff, *The Great Retreat*, 192–203, 319–21. On the abortion debate, see Wendy Goldman, 'Women, Abortion, and the State' in Barbara E. Clements, Barbara A. Engel, and Christine D. Worobec (eds.), *Russia's Women: Accommodation, Resistance, Transformation* (Berkeley, Calif., 1991), 243–66.

20. For an intriguing thesis on Soviet 'Philistinism' in the Stalin period, see Vera S. Dunham, *In Stalin's Time. Middle-class Values in Soviet Fiction* (Cambridge, 1976).

21. Independence and self-assertion on the part of 'backward' women (peasants, national minorities) was still strongly endorsed by the regime: see Fitzpatrick, *The Cultural Front*, 233–5, and Yuri Slezkine, *Arctic Mirrors: Russia and the Small Peoples of the North* (Ithaca, NY, forthcoming 1994).

22. *Vsesoiuznoe soveshchanie zhen khozyaistvennikov i inzhenerno-tekhnicheskikh rabotnikov tyazheloi promyshlennosti. Stenograficheskii otchet, 10–12 maya 1936 g.* (Moscow, 1936).

23. Trotsky, *The Revolution Betrayed*, 102–5; *Sto sorok besed s Molotovym*, 410–11.

24. Milovan Djilas, *The New Class. An Analysis of the Communist System* (London, 1966); Robert C. Tucker, *Stalin in Power* (New York, 1990), 319–24.

25. For an elaboration of this point, see Sheila Fitzpatrick, 'Becoming Cultured: Socialist Realism and the Representation of Privilege and Taste,' in Fitzpatrick, *The Cultural Front*, 216–37.

26. Thomas Carlyle, *The French Revolution* (London, 1906), ii. 362.

27. *Izvestiia TsK KPSS*, 1989 no. 8, 115.

28. These trials are vividly described in Robert Conquest, *The Great Terror. Stalin's Purge of the Thirties* (London, 1968), updated as *The Great Terror: A Reassessment* (New York, 1990).

29. See e.g. the exchange between Rykov and Vyshinsky in *Report of Court Proceedings in the Case of the Anti-Soviet 'Bloc of Rights and Trotskyites', Heard before the Military Collegium of the Supreme Court of the U.S.S.R., Moscow, March 2–13, 1938* (Moscow, 1938), 161–2.

30. From the Indictment in ibid., 5–6.

31. Molotov, in *Bol'shevik*, 1937 no. 8 (15 Apr.), 21–2.

32. The minutes of this plenum were published for the first time in *Voprosy istorii*, 1992 nos. 2–3 and subsequent issues.

33. *Khrushchev Remembers*, trans. and ed. by Strobe Talbott (Boston, 1970), 572; Graeme Gill, *The Origins of the Stalinist Political System* (Cambridge, 1990), 278.

34. Politburo resolution of 2 July 1937 'On Anti-Soviet Elements', signed by Stalin, and operational order of 30 July signed by Ezhov (head of the NKVD), *Trud*, 4 June 1992, 1.

35. Data from V. N. Zemskov, in *Sotsiologicheskie issledovaniya*, 1991 no. 6, 14; N. Dugin, in *Na boevom postu*, 27 Dec. 1989, 3; J. Arch Getty, Gabor T. Rittersporn, Viktor N. Zemskov, 'Victims of the Soviet Penal System in the Prewar Years: A First Approach on the Basis of Archival Evidence', *American Historical Review*, Oct. 1993.

36. For another perspective on the party *chistki*, see J. Arch Getty, *Origin of the Great Purges. The Soviet Communist Party Reconsidered, 1933–1938* (New York, 1985).

37. Eikhe, in discussion at Feb.–Mar. plenum of the Central Committee, *RTsKhIDNI*, f. 17, op. 2, d. 612, l. 16.

38. On denunciations, see Fitzpatrick, *Stalin's Peasants*, ch. 9.

39. *Zvezda* (Dnepropetrovsk), 1 Aug. 1937, 3; *Krest'yanskaia pravda* (Leningrad), 9 Aug. 1937, 4. On the popular dimension of the Great Purges, see also J. Arch Getty and Roberta Manning (eds.), *Stalinist Terror: New Perspectives* (New York, 1993), esp. articles by Gabor Rittersporn and Robert Thurston.

40. On Ezhov's role and removal, see Getty and Manning, *Stalinist Terror*, 21–39, and *Sto besed s Molotovym*, 399, 401–2.

41. Stalin, *Works*, ed. Robert H. McNeal, i. (14), 368–9.

42. Dmitri Volkogonov, *Stalin. Triumph and Tragedy*, trans. by H. Shukman (London, 1991), 279;, or, in the more detailed Russian edition, *Triumf i tragediya. Politicheskii portret Stalina* (Moscow, 1989), bk 1, pt 1, 51, and pt 2, 201.

43. On Stalin's angry reaction to reading Trotsky's *The Revolution Betrayed*, where this charge is made, see Volkogonov, *Stalin*, 260.

Select Bibliography

ANWEILER, OSKAR, *The Soviets: The Russian Workers', Peasants' and Soldiers' Councils, 1905–1921* (New York, 1974).

ASCHER, ABRAHAM, *The Revolution of 1905*, i: *Russia in Disarray* (Stanford, Calif., 1988); ii: *Authority Restored* (Stanford, Calif., 1992).

AVRICH, PAUL, *Kronstadt, 1921* (Princeton, NJ, 1970).

BENNETT, JOHN W., *Brest-Litovsk. The Forgotten Peace* (London, 1938).

BENVENUTI, F., *The Bolsheviks and the Red Army, 1918–1922* (Cambridge, 1988).

BORKENAU, F., *World Communism. A History of the Communist International* (Ann Arbor, Mich.). First published 1938.

BROVKIN, VLADIMIR N., *The Mensheviks after October: Socialist Opposition and the Rise of the Bolshevik Dictatorship* (Ithaca, NY, 1987).

BROWDER, ROBERT P. and KERENSKY, ALEXANDER F. (eds.), *The Russian Provisional Government, 1917* (3 vols., Stanford, Calif., 1961).

BUKHARIN, N. and PREOBRAZHENSKY, E., *The ABC of Communism*, trans. by E. and C. Paul, introduction by E. H. Carr (London, 1969). Written in 1919.

BURBANK, JANE, *Intelligentsia and Revolution. Russian Views of Bolshevism, 1917–1922* (New York, 1986).

CARR, E. H., *A History of Soviet Russia* (London, 1952–78). Individual titles: *The Bolshevik Revolution, 1917–1923* (3 vols.; 1952), *The Interregnum, 1923–1924* (1954), *Socialism in One Country, 1924–1926* (3 vols.; 1959), *Foundations of a Planned Economy, 1926–1929* (3 vols., vol. 2 with R. W. Davies, 1969–78).

CHAMBERLIN, W. H., *The Russian Revolution* (2 vols., London, 1935).

—— *Russia's Iron Age* (London, 1935).

CHASE, WILLIAM, *Workers, Society, and the Soviet State. Labor and Life in Moscow, 1918–1929* (Urbana, Ill., 1987).

CLEMENTS, BARBARA E., *Bolshevik Feminist. The Life of Alexandra Kollontai* (Bloomington, Ind., 1979).

COHEN, STEPHEN F., *Bukharin and the Bolshevik Revolution. A Political Biography, 1888–1938* (New York, 1973).

COHEN, STEPHEN F. and TUCKER, ROBERT C., *The Great Purge Trial* (New York, 1965).

CONQUEST, ROBERT, *The Harvest of Sorrow. Soviet Collectivization and the Terror-Famine* (New York, 1986).

—— *The Great Terror: A Reassessment* (New York, 1990).

DANIELS, ROBERT V., *The Conscience of the Revolution. Communist Opposition in Soviet Russia* (Cambridge, Mass., 1960).

—— *Red October. The Bolshevik Revolution of 1917* (New York, 1967).

DAVIES, R. W., *The Industrialization of Soviet Russia*, i: *The Socialist Offensive. The Collectivisation of Soviet Agriculture, 1929–1930* (Cambridge, Mass., 1980); ii: *The Soviet Collective Farm, 1919–1930* (Cambridge, Mass., 1980); iii: *The Soviet Economy in Turmoil, 1929–1930* (Cambridge, Mass., 1989).

DEBO, RICHARD, *Revolution and Survival: The Foreign Policy of Soviet Russia, 1917–1918* (Toronto, 1979) and *Survival and Consolidation: The Foreign Policy of Soviet Russia, 1918–1921* (Montreal, 1992).

DEUTSCHER, ISAAC, *The Prophet Armed. Trotsky: 1879–1921* (London, 1954).

—— *The Prophet Unarmed: Trotsky, 1921–1929* (London, 1959).

—— *The Prophet Outcast: Trotsky, 1929–1940* (London, 1970).

FAINSOD, MERLE, *Smolensk under Soviet Rule* (London, 1958).

FERRO, MARC, *The Russian Revolution of February 1917*, trans. by J. L. Richards (London, 1972).

—— *October 1917: A Social History of the Russian Revolution*, trans. by Norman Stone (Boston, 1980).

FIGES, ORLANDO, *Peasant Russia, Civil War. The Volga Countryside in Revolution, 1917–1921* (Oxford, 1989).

FILTZER, DONALD, *Soviet Workers and Stalinist Industrialization. The Formation of Modern Soviet Production Relations, 1928–1941* (New York, 1986).

FISCHER, LOUIS, *The Soviets in World Affairs. A History of Relations Between the Soviet Union and the Rest of the World, 1917–1929* (Princeton, NJ, 1951).

FITZPATRICK, SHEILA, *The Commissariat of Enlightenment. Soviet Organization of Education and the Arts under Lunacharsky, October 1917–1921* (London, 1970).

—— (ed.), *Cultural Revolution in Russia, 1928–1931* (Bloomington, Ind., 1978).

—— *Education and Social Mobility in the Soviet Union, 1921–1934* (Cambridge, 1979).

—— *The Cultural Front. Power and Culture in Revolutionary Russia* (Ithaca, NY, 1992).

—— *Stalin's Peasants. Resistance and Survival in the Russian Village after Collectivization* (New York and Oxford, 1994).

—— RABINOWITCH, A., and STITES, R. (eds.), *Russia in the Era of NEP. Explorations in Soviet Society and Culture* (Bloomington, Ind., 1991).

FLORINSKY, MICHAEL T., *The End of the Russian Empire* (New Haven, Conn., 1931).

FÜLÖP-MILLER, RENÉ, *The Mind and Face of Bolshevism. An Examination of Cultural Life in Soviet Russia* (London, 1927).

GALILI, ZIVA, *The Menshevik Leaders in the Russian Revolution: Social Realities and Political Strategies* (Princeton, NJ, 1989).

GETTY, J. ARCH, *Origins of the Great Purges. The Soviet Communist Party Reconsidered, 1933–1938* (New York, 1985).

—— and MANNING, ROBERTA (eds.), *Stalinist Terror: New Perspectives* (New York, 1993).

GETZLER, ISRAEL, *Kronstadt, 1917–1921. The Fate of a Soviet Democracy* (Cambridge, 1983).

GILL, GRAEME, *Peasants and Government in the Russian Revolution* (London, 1979).

GLEASON, A., KENEZ, P., and STITES, R. (eds.), *Bolshevik Culture. Experiment and Order in the Russian Revolution* (Bloomington, Ind., 1985).

HAIMSON, LEOPOLD, *The Russian Marxists and the Origins of Bolshevism* (Cambridge, Mass., 1955).

—— 'The Problem of Social Stability in Urban Russia, 1905–1917,' *Slavic Review*, 23: 4 (1964) and 24: 1 (1965).

—— *The Mensheviks. From the Revolution of 1917 to World War II* (Chicago, 1974).

HASEGAWA, TSUYOSHI, *The February Revolution: Petrograd, 1917* (Seattle, 1981).

HULSE, JAMES W., *The Forming of the Communist International* (Stanford, Calif., 1964).

HUSBAND, WILLIAM, *Revolution in the Factory. The Birth of the Soviet Textile Industry, 1917–1920* (New York, 1990).

KATKOV, GEORGE, *Russia, 1917: The February Revolution* (London, 1967).

KEEP, JOHN, *The Russian Revolution. A Study in Mass Mobilization* (New York, 1976).

—— *The Debate on Soviet Power. Minutes of the All-Russian Central Executive Committee of Soviets: Second Convocation, October (1918)* (Oxford, 1979).

KENEZ, PETER, *Civil War in South Russia, 1918* (Berkeley, 1971).

KENEZ, PETER, *Civil War in South Russia, 1919–1920* (Berkeley, 1977).

—— *The Birth of the Propaganda State. Soviet Methods of Mass Mobilization 1917–1929* (Cambridge, 1985).

KENNAN, GEORGE F., *Soviet-American Relations, 1917–1920*, i: *Russia Leaves the War* (Princeton, NJ, 1956); ii: *The Decision to Intervene* (Princeton, NJ, 1958).

KOENKER, DIANE, *Moscow Workers and the 1917 Revolution* (Princeton, NJ, 1981).

—— and ROSENBERG, W. G., *Strikes and Revolution in Russia 1917* (Princeton, NJ, 1989).

—— ROSENBERG, W. G., and SUNY, R. G. (eds.), *Party, State, and Society in the Russian Civil War: Explorations in Social History* (Bloomington, Ind., 1989).

KUROMIYA, HIROAKI, *Stalin's Industrial Revolution: Politics and Workers, 1928–1932* (Cambridge, 1988).

LAZITCH, BRANKO and DRACHKOVITCH, MILORAD M., *Lenin and the Comintern*, i (Stanford, Calif., 1972).

LEGGETT, GEORGE, *The Cheka. Lenin's Political Police* (Oxford, 1981).

LEWIN, MOSHE, *Lenin's Last Struggle* (New York, 1968).

—— *Russian Peasants and Soviet Power* (London, 1968).

—— *The Making of the Soviet System: Essays in the Social History of Interwar Russia* (New York, 1985).

LINCOLN, W. BRUCE, *Red Victory: A History of the Russian Civil War* (New York, 1989).

MALLE, SILVANA, *The Economic Organization of War Communism, 1918–1921* (Cambridge, 1985).

MALLY, LYNN, *Culture of the Future: The Proletkult Movement in Revolutionary Russia* (Berkeley, Calif., 1990).

MANDEL, DAVID, *The Petrograd Workers and the Fall of the Old Regime* (London, 1983).

—— *The Petrograd Workers and the Soviet Seizure of Power* (London, 1984).

MCAULEY, MARY, *Bread and Justice. State and Society in Petrograd, 1917–1922* (Oxford, 1991).

MAWDSLEY, EVAN, *The Russian Revolution and the Baltic Fleet. War and Politics, February 1917–April 1918* (New York, 1978).

—— *The Russian Civil War* (Boston, 1987).

MEDVEDEV, ROY A., *The October Revolution* (New York, 1979).

—— *Let History Judge. The Origins and Consequences of Stalinism* (rev. edn.; New York, 1989).

MELGUNOV, S. P., *The Bolshevik Seizure of Power* (Santa Barbara, Calif., 1972).

PETHYBRIDGE, ROGER, *Witnesses to the Russian Revolution* (London, 1964).

—— *The Social Prelude to Stalinism* (London, 1974).

PIPES, RICHARD, *The Formation of the Soviet Union. Communism and Nationalism, 1917–1923* (Cambridge, Mass., 1954).

—— *The Russian Revolution* (New York, 1990).

RABINOWITCH, ALEXANDER, *Prelude to Revolution. The Petrograd Bolsheviks and the July 1917 Uprising* (Bloomington, Ind., 1968).

—— *The Bolsheviks Come to Power. The Revolution of 1917 in Petrograd* (New York, 1976).

RADKEY, OLIVER H., *The Agrarian Foes of Bolshevism. Promise and Default of the Russian Socialist Revolutionaries, February to October 1917* (New York, 1958).

—— *The Sickle under the Hammer: The Russian Socialist Revolutionaries in the Early Months of Soviet Rule* (New York, 1963).

—— *The Unknown Civil War in Soviet Russia. A Study of the Green Movement in the Tambov Region, 1920–1921* (Stanford, Calif., 1976).

—— *Russia Goes to the Polls. The Election to the All-Russian Constituent Assembly, 1917* (Ithaca, NY, 1989).

RALEIGH, DONALD J., *Revolution on the Volga: 1917 in Saratov* (Ithaca, NY, 1986).

READ, CHRISTOPHER, *Culture and Power in Revolutionary Russia: The Intelligentsia and the Transition from Tsarism to Communism* (New York, 1990).

REED, JOHN, *Ten Days that Shook the World* (London, 1966).

REIMAN, MICHAL, *The Birth of Stalinism. The USSR on the Eve of the 'Second Revolution'*, trans. by George Saunders (Bloomington, Ind., 1987).

REMINGTON, THOMAS F., *Building Socialism in Bolshevik Russia: Ideology and Industrial Organization, 1917–1921* (Pittsburgh, 1984).

RIGBY, T. H., *Lenin's Government, Sovnarkom. 1917–1922* (Cambridge, 1979).

ROSENBERG, WILLIAM G., *Liberals in the Russian Revolution* (Princeton, NJ, 1974).

—— *Bolshevik Visions. First Phase of the Cultural Revolution in Soviet Russia* (2nd edn., 2 vols.; Ann Arbor, Mich., 1990).

SAKWA, RICHARD, *Soviet Communists in Power: A Study of Moscow During the Civil War, 1918–1921* (New York, 1988).

SCHAPIRO, LEONARD, *The Origin of the Communist Autocracy. Political Opposition in the Soviet State: First Phase, 1917–1922* (Cambridge, Mass., 1955).

SCOTT, JOHN, *Behind the Urals. An American Worker in Russia's City of Steel* (Boston, 1942).

SERGE, VICTOR, *Memoirs of a Revolutionary* (Oxford, 1963).

SERVICE, ROBERT, *The Bolshevik Party in Revolution. A Study in Organizational Change, 1917–1923* (London, 1979).

—— *Lenin: A Political Life*, i and ii [to 1918] (Bloomington, Ind., 1985–1991).

SIEGELBAUM, LEWIS H., *Soviet State and Society between Revolutions, 1918–1929* (Cambridge, 1992).

SLUSSER, ROBERT M., *Stalin in October. The Man who Missed the Revolution* (Baltimore, 1987).

SMITH, STEPHEN A., *Red Petrograd: Revolution in the Factories, 1917–1918* (Cambridge, 1983).

SOLZHENITSYN, ALEKSANDR I., *The Gulag Archipelago 1918–1956*, trans. by Thomas P. Whitney (New York, 1973).

STEINBERG, I. N., *In the Workshop of the Revolution* (New York, 1953).

STITES, RICHARD, *The Women's Liberation Movement in Russia. Feminism, Nihilism, and Bolshevism, 1860–1930* (Princeton, NJ, 1978).

—— *Revolutionary Dreams. Utopian Vision and Experimental Life in the Russian Revolution* (Oxford, 1989).

STONE, NORMAN, *The Eastern Front 1914–1917* (New York, 1975).

SUKHANOV, N. N., *The Russian Revolution 1917* (2 vols., ed. and trans. by Joel Carmichael; New York, 1962).

SUNY, RONALD G., *The Baku Commune, 1917–1918. Class and Nationality in the Russian Revolution* (Princeton, NJ, 1972).

TIMASHEFF, NICHOLAS S., *The Great Retreat. The Growth and Decline of Communism in Russia* (New York, 1946).

TIRADO, ISABEL, *Young Guard! The Communist Youth League, Petrograd 1917–1920* (New York, 1988).

TROTSKY, L., *The Revolution Betrayed* (London, 1937).

—— *The History of the Russian Revolution*, trans. by Max Eastman (Ann Arbor, Mich., 1960).

TUCKER, ROBERT C., *Stalin as Revolutionary, 1879–1929* (New York, 1973).

—— *Stalin in Power: The Revolution from Above, 1928–1941* (New York, 1990).

—— (ed.), *Stalinism. Essays in Historical Interpretation* (New York, 1977).

TUMARKIN, NINA, *Lenin Lives! The Lenin Cult in Soviet Russia* (Cambridge, 1983).

ULAM, ADAM B., *The Bolsheviks. The Intellectual and Political History of the Triumph of Communism in Russia* (New York, 1965).

—— *Stalin. The Man and his Era* (New York, 1973).

ULLMAN, RICHARD H., *Anglo-Soviet Relations, 1917–1921* (3 vols., Princeton, NJ, 1961–73).

VAKSBERG, ARKADY, trans. by Jan Butler, *The Prosecutor and the Prey: Vyshinsky and the 1930s Moscow Show Trials* (London, 1990).

VALENTINOV, NIKOLAY (N. V. Volsky), *Encounters with Lenin* (London, 1968).

VIOLA, LYNNE, *The Best Sons of the Fatherland. Workers in the Vanguard of Soviet Collectivization* (New York, 1987).

VOLKOGONOV, DMITRI, *Stalin. Triumph and Tragedy*, ed. and trans. by Harold Shukman (London, 1991).

VON HAGEN, MARK, *Soldiers in the Proletarian Dictatorship. The Red Army and the Soviet Socialist State, 1917–1930* (Ithaca, NY, 1990).

WADE, REX A., *The Russian Search for Peace, February–October 1917* (Stanford, Calif., 1969).

—— *Red Guards and Workers' Militias in the Russian Revolution* (Stanford, Calif., 1984).

WARTH, ROBERT D., *The Allies and the Russian Revolution* (Durham, NC, 1954).

WILDMAN, ALLAN K., *The End of the Russian Imperial Army*, i: *The Old Army and the Soldiers' Revolt (March–April 1917)* (Princeton, NJ, 1980); ii: *The Road to Soviet Power and Peace* (Princeton, NJ, 1987).

ZEMAN, Z. A. B. (ed.), *Germany and the Revolution in Russia, 1915–1918: Documents from the Archives of the German Foreign Ministry* (London, 1958).

Index

Alekseev, General Mikhail 60
Aleksei, Tsarevich 37, 38, 44–5
Alexander II, Emperor 23, 25, 32
Alexandra, Empress 37, 38
America 6, 8, 41, 83, 129, 142
  intervention in Civil War 74
American Revolution 1
anarchism 55, 79
antisemitism 25
Army, Russian Imperial 32–3, 37–8,
  41, 44, 46, 47–8, 52, 53, 57,
  59–60, 66, 72–3, 75, 77, 89
  see also Red Army; White Armies
atheism 41, 142, 171
Austria-Hungary 72, 74

Bogdanov, Aleksandr 98
Bolshevik Party, see Communist Party
'bourgeois experts', see intelligentsia
Brest-Litovsk 69, 70, 72–3
Brezhnev, Leonid 7, 145
Brinton, Crane 2, 148, 149
Britain 15, 37, 120, 121, 123, 129,
  130, 140, 164, 165
  intervention in Civil War 73–4
Bukharin, Nikolai 73, 78, 84, 116,
  117, 121, 127, 128, 135, 159, 164
bureaucracy and administration 75,
  84–5, 87, 88, 89, 102–6, 136,
  156, 162, 165
  party 89, 91, 104–6
  state (soviet) 91, 102–3, 106, 109,
    122, 141, 144
  Tsarist 21, 23, 32, 38, 46

Cadets (Constitutional Democrats)
  33, 38, 44, 57, 59, 72, 97, 167
Carlyle, Thomas 166
Carr, E. H. 7
Central Committee of Russian (later
  Soviet) Communist Party 13, 58,
    62, 73, 87–9, 98, 100, 101, 104,
    105, 109, 125, 126, 146, 164, 165,
    168, 169
  Secretariat 87, 101–2, 104, 108–9,
    110
Chaadaev, Peter 171
Chamberlin, W. H. 5
Cheka 76–7, 87, 91, 94, 113, 121
  see also GPU, NKVD
children, homeless 84, 145, 163
China 26, 121, 142
Civil War 2, 4, 12, 31, 41, 44, 45, 51,
  70–8, 79, 84, 87, 88, 89, 90, 93,
  97, 100, 107, 110, 113, 136, 141,
  143, 148, 157, 165
  as model and myth 118–19, 120,
    125–6, 136, 142
class enemies 3, 10, 12, 25, 70, 76,
  90–1, 101, 118, 120, 136–7, 141,
  144, 147, 149, 165–6, 168, 169
Clemenceau, Georges 121
clergy, see priests
Cold War 6, 170, 171
collectivization 2, 112, 117, 120,
  130, 132, 135–41, 145, 146, 147,
  149, 150, 152–3, 165
  see also kolkhoz
Comintern 95, 96, 99, 115, 120, 127,
  128, 141
communism, see socialism
Communist Party 4, 7, 10, 30–1, 35,
  37, 54, 57, 60, 61, 66–7, 77,
  86–92, 95, 97, 99, 102, 106, 108,
  110–11, 114, 118–19, 122, 129,
  150, 152, 153, 156, 157, 160, 161,
  165, 168, 169, 172 n. 6
  and Civil War 2, 71, 75, 118–19
  and collectivization 126, 136–8,
    141
  factions in 73, 76, 89, 98–102, 108,
    109, 146, 167

Communist Party (*cont.*)
    intellectuals in 30, 85, 87, 90, 91,
        99, 100, 109, 141, 159
    and NEP 3, 96, 112–13, 141, 142
    party organization and discipline
        42, 89, 96–9, 104
    and peasantry 10, 31, 36, 81–3, 90,
        96, 112–13, 115–16, 150, 153
    as proletarian vanguard 6, 9, 10,
        30, 67, 162
    recruitment and membership 11,
        42, 52, 71, 90, 105–6, 174 n. 12
    and revolution 1, 2, 6, 9, 40–3,
        49–52, 64–5, 68, 88
    workers in 11, 52, 71, 87, 89,
        90–2, 100, 118, 141
    see also Central Committee, Old
        Bolsheviks, Oppositions,
        Politburo, purges
Conquest, Robert 7
Constituent Assembly 40, 41, 43–4,
    45, 57, 66–7
Constitutions:
    Russian Republic (1918) 91, 154,
        155
    USSR (1936) 154–5
Council of People's Commissars
    65–6, 76, 87, 88, 107, 128
Cubism 85, 87
Cultural Revolution 2, 11, 12, 141–5,
    147, 157, 159, 162, 165, 167
Czech Legion 74

Danilov, V. P. 138
Deutscher, Isaac 7
Djilas, Milovan 162
diplomacy, *see* foreign relations
'dual power' 40, 43–4, 46, 48, 49, 58
Duma 16, 33, 34–5, 37, 38, 44, 46
Dzerzhinsky, Feliks 113

education 22, 27–8, 86, 91, 96, 111,
    143, 145, 149, 157, 159
    higher 11, 109, 144–5, 155, 159
elections 48, 88
    Constituent Assembly 40, 66–7
    Duma 33–4, 35
    party 100, 104, 108–9, 129
    soviets 52, 65, 88, 155, 182 n. 11
    see also voting rights

Emancipation of serfs (1861) 15, 17,
    19, 21, 56
emigration 28, 35–6, 41, 49, 50, 51,
    93–4, 98, 123
Engels, Friedrich 26, 67, 84, 86
engineers 23, 81, 111, 122–3, 149,
    158, 161
Esperanto 87
Evtushenko, Evgenii
Ezhov, Nikolai 165, 169

factory committees 52, 54–5, 69, 81,
    91
family 27, 45, 82, 84, 86, 145, 157,
    160–1, 162
famine 32, 84
    of 1921–2 93, 97
    of 1932–3 13, 139, 145, 147, 152,
        163, 180 n. 22
First Five-Year Plan 2, 10, 110, 114,
    117, 120, 122, 124–6, 130–4,
    143, 144–5, 147, 148, 150, 151,
    152, 158
Fischer, Louis 5
foreign investment and ownership 26,
    36–7, 95–6, 112, 114
foreign relations 5, 32, 33, 69, 70, 89,
    115, 120–1, 122–3, 147, 162
France 15, 24, 36, 37, 74, 123, 130,
    164
French Revolution 1, 3, 5, 30, 107,
    118, 122, 171, 179 n. 2
    see also Napoleon; terror;
        Thermidor
Frumkin, Moshe 126
Futurism 85

Gapon, Father 32
Germany 4, 6, 15, 29, 37, 41, 50, 52,
    57, 58, 59–60, 63, 66, 69, 70,
    72–3, 95, 162, 164, 165, 169
Gerschenkron, Alexander 19
Gogol, Nikolai 16
Gorbachev, Mikhail 13, 117, 171
Gorky, Maxim 63, 143, 149, 164
GPU 76–7, 121–3, 137
    see also Cheka, NKVD
Great Purges 3, 4, 12–13, 145, 148,
    150, 161, 164–70, 173–4 n. 8,
    182 n. 11
Guchkov, Aleksandr 16, 47
Gulag 3, 7, 13, 147, 165, 166, 170

Hitler, Adolf 162

industrialists 38, 43, 45, 59, 123, 133
industrialization 2, 9–10, 15, 19,
    23–4, 26, 109–10, 113–14,
    116–17, 120, 123, 124, 126,
    129–34, 135, 139–40, 147, 149,
    151, 162
industry 20, 36, 63, 70, 79–80, 91,
    93, 95, 111, 112, 113, 116, 124,
    129–34, 139, 151, 152, 164, 165
  nationalization 78–80, 95
intelligentsia 2, 6, 10, 13, 22–31, 81,
    85, 86, 147, 154, 162, 165
  'bourgeois' 89, 96, 103, 118,
    122–3, 126, 132, 141, 144, 159,
    162, 165, 167
  new Soviet 144, 156
Italy 99, 107, 143
Ivan the Terrible 159

Japan 32, 130, 164
  intervention in Civil War 74
Jews 30, 41, 70
  in Bolshevik Party 30, 110, 115
  see also antisemitism
July Days 43, 49, 57–8, 62, 94

Kaganovich, Lazar 128, 134
Kamenev, Lev 63, 107, 109, 164
Kerensky, Aleksandr 45, 57, 59, 60,
    63, 64, 73
Khrushchev, Nikita 7, 118, 145, 159,
    165
Kirov, Sergei 163, 164
Koestler, Arthur 6
Kolchak, Admiral Aleksandr 73, 74
kolkhoz 83, 137–40, 142, 145, 150,
    153, 163, 168, 170, 182 n. 13
Kollontai, Aleksandra 86
Komsomol (League of Communist
    Youth) 86, 137, 142–3, 168
Kornilov, General Lavr 40, 43,
    59–61, 63
Kosygin, Aleksei 145
Krasnov, General Petr 72
Kronstadt sailors 48, 57, 58, 94
  revolt 10, 94–5
Krupskaya, Nadezhda 108
Krymov, General Aleksandr 60
Krzhizhanovsky, Gleb 131
kulaks 10, 12, 91, 113, 115, 116, 120,
    123, 125, 126, 135–9, 145, 153,
    154, 164, 166, 168
  deportation of 137–9, 145

landowners 10, 18, 20, 21, 34, 51,
    55–7, 59, 78
  see also nobility
law, lawyers 22–23, 25, 35, 45, 77,
    85, 89, 90, 105, 112, 143
'legal Marxists' 28–9
leadership, theories and styles of
    30–1, 102, 106–8, 110–11, 118,
    127, 133, 145, 146, 158–9
Lenin, Vladimir 3, 7, 13, 20, 26–31,
    36, 37, 50–52, 68, 69, 73, 75, 78,
    86, 88–90, 91, 94, 105, 106, 108,
    110, 113, 117, 119, 126, 154, 157,
    159, 171, 179 n. 18
  on bureaucracy and administration
    84, 103
  on factions and opposition 89,
    97–102, 166–7
  as 'German agent' 41, 50, 58
  illness and death 107, 108, 110, 127
  and NEP 3, 95–7, 116–17, 129
  on the party 29, 30–1, 42, 71,
    98–9, 110
  and revolution 31, 35, 58, 61–6,
    111, 114, 117
  and terror 76, 96–8, 166
Lenin cult 110–11
'Lenin levy' 106
Leningrad *see* Petrograd
liberalism, liberals 15, 20, 22, 24, 27,
    28, 32–4, 40, 41, 44, 45, 47, 49,
    59, 161
  see also Cadets; Liberation
    movement; Octobrists
Liberation movement 27, 29, 32
literacy 18, 27, 111, 143, 149,
    181 n. 3
Louis Philippe, King 32
Lunacharsky, Anatolii 87
Luxemburg, Rosa 51
Lvov, Prince George 45, 57

Magnitogorsk 130, 133, 145, 152
Makhno, Nestor 94
Martov, Yulii 29, 30, 65
Marx, Karl 26, 31, 84, 105, 115, 140,
    157, 169

Marxism, Marxist theory 5, 6, 9–10, 11, 12, 19–20, 27, 28, 30–1, 40, 47, 53, 78–9, 82, 83–4, 108, 111, 114, 116, 127, 145, 150, 154, 156, 159, 161–2
  in prerevolutionary Russia 9, 24–31, 56
Mayakovsky, Vladimir 85
Medvedev, Roy A. 7
Menshevik Party 30–1, 33, 37, 41, 47, 49, 50, 60, 65, 68, 97, 98, 99, 111, 132, 143, 167
Menzhinskii, Vyacheslav 123
Meyerhold, Vsevolod 85
Michael, Grand Duke 45
Mikoyan, Anastas 100
Milyukov, Pavel 38, 45, 48
mir 17, 24, 25, 36, 56, 82, 112, 138
modernization 9–10, 23, 26–7, 28, 111, 114, 129, 151, 160
Molotov, Vyacheslav 50, 89, 100, 101, 102, 128, 131, 161, 165, 169
Moscow 10, 16, 19–20, 54, 66, 68, 74, 75, 87, 95, 96, 98, 99, 103, 129, 138, 146, 148–9, 163
  party organization 52, 107, 126, 127–8
  Soviet 33, 61
Mussolini, Benito 107

Napoleon, Emperor 1, 3, 107, 111, 159
national question, nationalities 69–70, 91, 115, 183 n. 21
  self-determination 69
national strength 114–15, 130, 151, 154, 171
NEP (New Economic Policy) 2, 3, 4, 10, 78, 95–7, 112, 114, 116–18, 120, 126–9, 131, 135, 141, 142, 148, 152
Nepmen 112, 115, 118, 131, 141, 145, 168
Nicholas II, Emperor 2, 15, 16, 20, 23, 32, 33, 34, 35, 36, 37, 44–5, 55
NKVD 164, 165, 166, 167, 169
  see also Cheka, GPU, Gulag

nobility 12, 21–2, 27, 32, 34, 38, 55, 90
  see also landowners

Octobrists 33
OGPU, *see* GPU
Old Bolsheviks 3, 6, 71, 99, 108, 114, 131, 133, 157, 159, 161, 164, 165, 167
Opposition 100–2, 121, 129, 146, 164, 167, 178 n. 17
  see also Communist Party, factions in
  Left (Trotskyite-Zinovievite) 12, 108–9, 118, 125, 126, 127, 133, 146, 152, 164
  Right 124, 126–9, 132, 133, 141, 146, 152, 167
  Workers' 100–2
Ordzhonikidze, Sergo 130, 164
Orthodox Church 56, 97–8, 137
Orwell, George 6, 84–5

passports, internal 18, 139
peasants 6, 10, 15, 17–18, 20–1, 24–5, 31, 36, 48, 51, 55–6, 66, 75, 77–8, 80, 81–3, 93–4, 96, 112–13, 115–16, 121, 124–6, 135–41, 145, 146, 150, 152–3, 154, 155, 163
  class differentiation issue 82, 113, 126, 135
  departure from village 18–19, 21, 36, 137, 138, 140–1, 145
  land seizures and redistribution 55–7, 78, 82
  revolts 20–1, 34, 94–5
  see also collectivization
'People's Will' 25–6
Peter the Great 147, 160
Petrograd (Leningrad, St Petersburg) 10, 16, 18–20, 32, 36, 43, 44, 53–4, 57, 60, 63, 73, 74, 75, 94, 107, 138, 163
  party organization 52, 107, 163, 164
  Soviet 33, 40, 43, 46–9, 50, 51, 52, 53, 58, 60–3
planning, economic 69, 81, 113, 114, 131–4, 149, 152, 158, 170
  see also First Five-Year Plan

Plekhanov, Georgii 26, 29, 30, 51
Pokrovsky, Mikhail 159
Poland, Poles 70, 84, 130, 164
police, secret 68, 147
    Soviet, *see* Cheka; GPU; NKVD
    Tsarist 27, 68, 77
police state 25, 31, 35
Politburo 13, 87-9, 101, 104, 107,
    108, 109, 110, 121, 122, 123, 125,
    126, 127-8
population 13, 15-16, 18, 111, 112,
    140, 145, 146
Populists 9, 24-5, 27, 28, 82, 144
Preobrazhensky, Evgenii 78, 84, 116,
    135
priests 15, 32, 91, 96, 97-8, 137,
    145, 168
professionals 15, 21, 22-23, 27, 32-3,
    105, 156, 162
    see also intelligentsia
proletariat 6, 7, 9, 10, 20, 24, 27, 28,
    31, 36, 43, 51, 53, 71, 86, 90, 91,
    93, 94, 105, 116, 117, 140, 142,
    143-4, 156
    cultural hegemony of 141, 144
    dictatorship of 55, 68-9, 76, 87-8,
    90, 92, 94, 105, 106, 154, 156,
    157
    see also workers
Provisional Government 2, 40, 43,
    45-9, 51-65 *passim*, 76, 80, 87,
    88
Pugachev revolt 20, 34
purges 128, 144, 145, 147, 159
    party 12, 101, 128, 167-8, 169,
    173-4 n. 8, 178 n. 9
    see also Great Purges
Pushkin, Aleksandr 162
Pyatakov, Yurii 136, 164

RAPP (Russian Association of
    Proletarian Writers) 142-4
Rasputin, Grigorii 37-8
rationing 80, 81, 120, 139, 146, 163
Red Army 6, 71, 75-8, 81, 84, 87,
    89, 91, 93, 94, 96, 107, 109, 125,
    131, 159, 161
Red Guards 61, 72, 75, 142
Reed, John 5
religion 27, 86, 96, 137, 166, 169
    see also atheism; Orthodox Church

requisitions 81, 93, 95, 125
revolution 1-2, 8-9, 26, 148, 149,
    150, 156-7, 166, 171
    of February 1917 2, 4, 40-1, 43,
    44-6, 48, 49, 51, 53, 58, 98, 148
    'from above' 2, 3, 4, 120, 128, 138
    international 69, 70, 84, 94, 95,
    111, 114
    of 1905 15, 20, 31, 32-5, 39, 40, 55
    of October 1917 1-2, 4, 6, 41-2,
    61-5, 62, 66, 70, 72, 80, 85, 88,
    93, 94, 111, 114, 118, 148, 154,
    157
    'permanent' 31
    Russian 1-4, 5-8, 148-50, 170-1,
    172 n. 1
    see also American Revolution;
    French Revolution
Rigby, T. H. 101
Robespierre, Maximilien 169, 170
Rostow, Walt 151
Russia (Soviet Union) and the West
    9, 15, 23-4, 26, 69, 111, 115,
    130, 134, 170-2
Russian Social-Democratic Labour
    Party 28-31, 173 n. 6
    see also Communist [Bolshevik]
    Party; Menshevik Party
Rykov, Aleksei 107, 117, 121, 125,
    127-9, 164

St Petersburg, *see* Petrograd
service, service class 21, 22, 162
    see also bureaucracy
sexual morality 86-7, 160
Shakhty trial 122, 127, 141, 144,
    165
Shlyapnikov, Aleksandr 100
show trials 122, 147, 164-5
    see also Shakhty trial
Shvernik, Nikolai 134
Siberia 45, 50, 73, 74, 125-6, 137
social mobility 21, 28, 159
    'promotion' of workers and peasants
    11, 91-2, 106, 140, 144-5, 156
socialism 3, 9, 24-6, 78-9, 80, 83,
    84, 131, 143, 150-1, 154-6, 170
    'building of' 9-10, 111, 113, 114,
    136, 149, 153-4
    'in one country' 114-15
    see also Marxism

socialist and Communist parties,
    European 29, 36, 37, 51, 95, 99,
    170
Solzhenitsyn, Aleksandr 7, 41
soviets 20, 33, 49, 51–2, 54–5, 57,
    61, 64–5, 68, 70, 74, 79, 87, 88,
    94, 102, 104, 154, 182 n. 11
    see also bureaucracy, state
spies 8, 120, 122, 127, 164, 168–9
SR (Socialist-Revolutionary) Party
    27, 47, 49, 50, 60, 66, 68, 97, 98
    left SRs 66, 73, 88
Stakhanovite movement 158
Stalin, Iosif 2, 4, 5, 6, 7, 13, 50, 104,
    120–4, 131, 141, 143, 144, 145,
    147, 148, 149, 156, 163, 168,
    184 n. 43
    and collectivization 125–6, 135–41
        passim
    and 'great retreat' 154, 157–61,
        162
    and industrialization 114, 129–31,
        133–4
    and Lenin 3, 7, 89, 100, 102, 108,
        110, 114, 116–17, 146, 157, 159
    and Right Opposition 73, 124–9,
        141
    in succession struggle 107–10, 115
    and terror 4, 165, 166, 169–70
Stalin cult 131, 146
Stalinism 4, 7, 71, 155
state farms (*sovkhozy*) 83, 135
Stolypin, Petr 36, 77
    agrarian reforms 36, 56, 82, 112,
        138, 177 n. 14.
strikes 20, 28, 32, 36, 44, 94
Struve, Petr 28–9, 32
Sukhanov, Nikolai 47, 48, 108
Supreme Economic Council 79, 113,
    130
Syrtsov, Sergei 125

Tarlé, Evgenii 159
taxation 95, 96
teachers 23, 86, 137
terror 11, 77, 173 n. 5
    French Revolution 4, 11, 13, 77,
        118, 163, 166, 169–70
    Russian Revolution 3, 4, 9, 10,
        12–13, 76–7, 165, 166–7, 169–70
    see also Great Purges

terrorism:
    anti-Soviet 121, 164
    revolutionary 22–3, 25, 32
Thermidor 2, 4, 5, 118, 148, 150,
    170, 173 n. 3, 179 n.26
Timasheff, Nicholas S. 148, 150
Tomsky, Mikhail 107, 128, 145
totalitarianism 4, 6, 42, 166
tractors 130, 132, 133, 134, 138, 151,
    152, 153
trade and distribution 78, 80, 95,
    112, 116, 120, 124, 126, 131, 132,
    146, 161–3, 164
trade unions 33, 35, 54, 60, 69, 81,
    107, 128, 144, 145, 158
    debate on 99–100
Trotsky, Lev 5, 6, 7, 30, 31, 33, 41,
    58, 69, 90, 100, 101, 107, 117,
    136, 143, 148, 150, 152, 164, 165,
    167, 171
    in Civil War 72–3, 75, 76, 107
    in October Revolution 62, 64–5,
        176 n. 17
    in succession struggle 104, 107–10,
        114–15, 121
    The Revolution Betrayed 5, 157,
        161, 170, 184 n. 43
Tucker, Robert C. 162
Tukhachevsky, Marshal Mikhail 164

Uglanov, Nikolai 126, 128
Ukraine, Ukrainians 16, 19, 25, 54,
    66, 70, 72–3, 74, 94, 128, 130,
    133–4, 138, 139
Ulam, Adam B. 10
unemployment 54, 55, 59, 96, 118
United States, *see* America
Urals 45, 74, 125, 126, 129, 130,
    133–4, 137, 146
utopianism 8, 24, 25, 83–7, 143, 157

Volga region 74, 93, 126, 139
Voroshilov, Klim 161
voting rights 34, 91, 113, 155

wages and salaries 10, 20, 29, 53, 80,
    86, 145, 157, 158, 161, 164
war 31–2, 39, 51, 73, 84, 120, 124,
    166
    First World War 16, 18, 19, 20,

37–9, 41, 48, 49, 52, 53, 57, 59,
63, 70, 73, 74, 93, 94, 121
Second World War 4, 5, 6, 124
war scare (1927) 120–2, 127
see also Civil War
War Communism 78–83, 84, 93, 94,
95, 117, 120, 126, 131, 136
War Industries Committee 38, 46
Weber, Max 105
White Armies 70, 73–8, 81, 88, 91,
94, 164
Wildman, Allan K. 53, 175 n. 10
Witte, Count Sergei 23, 26, 33, 36,
129
women 18, 21, 44, 53, 86, 137, 145,
160–61, 183 n. 21
workers 15, 18–21, 32–3, 35, 36,
53–5, 60–1, 63, 70, 71, 73, 75,
79, 81, 90, 91–2, 93–5, 111, 112,
118, 122, 138, 145, 154, 155, 156,
158, 164, 168

and Communist party 10–11, 30,
67, 77, 105–6, 145
and Russian Marxists 27–8, 30
self-betterment and upward
mobility 11, 28, 91–2, 93, 141,
144–5, 156, 159
see also proletariat; strikes; workers'
control
'workers' control' 54–5, 69, 81
Workers' Opposition, *see* Opposition,
Workers

xenophobia 70, 147

Yagoda, Genrikh 164
Young Pioneers 86, 169
Yudenich, General Nikolai 74

Zamyatin, Evgenii 84
zemstvos 23, 27, 32, 33, 38, 45, 46,
104
Zinoviev, Grigorii 41, 58, 63, 108,
109, 115, 133, 164